The King Arthur Mysteries

The King Arthur Mysteries

Arthur's Britain and Early Mediaeval World

Timothy Venning

First published in Great Britain in 2021 by
Pen & Sword History
An imprint of
Pen & Sword Books Ltd
Yorkshire – Philadelphia

ISBN 978 1 52678 390 5

A CIP catalogue record for this book is available from the British Library.

Typeset by Mac Style
Printed and bound in UK by CPI Group (UK) Ltd, Croydon, CRO 4YY

Pen & Sword Books Limited incorporates the imprints of Atlas, Archaeology, Aviation, Discovery, Family History, Fiction, History, Maritime, Military, Military Classics, Politics, Select, Transport, True Crime, Air World, Frontline Publishing, Leo Cooper, Remember When, Seaforth Publishing, The Praetorian Press, Wharncliffe Local History, Wharncliffe Transport, Wharncliffe True Crime and White Owl.

For a complete list of Pen & Sword titles please contact

PEN & SWORD BOOKS LIMITED
47 Church Street, Barnsley, South Yorkshire, S70 2AS, England
E-mail: enquiries@pen-and-sword.co.uk
Website: www.pen-and-sword.co.uk

Or

PEN AND SWORD BOOKS
1950 Lawrence Rd, Havertown, PA 19083, USA
E-mail: Uspen-and-sword@casematepublishers.com
Website: www.penandswordbooks.com

Contents

Introduction: The Need for King Arthur

The Arthurian story, the 'Matter of Britain', has long exercised a fascination over writers and their public – a career of over eight hundred years in the English imagination and longer in Wales. But it has equally been a matter of controversy among 'serious' historians, who have been at odds with the literary romancers at least since the time around 1125 when the monastic chronicler William of Malmesbury was separating the 'real' Arthur from the literary edifice created around him. Already at this point the implausibilities in the myths surrounding the warrior-king were being used to suggest that he had never existed. Unlike the parallel 'Matter of France' surrounding the career and exploits of the late eighth-century Frankish hero-king Charles 'the Great', a.k.a. 'Charlemagne' (crowned Emperor in 800), Arthur had no definitive place in the history and royal genealogies of his people. He had not founded a verifiable empire and long-lasting dynasty as Charles had done, and even his exact dates were uncertain. When he first emerged in the historical consciousness of the new Anglo-Norman kingdom of England in the early twelfth-century, romancers presented him as a ruler of 'Britain' (and an ever-wider empire like Charles') in the period following the end of Roman rule in AD 410. Even in the context of Welsh oral and literary myth where he was a major figure from the ninth-century onwards, he was not given a precise geographical context or clear career as a 'fixed' member of a prominent dynasty. He was a hero fighting monsters and Otherwordly foes in Welsh myth as well as in mediaeval knightly tales – a fact which recent 'debunkers' have enthusiastically latched onto.

Unlike France where Charles' empire was the verifiable forerunner of the contemporary French kingdom and he was the ancestor of its kings, Arthur's 'Britain' was separated from contemporary Britain by a gulf of time and culture. Not only was Arthur seen as ruling around 600 years before William's time, 300 years before Charles, but 'his' Britain had been a conglomerate of obscure post-Roman kingdoms subsequently conquered by the ancestors of the English. The 'Anglo-Saxon' peoples conquered by the Normans in 1066, whose coming to Britain from north-west Germany in Arthur's time was chronicled by Bede in the 730s, had no political or cultural/'ethnic' connection to Arthur and his subjects, unlike the twelfth-century French had with Charles and his empire. Indeed, there was no mention of Arthur in Bede's meticulously detailed account of the foundation of the Anglo-Saxon kingdoms; details of his exploits in battle against the Anglo-Saxons had only survived in the patchy chronicles and later mythologizing of the conquered British. These peoples, referred to as the 'Welsh' ('foreigners') by the Anglo-Saxons, had not even spoken the same language as the Germanic incomers and were believed to have been driven out of what became 'England' into the western hills of Cornwall and Wales. Bede was dimly aware of the British 'fight-back' against the Anglo-Saxons, their leader Ambrosius Aurelianus, and their victory at 'Mount Badon'; and the 820s Welsh Church writer Nennius was aware of the legendary wars of 'Hengest' in fifth-century Kent. But no such common agreement as to perceived 'fact' involved Arthur.

So the new 'Matter of Britain' presented a major problem from its creation; its hero had fought against, not for, the ancestors of the majority of its readership in twelfth-century England. It was noticeable that English interest in Arthur only became apparent after the Norman Conquest, as the new Europe-wide literary culture of knightly 'chivalry' (centred on France) took hold in England. Before 1066, the secular national literary culture in Anglo-Saxon England seems to have centred on heroic Germanic poetry on Northern Continental themes – as with the epic of Beowulf, presented as a king of the Swedish 'Geats' in the early sixth-century. Religious literary culture was centred on the 'foundation-myth' of the English Church as transmitted by Bede – a picture in which Christianity came to a pagan England from Papal Rome in 597 and there was no mention of post-Roman Christian Britain or its kings. Cultural contact with the actual political heirs of 'Arthurian' Britain, the Welsh kingdoms of the West, was minimal and marked by incomprehension and hostility. Coincidentally or not, the Norman conquest of 1066 not only saw lowland Britain's conquerors conquered in turn; it brought to England an important group of Breton lords and knights in Duke William's train, from a people descended from British expatriates of Arthur's time who had settled in Brittany. Interest in Arthur and pre-Saxon Britain escalated under the new Norman kings and ruling class, not least as they launched a comprehensive conquest of lands in Wales which brought the new rulers and settlers of the 'March' there into close contact with the Welsh. The first great fabulator of Arthurian stories in the twelfth-century, Geoffrey of Monmouth, came from this area of cultural mix – and may have had Breton blood; and the other great twelfth-century creator of new 'Arthur' stories in a contemporary setting, Chretien de Troyes, may also have had access to Breton legends in northern France.

Equally importantly, the idea of a powerful British king ruling over many sub-kings – and in due course Continental lands – was to answer the political needs of the Anglo-Norman kings of the early twelfth-century. The creation of a joint rule of the kingdom of England with his ancestral Duchy of Normandy in 1106 brought Henry I a realm straddling the Channel and the first beginnings of a Continental dominion which was to endure until the loss of Calais in 1558. The Duke of Normandy (and later the Count of Anjou and Duke of Aquitaine), the English kings' Continental titles, remained titular vassals of the King of France, descendant of Emperor Charles. Creating the idea of an equally powerful and wide-ruling ancestor for the English Kings to match Charles was a valuable asset, even if it so happened that 'Arthur' was not 'English' at all. Equally, in linguistic terms he was not unambiguously a 'King' to the first Welsh writers to mention him. e.g. 'Nennius' c.829. The use of this term to denote sovereignty was Germanic and only came into existence after the Anglo-Saxon political and linguistic takeover of his realm. Assuming that he had had royal status at all (which the Welsh literary sources left ambiguous), his royal title would have been expressed in Latin or a British language and in fourth/fifth-century Late Roman terminology.

The differences between the mythical and any 'original' Arthur

Arthur was primarily seen as the epitome of a mediaeval chivalric order by the most detailed writers and poets to cover his career, from Geoffrey of Monmouth in the 1130s to Sir Thomas Malory in the 1460s. Writers thought of him in contemporary terminology, without a thought about any concept of anachronism. A paragon of kingly virtues and arguably developed as a British counterpart to the great French hero-king (and multi-national ruler) 'Charlemagne', he was the British member of a select body of mediaeval Christian heroes, the chivalric 'Seven Worthies'. The updating of his setting to a contemporary one was not an unusual phenomenon either, as seen by the French treatment of Charlemagne and his nephew as proto-leaders of the 'Reconquista' in Spain. The centrepiece of Arthur's literary presentation was his magnificent and well-attended court, from the mid-twelfth-century placed at 'Camelot' – though by French writers but at Caerleon by the better-informed 'local' Geoffrey of Monmouth. Initially Arthur's military career was the centrepiece of the stories, with Geoffrey presenting him as conqueror of much of Europe and defeater of the Romans. The French writers from Chretien de Troyes moved attention to the knightly virtues that predominated at his court and told tales of his knights' exploits, many of them symbolic and/or involving magic and Otherworldly figures. The 'Round Table', first referred to in the mid-twelfth-century by Jersey mythographer Wace (see Chapter Three), came to be the lynchpin for a chivalric order of knights dedicated to using their prowess to aid women, the poor, and the downtrodden against injustice – and thus served as a template of an ideal for contemporary knights to follow in the 'Age of Chivalry'. To add to the identification of Arthur with what his twentieth-century interpreter T.H. White called 'the Middle Ages as they should have been', the visual imagery presented by the illustrators of Arthurian romances also showed his Court in contemporary clothing and buildings. The concept of anachronism was not one with which such writers were familiar – or which they saw any need to correct. This contrast between the 'real' and the literary Arthur has continued to the present day.

All of this was of course not the world of a real ruler of the late fifth or sixth-century, the period in which the few historical references placed the 'real' Arthur. It was accepted that Arthur's place in history belonged in the fifth-century after the fall of the Western Roman Empire, but where real people were used they were shadowy figures from the post-Roman origins of mediaeval dynasties. The errors and fabulations began early, and cannot be blamed on the example set by Geoffrey of Monmouth; before him William of Malmesbury was already complaining of this.[1] It is now argued that even the early Welsh references to Arthur (none contemporary) were as much affected by the need to 'create' an inspiring hero for the writers' own times as were the twelfth-century and later literary effusions. Their Arthur was as divorced from fifth-century and sixth-century reality as much as Malory's. The search for a 'real' Arthur thus has its problems, principally of the objectivity of all the authors who wrote about him. The search is less straightforward than used to be assumed when twentieth-century enthusiasts believed that the real ruler could be found by ignoring the anachronistic mediaeval stories in favour of 'genuinely historical' early Welsh writings. This scenario was gleefully savaged by literary experts who had more knowledge of what these early authors' 'mindsets' were. But in any case even the written evidence we have on the late fifth and early sixth-century, presumed to be Arthur's correct dating from the early stories of his wars with the invading 'Anglo-Saxons', is mostly later although one near-contemporary poem, the *Goddodin* of the early seventh-century, refers to him as a figure already known as a great warrior.[2] Sceptics have long been able to make the most of the omission of Arthur's name from the one 'historical' – though polemical – work on his presumed era of the early sixth-century, by Gildas (either British or Breton in location). The first written account of his activities, undated but placed some time in the later fifth-century by inference, is in the Welsh '*Historia Brittonum*', attributed to the early ninth-century Gwynedd cleric Nennius.[3] The first dating of Arthur's military career is a brief statement in the mid-tenth-century *Annales Cambriae*, a patchy chronicle of important events through the post-Roman period, where it is stated that he won a major victory over the Saxons at 'Mount Badon' in 516/18 and was killed at Camlann with 'Medraut' twenty-one years later.[4] The context of the reference in a mainly ecclesiastical work, full of transcribed Irish rather than local Welsh detail, has also led to sceptics doubting its authenticity. Was it a direct copy of 'Nennius'? The greater detail given earlier about Arthur's wars by 'Nennius' has been re-assessed recently as being as much a piece of political propaganda as the twelfth-century writings of Geoffrey of Monmouth. (See the analyses by Oliver Padel, 1994 and 2000, and Nicholas Higham, 2000.) In addition, the space that Nennius gave to miraculous phenomenena in his 'Mirabilia' suggested that he was a mythographer, not a historian (as we would see the term). But any consideration of the 'real' Arthur and the myths constructed around him must first consider the politico-military context – the decades following the end of Roman Britain in AD 410.

In recent decades much of what we thought we 'knew' about this period has been reassessed, not least the question of the Anglo-Saxon 'invasions'. Was there really a wholesale invasion and takeover of what is now England by waves of settlers from north-west Germany, as claimed by the nearest contemporary writer Gildas around 540? The DNA for southern Britain shows some (but not overwhelming) Continental presence – but not if this is pre- or post-Roman. And does the archaeological and linguistic evidence of a new Germanic culture in Britain from the fifth-century justify accepting the literary stories of a mass-migration and over a century of struggle between Britons and Anglo-Saxons, in which Arthur played a crucial role? Some enthusiasts for a 'positive' interpretation of history would even claim that the concept of mass-invasions by Germans is wrong and change was due to trade/'fashion', though this appears to be too radical. Establishing evidence of continuity and analysing the motives of apocalyptic contemporary historians is not proof that the traditional picture is totally inaccurate. There is abundant evidence of material decline in living-standards throughout the West, and evidence of a new 'German' culture in Britain – especially language – surely indicates political disruption. There is still a place for a British warlord fighting the Saxons and impressing his inheritors enough to be celebrated for centuries in literary culture.

Chapter 1

Arthur In History: Arthur's Real Context: The End of Roman Britain

(i) Overview: the end of one (Romano-British) culture and the emergence of another (German)

The context for Arthur's traditional 'timeline', in Britain after the end of Roman rule, was long accepted by mainline historians as a basic story of the replacement of one politico-social/ethnic culture (Romano-British) by another ('Anglo-Saxon' ie Germanic) in lowland Britain between 400 and 650 (Common Era/AD). Nowadays that is being challenged, and suggestions have been made that there was no major replacement of one ethnic grouping by another – traditionally by invasion – but a case of a different culture emerging by a mixture of immigration, trade and 'fashion'. This would undermine the very idea of Arthur as a Romano-British military leader fighting to hold back apparent 'hordes' of invading Anglo-Saxons, which has been seen as the reason for his fame from the time of ninth-century (?) Welsh monastic author 'Nennius' onwards. This is still contentious, as the language of post-Roman society in Britain certainly became Germanic ('Old English') even if modern studies of DNA seem to indicate that the notion of 'ethnic cleansing' by incoming Germans has been over-emphasised. But the history of post-Roman Britain is certainly an area of major contention, not least from the lack of definite and unchallengable 'facts'.

The former province of Britain, divided into two by Emperor Septimius Severus around 208 and into five in Diocletian's reforms in the 290s, owed allegiance to that Emperor ruling the extreme West of the Empire until 410. The Empire had been divided into two by Diocletian, with its capitals eventually being fixed at Rome/Milan for the west and Constantinople for the East. However there was at times a further division of sovereignty in the west, with a separate ruler at Trier governing west of the Alps, and in those cases he was the man recognised in Britain. The end of Roman rule in Britain is traditionally dated at 410, due to a letter which the Western Emperor Honorius sent to the civic authorities of a province – probably Britain, though Bruttia in Italy has been suggested. They were seeking to resume recognition of him as legitimate ruler and asked for troops, having given allegiance to the usurper Constantine III in 407, but were told to look to their own defences as the Empire had enough of a crisis at home in Italy with the invading Goths. From this point – or arguably from the rebellion of Constantine III in Britain in 407 – the island was detached from the rest of the west and did not owe allegiance to the current Western Emperor. Roman administration however continued in Northern Gaul across the Channel into the 450s, with the Western commander-in-chief Aetius (in power from 433–54 under Valentinian III) campaigning there at times against marauding Germans who had been at large west of the Rhine since a mass-crossing in the winter of 405–6. The question of what Roman political or commercial influence, if any, was retained in Britain after the Western Empire restored order to its nearest region (northern Gaul) in the early 410s is unclear. But no coins of the post-410 Emperors have been found in Britain, and it is logical that the end of a former system whereby estates in Britain supplied corn to the Roman army on the lower Rhine caused economic distress to the suppliers – the larger southern British 'villa' estates. In literary tradition in the Romano-British 'successor states' in Wales, however, the decisive break was seen as coming with rebel Emperor Magnus Maximus taking the army to Gaul in 383, not Constantine III (who was forgotten).

In 451 the invasion of Gaul by Attila the Hun, overlord of a vast 'empire' of tribes from the Rhine to the Ukrainian steppes, was met by a coalition of Aetius' Romans and local Germanic settlers (principally the West Gothic kingdom of Toulouse, established in 418) and defeated in battle at the 'Campus Mauriacus' near Chalons in Champagne. Roman rule of Northern Gaul ended after Aetius was murdered by his jealous sovereign Valentinian III in autumn 454 and the Empire's authority in the province collapsed, though Aetius' former lieutenant Aegidius and his successor Syagrius maintained a semi-Roman kingdom based at Soissons until Clovis' Franks overran it in 486. Roman rule in Southern Gaul lasted into the late 460s, threatened by the expanding Gothic kingdom in Aquitaine, and it will be seen that a British army (led by one candidate for the role of 'Arthur') was campaigning against the

Germans in alliance with the Western Empire around 468. The careers of Aegidius and Syagrius as post-Roman warlords leading a Roman-trained, Roman-style army (much of it cavalry) to keep the world of Romano-Gallic civilization free of 'barbarian' German invaders is a template for historians' and writers' guesses about what happened in Britain, where written evidence is much more sketchy. Plausibly, the mid-late fifth-century British war-leader Ambrosius – called 'last of the Romans' and of 'noble Roman blood' by Gildas – was similar to these two commanders; but was 'Arthur'?

Literary sources and archaeology agree that Roman 'civilization' in Britain did not come to a sudden end although formal, Imperial authority did. The pattern of Late Roman urban and rural life continued without major disruption probably to the 440s; in fact the size and presumed prosperity of towns had been shrinking though the later fourth century and no new urban buildings can be dated to this period. (Some historians argue that 'urban' civilization was never an organic 'British' institution but only a forcible Roman cultural import, alien to the majority of the elite as well as the rural farming majority who continued to live under Rome as before, and quickly declined.) The heavy Late Roman tax-burden for an inflated army and civil service has been blamed for causing a 'flight to the countryside' by the rich, who had previously been responsible for constructing and maintaining civic buildings. The main difference after 407/410 seems to have been that the Late Roman British agricultural economy had been geared to providing corn (and other supplies?) for export to the rest of the Empire, in particular for the huge army based on the Rhine. This ceased with the Roman loss of control of the area from the invasions of 406, and increased insecurity in German-ravaged Gaul impeded all trade with the Continent. The later fourth and early fifth-century saw the decline of the great rural 'villa' estates in southern Britain and the abandonment of their sprawling residential complexes, some of them quite late in building-date (e.g. the villa at Lullingstone in Kent with its Christian mosaics). The abandonment of these estates used to be linked to the caches of coin-hoards found across the region and the literary evidence of ravaging by Saxons, Irish, and Picts found in Gildas. It was presumed that most had been either burnt down by raiders or abandoned. The West Saxons' later, ninth-century *Chronicle* noted that in 418 the Britons had 'assembled all the gold-hoards that were in Britain, and hid some in the earth so that nobody could find them, and the rest they took with them into Gaul'.[1]

This evidence, backed up by signs of fire at some villas, could be interpreted as meaning a wave of raids by hordes of invading 'barbarians' and a collapse of civilization, with villas and their leisured aristocratic lifestyle abandoned. Accordingly, early and mid-twentieth-century historians could create a comprehensive picture of the collapse of an entire civilization of Roman Britain in the years after the great triple raid of Saxons, 'Picts' from Scotland, and Irish on Britain testified to by Ammianus Marcellinus for 367.[2] This had been fought off by Roman troops sent from the Continent, but only after serious military losses and apparent looting of the countryside (and some less-well-defended towns?). Ravening bands of pirates were supposed to have systematically ruined rural Britain by burning all its villas, and illustrations were duly created for textbooks of such sackings to show the end of Roman civilization. A whole edifice was created on the assumption that every fire in the later fourth-century was the work of invaders, although villas built of wood as well as stone would logically have been vulnerable to accidents. Nowadays the latter fact is given due recognition, although the undeniable existence of a multiplicity of hoards of coins and silverware testifies to a much larger degree of political and military instability around 400 in which wealthy people found it advisable to hide their valuables and could not always reclaim them. Meanwhile, more is made of the number of smaller, 'Iron Age'-style farms (the 'norm' in north and west) across Britain, the signs of continuity in land-use into the fifth-century, and the lack of evidence of mass-burnings in town or countryside.[3] The use of round-huts and circular enclosures of farm-buildings was similar to that used in pre-Roman sites, so this was assumed to be an indigenous form of building which was eclipsed by the more 'advanced', Italian-style Roman buildings with rectangular houses and larger villas.

The ending of political control from the Continent at the time of Constantine III's revolt in 407, coupled with the insecurity caused by wandering bands of Germanic peoples across Gaul once the Rhine was crossed at New Year 406, meant that access to metals was restricted. Once the useable mines in Britain had been exhausted, or the ability of Britain's rulers to recruit miners and moneyers ended, coins could not be struck. Moreover, it had been the Imperial government that owned and manned the mines, providing the impetus to dig, and the army and bureaucrats who were paid in the coins. Once central political authority collapsed and governance was a much more localised affair, it seems that nobody was interested in maintaining the mines. Trade must have been by barter, and was probably local from the lack of any post-410 Roman coins from Gaul in circulation. What is very noticeable is that no coins have been found in Britain bearing the names of Roman Emperors after Honorius (probably) instructed the British civic authorities to look to their own defences in 410, or the names of British rulers. The sudden break implies an atomisation of the political structure and a narrowing of political horizons.

But it is not certain that the absence of coinage in finds shows a precise date for the abandonment of coins as a means of trade or expressing political control and propaganda. The most that can be said is that coins were in use until 407/10 at the earliest, and that the balance of probability is in favour of people using near-contemporary coins for at least some transactions. Sites still in use until c.410 should have at least a few late fourth-century coins, even though some earlier ones may have been in use as greater political insecurity meant a decline in production of new ones. If no coins from after c.380 are found at a site, it was probably not still in use twenty to thirty years later. If coins dating from c.407–10 are found at a site, logically the residents would not have been using these coins more than a couple of decades later. As far as villas geared to large-scale agricultural production for the Roman army are concerned, the numbers of troops on the Rhine and thus the amount of food-supplies needed may have already been in decline before 400 – particularly after the civil wars of 383–8 and 392–4 when rebel Western emperors in Gaul (the first a commander from Britain, Magnus Maximus) challenged the Emperors ruling in Italy. The economic usefulness of the villas as centres of agricultural production was therefore declining at this time, even without 'barbarian' raids. Logically, the decline in prosperity would mean that new buildings from after c.383–400 would be smaller and cheaper; there were not adequate resources to build on the scale of earlier decades once the villa-estates were no longer supplying the Rhine armies. Building would be in wood not stone, and even without the insecurity caused by seaborne raids it would be more difficult to find or pay skilled stonemasons in post-Roman Britain. Did a decline in skills as well as lack of need affect building as well as the making of coins? On the available evidence of Continental developments after the parallel end of Roman rule there, the scale and skill of building suffered a substantial decline in the later fifth-century.[4] In Britain, it is now suggested that the development of post-Roman wooden 'hall'-buildings at rural sites was as much the work of British craftsmen in the fifth-century as the incoming 'Anglo-Saxons' who were traditionally supposed to have built in wood as a new departure from Romano-British practices. There are large wooden structures in towns still in British hands around 500, principally Viroconium (Wroxeter) in the upper Severn valley.[5] Thus we cannot now use the discovery of wooden buildings ascribed to an approximate date to say that these 'must' have been Germanic rather than British in origin, and the approximate 'frontiers' between Briton and Anglo-Saxon drawn up by twentieth-century historians using archaeological evidence now seem even less accurate.

The hiding of coin-hoards at residential sites certainly implies insecurity, probably due to the attacks to which 540s (probably) monastic writer Gildas testifies, and so does the finding of Late Roman collections of gold and silver objects as at Mildenhall. It is significant that even if local society did survive well into the fifth-century no more coins were issued on behalf of whoever ruled in Britain. The will or the technology had been lost, and trade within British society must have been carried on satisfactorily by barter. The question of a declining population needing less trade or foreign imports is less clear, as we cannot even be certain of the size of the Late Roman population – three to five million? The literary 'evidence' of mass-slaughter is problematic, as will be seen later, though some substantial exodus seems to have taken place to Armorica/Brittany by the 460s. (The specific number of 12,000 given for the menfolk of 'Riothamus' British or Breton following in 469 is the only contemporary calculation of the size of 'British' manpower).[6] Nor is it clear how badly the population of Britain was affected by the catastrophic plague of the late 540s, which in comparable societies caused major disruption in Ireland and the loss of half the population of Constantinople, the East Roman capital.[7] The East Roman historian Procopius had acquired some garbled information in the 550s about an island in the British Isles being abandoned by the living[8] – was this a reference to the plague, or just local myth? Was this epidemic the crucial blow to a relatively populous and economically flourishing Britain of the fifth-century and early sixth-century, in which the end of Roman rule and coinage did not imply chaos and mass-slaughter as per Gildas? Was the real break in socio-cultural continuity the plague in the 540s, not the end of Roman political control? On a local level, the basic regional agricultural economy – which fed into local not international export – would have suffered more from a serious loss of population than from an end to exports to Gaul and Italy. Is it a coincidence that the next major series of Saxon advances in southern England recorded by the ninth-century *Anglo-Saxon Chronicle*, e.g. of the 'Gewissae' of Wessex in Wiltshire, occurred in the 550s – after plague had weakened their enemies? All this has implications for the understanding of British society in the era to which 'Arthur' and his wars have been connected.

British rulers and towns

Were these post-Roman states ruled by 'kings' – in the sense of single rulers, who would have used the Brittonic word 'brenin' or Latin 'rex'? (Technically any 'Arthur' as a sovereign in British-ruled territory would have been called 'Brenin' or 'Rex' not the Anglo-Saxon 'Konung' ie 'King'.) Was there any surviving authority above the level of the small Late Roman provinces – most probably some form of military co-ordination by a successful commander such as the most logical role for an 'Arthur'? Can any trust be placed in the later literary stories of post-Roman British kings, which were implicitly believed for centuries but are now savaged by historians as answering mediaeval political needs, not being 'real' history?[9] Around 540 the polemicist Gildas, the first British 'historian', wrote that the Britons had taken up arms to defeat the combined threats of Picts, Irish, and Germanic raiders immediately after the end of Roman rule and been successful: 'the British peoples took up arms, bore the brunt of the attack, and freed their cities from the barbarian threat'.[10]

This left open the possibility of a revival of the mobile 'field army' that the overall commander of the five Roman provinces in Britain, the 'Count of Britain', was recorded as possessing in the later fourth-century. This army would have needed a commander, but did he have any civil authority too? Co-ordination of successful defence could then translate into some form of civil authority, as in Northern Gaul after the end of direct Roman rule in 455 when the 'field-commander' Aegidius succeeded to rule of a 'kingdom' which lasted for several decades. This sort of super-provincial authority might lie behind the early mediaeval British (and later Anglo-Norman) stories of a succession of 'High Kings' ruling in Britain from c.410.

Did any surviving Roman officials retain control of their provinces, particularly in the more settled and urban south-east? Or did the civic authorities rule autonomous local towns where these were wealthy enough to survive as independent institutions? There were provincial 'councils' of aristocrats to assist the governors across the Empire, the joint council of the Gallic provinces lasting into the 470s despite the loss of control of parts of the area to local Germanic 'kingdoms' from 418 onwards and growing brigandage from incoming Germans and bands of rootless peasant brigands ('Bacaudae'). A joint council of senior figures in the five British provinces in and after 410 is logically possible, and is implied by what Gildas says about decisions by the local authorities to fight the Saxon, Pictish, and Irish raiders after the end of central authority from Rome. But he also has kings who were 'anointed… and soon afterwards slain' by their supporters,[11] an indication of tradition by c.545 believing that (unstable) royal rule dated to soon after the end of Roman rule. Gildas notably says that civil wars had continued after the British defeated the Saxons at 'Mount Badon',[12] implying that there was inter-state instability whenever and wherever he was writing rather than a region at peace. On an archaeological level, the construction of the post-Roman 'Wansdyke' ditch in northern Somerset and Wiltshire – facing north and probably protecting a kingdom to its south, in the territory of the 'Dumnonii' – could imply a local threat from the north, possibly a kingdom in the Cotwolds where there were no 'Anglo-Saxon' farms or villages this early so its rulers were presumably post-Roman Britons.

On a lower level, each Roman 'civitas' had its own council of wealthy citizens, many of them landed aristocrats whose wealth lay in the countryside but who had 'town houses' too – to administer its affairs and its rural hinterland. This system of 'low-level' autonomy was one on which the poorly-staffed central government had relied for much of its control by local elites under the Early Empire. Since the reforms of the 280s additional layers of bureaucracy had been created at the provincial level, along with more, smaller provinces and a new level of 'vicarates' (groups of provinces) between the provinces and the central government. The civic elites, as a privileged but burdened legal entity which maintained the physical structure of the towns from their own resources, corporately provided the necessary tax-revenues for the central government – which grew increasingly burdensome under the Later Empire with far more officials and a huge army (c.300,000 according to some estimates) to sustain. The exorbitant cost to the civic classes – already reduced in numbers by plague and ruinous plundering by third-century raiders and civil wars – has been cited as one reason for the decline of urban civilization in the fourth-century and fifth-century, at least in the West which had fewer towns to share the cost than the longer-urbanised East. But Britain had largely escaped ravages by Germanic marauders or being fought over in the mid-third-century, when it formed part of the 'breakaway' empire of Postumus and Tetricus in the west from 260–73 and was not fought over except in 296, and was prosperous and settled in the fourth-century as shown by the large south-eastern British villas. It had provided large-scale agricultural supplies to the army on the Rhine, although the effects of Saxon, Pictish, and Irish raids in the 360s – particularly a joint attack in 367 – were regarded as serious by the contemporary historian Ammianus Marcellinus. But the increased level of raids on coastal areas need not have caused major disruption to civic or rural life outside the affected areas, and nowadays is regarded as less serious than it once was. Towns were walled and the countryside could recover from raids, as it had in Gaul after major ravages in the third-century, though there were long-term effects of any major disruption (as in 367) in terms of abandoned estates reducing prosperity. The economic realities of the end of supplies to the Roman army on the Continent after the abandonment of the Rhine frontier in 406 would probably have been a more decisive blow to large-scale production of agricultural surpluses by large villa-estates. The insecurity caused by roaming bands of Germans, rebellious peasants, and opportunistic brigands across Gaul from then onwards would have decreased 'export' trade from British towns and the countryside, even when nominal Roman control of most of Gaul had recovered in the mid-410s.

It is uncertain to what extent trade may have developed with the Germanic peoples in North-West Europe to compensate for this. Nowadays it is argued that the growth in Germanic goods found at sites in Eastern Britain could reflect trade as much as the presence of Germanic settlers. The same settlers could have moved into the region before rather than after 410, if the so-called 'Saxon Shore' in south-eastern England (with its chain of coastal fortresses in use in the later third and fourth-century) meant shore settled by Germanic mercenaries in Late Roman Imperial service rather than one threatened by Saxons. Certainly, some of the earliest 'Germanic' sites exacavated for the fifth century (featuring distinctive non-'Roman' forms of burial and cruciform brooches of non-Roman design similar to those from Germany) were not on the coast. Groupings of sites quickly developed in eastern England in south-western Norfolk, the Fens, Lincolnshire, and the east of Leicestershire as well as on the Essex and Kent coasts, with an apparent link to the Icknield Way road South-West from the Wash. By the mid-late fifth-century there were 'Germanic' villages in southern Oxfordshire far inland, around Sutton Courtenay and Wallingford on the upper Thames. Were these the homes of traders or mercenaries who had been allowed to move there by allied locals or who had seized land? Or, as some would now argue, the homes of long-resident 'British' who had just happened to adopt 'Germanic' clothing, decoration and household objects for everyday use – presumably from Germanic traders who had replaced ones from Roman Gaul.

The modern notion of a peaceful acculturation of fifth-century Britons to new Germanic fashions seems rather optimistic, and begs the question of why these 'fashions' were adopted from a people who were still 'pagan' in religion (unlike the British elite) and spoke a different language. There had indeed been many – usually Christianised – Germans in the service of the Later Roman Empire in the fourth-century and fifth-century, including great generals such as Stilicho (a Vandal). But there is no literary sign of trade between pre-410 Britain and the Germanic peoples; where the two inter-act this is exclusively violent, as in the 367 Saxon/Pictish/Irish attacks on Britain. There is no indication of the local 'Romanised' peoples of the Western Empire wanting to adopt Germanic goods and manners, rather of Germans attempting to become Romanised. After the Germanic invasions of the West and the transfer of power to new German leaders it was said that the rich Goths wanted to copy the Romans and only the poor Romans wanted to copy the Goths.[13] There is no written evidence of this assumed trade, which would have had to be large-scale for decades to produce a widespread adoption of 'German' culture by the

British. 'Cross-cultural' Romano-British influence on the Germans in the fifth and sixth-century was small – most crucially in the field of religion. The Roman Empire of the fourth-century had been a magnet for ambitious German warriors and refugee farmers (most notably the Goths after the seizure of their lands on the trans-Danube steppes by the Huns c.376). In return the Roman Church had sought to convert these pagans to Christianity, causing generations of religio-political problems to the new fifth-century German kingdoms as the 'Arian' theology professed by the men who converted them resulted in 'Arian' German kings being alienated from their Catholic subjects in the former Western Empire. But even if the post-Roman British did trade with the Germans and import their 'high-status' goods, found in graves across Eastern England, it had no impact on the Germans' resolute adherence to their ancestral religion in their new settlements in Britain. The Romano-British Christians and their Irish co-religionists made no known effort to convert the Germans – surely they would have done so had they been regular and friendly trading-partners? The Church in Gaul, after all, made a conscious effort to convert the leadership of their new neighbours-cum-overlords, the Frankish Merovingian kingdom north of the Loire under Clovis (d. 511), in the late fifth-century. There is no evidence of a parallel move to 'civilise' the new Anglo-Saxon polities in Britain. The Anglian Church historian Bede (d. 735) may have 'down-played' the survival of local British Christians in Jutish Kent as of 597, to increase the glory of his Roman missionary hero St Augustine in carrying out conversions there. But the one reference to Augustine meeting some British clerics has him travelling a long distance West, traditionally to Aust near Bristol (via Cerne Abbas in Dorset?), and having a hostile reception as the clerics interpreted his refusal to stand up when they arrived as evidence of typical Roman Church arrogance.[14]

Continuity between 'Roman' and 'Anglo-Saxon' worlds despite the literary evidence?

The abandonment of the large 'Romanised' villas around 400, some after fires which were automatically put down to hostile action by raiding Germans or revolting tenants, used to be assumed as graphic and conclusive evidence of a 'collapse' of Roman civilization across Britain caused by warfare. But the latest analysis of the countryside of Late Roman Britain is less pessimistic, pointing out that the number of large villas was not that great even in the South-East; most agricultural properties were smaller, traditional farms (which in a worst-case scenario were easier to rebuild and resume functioning after attacks than the complex and expensive villa-estates). Large-scale villas were few, and the traditional Iron Age 'round-houses' used in smaller farms continued to be built through the Roman era. There is no evidence of any abandonment of these farms to Germanic raiding in the early fifth-century, with most of the British countryside continuing to function as normal – and continuity in the use of certain sites, e.g. around Peterborough and in Essex (Mucking), directly into 'Anglo-Saxon' farms with no evidence of violence.[15] The end in use of the larger villas can be explained as a pragmatic reaction to the fact that the large Roman army on the Rhine (and Roman administration) had ceased to exist and thus their produce, corn in particular, was no longer needed for export. (See above.) The wealthy landed classes of post-Roman Britain thus could have been intact to provide local leadership well after 410, even if living in smaller residences. Equally, the main towns of Roman Britain seem to have been functioning in the early fifth-century, as administrative as well as residential centres, albeit on a smaller scale than in the prosperous days of the second century. Their physical survival is shown by the fact that so many of them re-emerged as administrative and trading-centres under the 'Germanic' kingdoms by the seventh and eighth-century – the new kingdoms' 'county towns' were often Roman ones, such as Canterbury (Durovernum), Chichester (Noviomagus), Winchester (Venta Belgarum), Dorchester (Durnovaria), Exeter (Isca Dumnoniorum), Colchester (Camulodunum), Gloucester (Glevum), and Lincoln (Lindum).

Decline was gradual not dramatic, with damaged buildings not being repaired; the only signs of damage by fire, particularly near walls and gates so logically by invaders, was near the East coast – most noticeably at Caistor near Norwich.[16] Coincidently or not, Caistor never became a Saxon town and the new inhabitants' polities were based on Thetford (Norfolk) and around Rendlesham (Suffolk). Were towns with no archaeological evidence of violent attack despite a local Germanic presence (eg Venta Belgarum/Winchester) more likely to survive? These towns would logically have relied on a restricted degree of local trade, with food-supplies coming in from the country estates of the wealthier inhabitants, in place of the cross-Empire trade of the decades before instability hit Gaul after 406. Their upper classes would have continued to provide civic and religious leadership, as with the parallel of immediately post-Roman Gaul in the 470s testified to in the writings of Sidonius Apollinaris. In that parallel situation the local aristocrats of Sidonius' Auvergne organised private armies to hold back raiding Germans, including cavalry mounted on horses provided from their estates. Is this what Gildas implies took place in Britain after 410, and so should we look for a cavalry-commanding 'Arthur' doing this? Nor should we assume that just because the names of post-Roman civic leaders and bishops have not survived there were no such men. Gildas was writing a literary polemic about wicked rulers not a historic record of fact, and is noticeably lacking in giving names (even of rulers). Nor was the next historian to write on post-Roman Britain, Bede in the 730s, interested in giving an account of what had transpired in politics and religion until the coming of the English settlers (from '449') and the Catholic missionaries (from 597).

The Romans had often divided up provinces into administrative districts based on the local tribal entities which had existed before their conquest, as with those of the Treveri (around Trier, 'Augusta Treverorum') and Parisii (around Paris) in northern Gaul.

Logically this would have been the same in Britain, where the re-emergence of the territory of the 'Cantii' who had faced Caesar in Kent in 55 BC as a distinct geographical/administrative area in the fifth-century shows that such divisions had been preserved through the Roman era. By this logic, it is probable that in the post-Roman south-east the main civic authorities would have been based at the earlier Roman towns that had been 'capitals' of local administrative districts – e.g. Noviomagus (Chichester) for the former lands of the '*Regni*', Venta Belgarum (Winchester) for the '*Belgae*', Calleva (Silchester) for the '*Atrebates*', Durnovaria (Dorchester) for the '*Durotriges*', Isca Dumnoniorum (Exeter) for the 'Dumnonii', Corinium (Cirencester) for the '*Dobunni*', Lindum (Lincoln) for the '*Coritani*', Isca (Caistor-by-Norwich) for the '*Iceni*', Caesaromagus (Chelmsford) for the '*Trinovantes*', and Viroconium (Wroxeter) for the '*Cornovii*'. Either Camulodunum (Colchester) or Verulamium (St Albans, now a major Christian shrine) would have served for the '*Catuvellauni*', former leaders of resistance to Caesar in 55–4 BC and Claudius in AD 43. The early nature of Anglian settlement in East Anglia – where archaeologists have found many fifth-century grave-sites containing Germanic artefacts – may have obscured a re-emerging 'Icenic' tribal-based polity after 410, or the destruction of the tribal identity and landed classes after the revolt of 60–1 may have 'atomised' society. Possibly the evidence of large, well-organised agricultural estates in the Fenland – drained by central government effort under the Empire – indicates Imperially-owned estates, producing grain for the Roman army on the Rhine, and thus no local aristocracy to take power after 410. The fact that the area around Verulamium remained British to c. 571 (the date of conquest in the *Anglo-Saxon Chronicle*) despite the nearby Germanic settlements may indicate a determined 'corporate' effort to maintain autonomy by the post-Roman 'Catuvellaunian' tribal landowners. Its survival as an entity also suggests that there was no determined, long-term effort by its 'Saxon' neighbours to east, north and west to eradicate it; the region was clearly a 'patchwork' of British and 'Germanic' political territories with no powerful state of either 'ethnic' affiliation able to overrun the area. This pattern may have been more common across Britain than was assumed in the simplistic adoption of Gildas' statements about widespread chaos and conquest by c. 545.

In South Wales, Venta Silurum (Caerwent) probably served as administrative centre of the Roman and post-Roman 'civitas' of the Silures. The three original Roman 'coloni' (settlements of soldiers granted autonomous civic status) – Camulodunum (Colchester), Glevum (Gloucester), and Eboracum (York) also had their own councils under Roman rule and would logically have assumed local authority after the end of central-appointed Imperial governorships. York in particular had the advantage of being the major Legionary fortress in the north since the 70s AD, and being the capital of the second British province established c.208 by Emperor Septimius Severus; it was the 'capital' of a British kingdom to c.580, and possibly the principal residence of the obscure kings of the realm of the 'Men of the North' created by Coel 'Hen' in the early fifth-century. The other two legionary fortresses, Caerleon and Deva/Chester, may also have been 'capitals' of two of the additional Late Roman provinces created by Diocletian though they were not apparently principal centres of post-Roman kingdoms; Caerleon was to be given the role of Arthur's capital by Geoffrey of Monmouth and Welsh legends.

Actual archaeological evidence of post-Roman use of these towns is thin on the ground, but this is only to be expected duc to the loss of centrally-directed authority and accumulations of men and materials for carrying out building. Work in stone was more difficult to fund or organise than in wood, and seems to have been abandoned in the fifth-century – where there is evidence of building (e.g. Viroconium/ Wroxeter) it is in wood, often re-using old sites on a smaller scale. Buildings would have been repaired where possible, and when it was no longer viable they would have been abandoned, rather than new work being carried out. The size of towns also decreased substantially, partly due to loss of trade. This is a more likely scenario than plague, which is not testified to as a major hazard until the 540s when a devastating epidemic spread across the Mediterranean world. At Corinium/Cirencester, in the agriculturally rich Cotswolds far from coastal Saxon or Irish raids so less likely than some towns to be affected by political turbulence, the fifth-century settlement relocated within the former Roman arena (presumably to use its walls for defence). Probably helped by a post-Roman administrative role, there seems to have been (wooden) building well into the sixth-century at Wroxeter; St Germanus' biographer Constantius testifies to St Albans being occupied c.418 and the *Anglo-Saxon Chronicle* to its being a British town as late as c.570,[17] while Chichester, Winchester, Exeter, and Lincoln survived to become important Saxon administrative centres. There was thus some continuity of occupation at these sites into Saxon times; the only major Roman administrative centres not to have re-emerged as Saxon settlement and/or county 'capital' were Wroxeter, replaced by Shrewsbury, and the abandoned Calleva/Silchester – which was noticeably on the borders of two counties so it was not a centre of local authority by the time that the Saxon counties were created.

Due to the lack of contemporary written evidence, we can only infer what sort of rulers who emerged after the end of Roman authority. But the only near-contemporary account, by Gildas c. 540, refers to legitimate rulers and magistrates in its denunciation of his contemporary and misruling kings as non-legitimate 'tyranni', implying that there had been properly-appointed rulers earlier. The Britons who he said had taken up arms to defeat attackers after the end of Roman rule evidently had militarily-competent and legally acceptable leaders. The tribal chieftains who had ruled the British lands before the Roman conquest had been suppressed and

Roman administration introduced, but did their equivalent re-emerge in the early fifth-century? The nature of the countryside would suggest that the pastoral economy would support hill-farms raising livestock. Their farm-buildings where discovered, e.g. in Cornwall, seem to continue in the 'round-house' tradition of pre-Roman farms with minimal Roman influence, and logically the inhabitants would include descendants of the earlier tribal aristocracy who could call on the allegiance – and military backing – of their tenants in times of crisis. It would be expected that a new body of local leaders would emerge to assume authority after the end of Roman rule, and set up local chieftainships – or even re-establish the old tribal lordships remembered from the first-century AD, as seems to have happened in Wales and Dumnonia (Devon and Cornwall). The name of 'Cornwall', indeed, is not that of any traditional local polity but of the midlands tribe of the 'Cornovii' – suggesting that some post-Roman authority moved a coherent elite of the latter, who continued to use their old name, to the region. 'Kings' would duly emerge as leaders of society, the men able to rally the local elites against the raiders who the literary sources testify troubled early fifth-century Britain – as stated by Gildas. New kingdoms lacking a long tradition of loyalty, in areas unaccustomed to such rulers as opposed to Imperial governors, would be at risk of overthrow – Gildas' claim to this effect is politically logical. Unlike in the south-east, there were no civic centres with their councils of landed gentry to dispute the authority of tribal kings in these areas.

The later Welsh sources date the early entries in the genealogies of post-Roman tribal kingdoms (e.g. Gwynedd, Powys, Dyfed, and Siluria/Morgannwg in Wales and Dumnonia in south-west England)[18] to this era, but are they trustable? It should be remembered that we have no extant pre-mediaeval documents containing these lists, and that the names of early rulers thus exist in writings complied up to 7–800 years after they lived – from which sceptics have hopefully asserted that they are inaccurate and/or legends. But this ignores the probability that earlier, now lost documents were copied by the writers of those which survived (how accurately is unknown); historians such as 'Nennius' (820s?) and William of Malmesbury (1120s) wrote that they used existing documents. Was this just a literary conceit to reassure their audience of their authenticity, or fact? Also, as in the modern tribal kingdoms of Africa and the Pacific, oral memories by 'professional' experts could keep up accurate 'king-lists' for many generations – if perhaps simplifying the 'descent' of kingship as always passing from father to son.

There is also the question of the much later literary 'evidence' of a central authority ruling over wider areas, a sort of 'High Kingship', as expounded by the Anglo-Norman romancer Geoffrey of Monmouth in the 1130s. He was writing with a view to contemporary issues and personalities not as a historian, and his work *The History of the Kings of Britain*[19] is riddled with inaccuracies and obvious inventions. Its use of twelfth-century names and terminology shows that it was designed for a contemporary audience as romance, not as a scholarly chronicle of history. Its notion of a 'kingdom of Britain' was not Geoffrey's invention, as this already existed in the early ninth-century work of 'Nennius' – who also refers to the eponymous dynastic 'founder' of the pre-Roman line of kings, 'Brutus' the supposed Trojan prince. The fact that 'Nennius' already knew of this legend would imply that it – and its use of a British derivation from the Roman legend of their own Trojan ancestors – was current by the 800s. Its treatment of the history of Roman Britain – where we can check it against Roman sources – bears little relation to the latter, and can be traced back to Gildas and the sources used by Nennius (below); he patriotically presents British kings ruling with or even successfully revolting against Roman governors in the first and second-century. Some of the names and episodes that he related had appeared earlier in the ninth-century Welsh *Historia Brittonum* attributed to 'Nennius',[20] although that too had probably been written with an eye to contemporary reviving 'national' pride by the new dynasty of Gwynedd. So at least Oliver Padel persuasively reckons.[21] Was there any truth behind the stories in these works of 'national' leadership among the post-Roman British? Three names stand out in particular – 'Vortigern' (a name meaning the 'over-king'), the 'last of the Romans' Ambrosius Aurelianus, and the enigmatic 'Arthur' who became the centre of a cycle of legends.

(ii) Maximus and the final decades of Roman rule: the template for later legendary creations of a post-Roman British 'Great King' ie Arthur?

The end of Roman rule in Britain was not one clear-cut break in government or military command. As early as 383 a substantial part of the five British provinces' garrison seems to have left the island to accompany Magnus Maximus, a commander (probably in Wales) claiming the throne of the Western part of the Empire. Rebelling against the young Emperor Gratian, Maximus – a former subordinate and possible Household official of Theodosius, the general who been sent from Rome to drive off a massive Saxon-Irish-Pictish attack in 367–8 – took over the British armies and landed in Gaul to confront Gratian. Deserted by his troops near Paris, Gratian fled south but was caught, arrested, and murdered at a banquet. Maximus then ruled the Western third of the Empire (Britain, Gaul, Spain, and the Rhineland) with the reluctant acquiescence of Eastern Emperor Theodosius, son of his old commander, while Gratian's half-brother Valentinian II kept the central third with Rome. In 387 Maximus took over Italy too and drove Valentinian to take refuge in the East, but he was defeated and killed by Theodosius at Aquileia in 388.[22] Nevertheless he seems to have made a profound impact on the British, as later Welsh legend remembered him as the great ruler 'Macsen Wledig' and Welsh dynasties claimed descent from him. As early as c.540, he is the last Roman ruler mentioned by name by Gildas.[23]

In the poem 'The Dream of Macsen Wledig' he was connected with the fortress at Segontium, later Caernarvon – a real Late Roman coastal fortress – where he supposedly dreamt that he saw a beautiful princess and duly sought her out.[24] This had an important enough literary 'reclame' for the conqueror Edward I to choose the site for the largest of his new castles at the Conquest in 1284, a building constructed by his Savoyard master-mason James of St George on the model of the Late Roman Imperial fortifications of Constantinople (built about thirty years after Maximus' reign). The literary picture created by the thirteenth century was however historically inaccurate, making Maximus a ruler of Rome who invaded Britain, not vice versa. In this version he was deposed during his long absence in Britain with his new wife Helen, and her brothers and their troops helped him to reconquer Rome; in real life he did not come to Britain as Emperor but as an officer under Count Theodosius (probably in 368, fifteen years before his revolt).

Gildas, our only early post-410 British writer and one using educated and elegant Latin, already shows signs of confusion about precise dates and names and lack of accurate knowledge, showing that it started early. His Maximus is not the Emperor of Roman historians' work, but the last Emperor to rule in Britain – a mistake by over twenty years. His sketchy account of the final decades of Roman rule may be due to his distance in place as much as in time – one mediaeval tradition has him living as a monk in Brittany, where there are churches dedicated to him. If he did have information to hand, oral memories or writings, the results as to accuracy are not impressive. But the physical survival to his time, c.140 years after the end of Roman rule, of some of what was available in writing (in Latin) about its history is probable. As shown by the archaeological evidence, the lurid picture in Gildas' story of mass-burning and sacking of almost all the Roman towns after 410 is a vast exaggeration. Books would thus have survived for him to consult, albeit mostly in monasteries given the collapse of leisured aristocratic literary culture in decades of turbulence and the physical decay of towns. (The 'Lives' of Saints such as Illtud, Samson, and Paul Aurelian show that by the early sixth-century the only schools were in monasteries, not secular ones in towns.) Literary teaching and the care of books would have been concentrated in monasteries and secular rulers would probably have been illiterate, but the church had no reason to 'weed out' history books from its libraries unless they were theologically heretical. Gildas would have been able to use whatever was available in an average monastic library. So why all his mistakes and omissions? Where is the ruler of Britain in 407, the military rebel Constantine III? From his account of the later fourth-century, we can see that a not entirely accurate view of Maximus as a British hero already loomed large in post-Roman British culture and/or dynastic traditions, at the expense of strict fact. It was only 160 years in the past, yet it had already passed into legend. It is clear that post-410 British writers and bards had a very limited knowledge of Roman history. This indicates that whatever literary records survived were not exhaustive 'histories' in the modern sense, or methodical chronicles. They were collections of stories that served a purpose, presumably 'political' or religious – and rulers that had left no impact were not remembered.

Maximus was remembered and Constantine III was not, though both took troops to Gaul and endeavoured to seize the Imperial throne in Rome – unsuccessfully. This suggests that Maximus played such crucial role in 'folk-memory' for another reason than his act of usurpation – and his long service in Britain before his revolt (c. fifteen years from Count Theodosius' campaign in 368?) and local marriage were obvious reasons to remember him and not Constantine III. The sceptics who sneer at the likely accuracy of the 'Maximus descent' in Welsh royal family trees need to consider why he, not another ruler like Constantine III, was used as the 'starting-point' for such pedigrees. Even if they remembered his political, not physical, heirs he was the choice of 'progenitor' for this 'family'. The linkage of a 'British' imperial ruler to a campaign in Gaul/France where he defeats the army of the current ruler of the Roman West was also crucial for the development of the Arthurian legend, where Geoffrey of Monmouth had Arthur invading Gaul to defeat and kill the 'procurator' Lucius Hiberius, viceroy for the Emperor Leo (who is presumably meant to be the Eastern Roman Emperor Leo I, ruled 457–74). Arthur then rules the Western Empire, as Maximus did (except for Italy). Did the idea for this come from Maximus overthrowing the Emperor Gratian in 383 – and get mixed-up with a later British expedition to Gaul to fight the German invaders in 469–70?

According to the stories Maximus had married a British 'princess', Helen 'Luyddog' ('of the Hosts'), daughter of the shadowy ruler 'Eudaf Hen'. Eudaf was the ruler at Segontium/Caernarfon in the 'Dream of Macsen Wledig', which would make him a local tribal dynast in North Wales – the pre-Roman land of the Deceangli, known to Roman history as 'Venedotia' and to Dark Ages Britain as 'Gwynedd'. Dark Ages genealogy, an inexact discipline owing much to contemporary political demands, however linked Eudaf not to Gwynedd but to the royal lines of south-east Wales, specifically 'Ewias' a.k.a. 'Ergyng' (between the upper Wye and lowland Gwent, centred on western Herefordshire). Eudaf, Maximus' father-in-law who rules at Caernarfon in the 'Dream of Macsen Wledig' in the 'Mabinogi' stories (of which the earliest document which survives is Peniarth Ms. 4 in the National Library of Wales, probably early thirteenth-century), becomes leader of the 'Gewissae' in South Wales by the time of Geoffrey of Monmouth, c. 1136.[25] The ninth-century 'Pillar of Eliseg', set up to commemorate a later king of Powys in mid-Wales, gave their dynasty's descent via Maximus and his daughter Severa[26] – suggesting that Maximus had inherited land in this region via his Welsh wife from her father. The (twelfth or thirteenth-century?) extant version of the legend of Macsen which places Helen's family at the fortress of Caernarfon may reflect a real connection – though it mistakenly made Maximus come to Wales as already Emperor in the fourth century. The

Roman fort of Segontium had defensive work done in around the 360s; it was a logical base for a Roman officer entrusted with defending the Welsh coast against Irish raiders. The Irish settled in Lleyn to the west, as seen by their 'ogham' stones, and Gwynedd had to be reconquered by the North British prince Cunedda (founder of the later royal line) some time after c.400 (or 440).[27] His family then divided up the region among themselves, at least as recorded by much later historians – which has led to a theory that this story was a contemporary 'political' creation to justify the divison of Gwynedd in 1170s, not accurate memory. By the 520s Cunedda's great-grandson Maelgwyn was supposedly the major ruler in Wales, and was remembered by Welsh legend as having been the 'wledig' (over-ruler?) of Wales – with a cautionary note that this detail was in the political interests of the twelfth-century kings of Gwynedd so it could have been played up then (or invented, say the sceptics). He played an important part in Gildas' story, who fulminated about his tyranny and moral lapses.[28]

Helen was legendarily connected with the network of Roman roads across Wales, linking the main fortresses, which by the mediaeval era were called 'Sarn Helen' after her. In reality the roads pre-dated her by centuries, and seem to have been built in the later first-century following the final conquest of the tribes of the Welsh uplands in the years after AD 61 – to move Roman troops quickly between disaffected areas. The fact that this British-based Roman Emperor's local wife had the same name as the mother of Constantine 'the Great' may well have led to a mix-up between the two. Helena, mother of Constantine, is recorded as the daughter of an Illyrian innkeeper but was by mediaeval times supposed to be the daughter of the British king 'Old King Cole' – in defiance of the facts.[29] She was even supposed to have brought the 'True Cross' to Nevern in Dyfed rather than to Rome, with documentation from the court of Hywel 'Dda' of Dyfed in the tenth-century (surviving in copies from c.1100 in British Library Harleian Mss. 3589) claiming the Cross had been hidden there.[30] This indicates a Welsh literary and religious interest in relics from Jesus' Palestine ending up in Britain as early as the tenth-century – which was to feed into the later idea of the 'Grail' in Britain. The real-life, unnamed wife of Maximus was recorded by contemporaries as being a friend and patron of the first monastic leader in Gaul, St Martin of Tours.[31]

The vital information preserved in the ninth-century 'Nennius' history that fifth-century British monks adopted the contemporary Eastern Roman practice of a 'perpetual choir'[32] shows there was Eastern influence on the British Church then. The three 'perpetual choirs' he names in Britain reflect that at a monastery on Mount Auxentius near Constantinople, founded c.400 at a time of heated evangelical enthusiasm led by Patriarch/St John 'Chrysostom'– which a ninth-century Welsh bishop would have been unaware of.

Literary myth or confusion? Maximus' wife and alleged sons: the 'Arthurian' dynasty

Welsh legend made the obscure fifth-century ruler Custennin (Constantine), who by the time of Geoffrey of Monmouth c. 1135 was supposed to have been Arthur's grandfather, the son of Maximus and Helen. But there is no contemporary literary or coinage evidence that Custennin son of Maximus even existed, as the records of Maximus' reign indicate that he had a son called Victor and an unnamed wife and younger children. Theodosius executed Victor, already Maximus' nominal co-emperor and enthroned at Trier by 388 so a political threat, but pardoned the latter.[33] It is also unclear if there is any genuine fact behind the later ascription to Maximus of another son called 'Anhun', probably 'Antonius', who is linked in legend to Galloway and/or the Isle of Man.[34] It is more likely that this ruler, if he ever existed, was a nominee of Maximus' later co-opted into his family by enterprising genealogists. In modern times the controversial scholars of early Welsh history, Baram Blackett and Alan Wilson, have made much of 'Andhun' as a possible progenitor for part of the 'Arthur' myth, citing the legendary Arthurian defeat of the Roman Emperor/tribune in Gaul as connected to Maximus' campaign in Gaul in 383. They suppose that Maximus' general Andragaithus, who defeated and captured the young Emperor Gratian, was 'Andhun' and also the model for this part of Arthur's career.[35] But there is no literary evidence for Andragaithus being Maximus' son, illegitimate or otherwise. If 'Andhun' existed at all, it was in the context of a dimly-remembered ancestral ruler of the kings of Galloway and/or Man who had some sort of link to Maximus. The 'Maximus' link may even have arisen later, as a source of dynastic 'respectability' for the local Galloway and Man princes as genealogically kin to the 'Maximus dynasties' of Wales. Nennius' employer, King Merfyn of Gwynedd, had paternal ancestors from Man.

A mysterious Owain 'Vinddu', 'son' of Maximus, was later known as one of the three most notable 'councillors' of Britain according to the *Triads* and linked to the 'Gewissae' ('confederates'?) by whatever source Geoffrey of Monmouth used c. 1135.[36]

(iii) After Maximus

Britain returned to the allegiance of the main Empire in 388, being awarded to Valentinian and later coming to Theodosius. According to later Welsh legend many of Maximus' troops were settled in Armorica (later to be called 'Brittany' or 'Little Britain' from the number of Britons there) under his brother-in-law, Cynan Meriadawc. The archaeological record seems to indicate a reduced use of the forts along Hadrian's Wall after the 380s, possibly indicating that there were not enough troops left to man them fully as the pressure of Germanic raids caused most of the Western army to be concentrated on the Rhine.[37] In the 390s the signal-stations set up along the Yorkshire coast (to give warning of Saxon and/or Pictish sea-raids) were destroyed by fire, probably due to attacks by seaborne raiders. Signs of attack, including piles of bodies, were found at at Huntcliff and Goldborough, and no coins date later than 394.[38]

The administrative record of the Late Imperial armed forces around 400, the *Notitia Dignitatum*, gives a long list of units in Britain as for other border-provinces, with special emphasis on troops in Yorkshire, Durham, and Westmoreland behind the line of the Wall (fourteen military units in all). The 'dux' of Britain was overall commander. The extant list was last brought up to date c.420, but its British section shows that that part must have been compiled before 407. But it is not clear if this is an outdated or idealised picture that did not reflect the situation on the ground even as of the years preceding 407.[39] It is incomplete, as it does not mention the Roman forts and units in Wales. The raiding from across the North Sea and the Irish Sea, and from less certain later literary evidence the Picts in Scotland, appears to have continued; the ninth-century references in 'Nennius' imply that the Picts and Irish were even more of a menace at the time than the Germans. The Irish settlement in Lleyn, Demetia, and western Cornwall – seen from place-names and ogham-inscriptions

– implies a loss of military control in these areas; Demetia even acquired a ruling dynasty linked to Leinster.It is unclear if the supposed death in battle of the Irish 'High King' Niall, nicknamed 'of the Nine Hostages', around 407 took place at the 'Muir nicht' (the sea of Ictis, possibly Vectis i.e. the Isle of Wight) or in 'Alba' which could be Scotland or the Alps.[40]

Was there a regional commander within Late Roman Britain to fight the threat of North Sea piracy – an office which could have descended to post-Roman generals like Ambrosius or 'Arthur'? There was undoubtably a regional coastal commander to fight the raiders in 367, when Ammianus reports him as being killed in a massive attack involving Irish, Picts, and Germans. Did this survive into the post-Roman era?[41] It is logical to assume that there was some such commander for all Britain, and that this was needed as much in the later fourth-century as in 367 so the office was kept in existence. Indeed, the fact that one of the 'Saxon Shore' fortresses guarding the South-Eastern coasts, Anderida (Pevensey), was to be stormed by the founding South Saxon king Aelle and its British inhabitants massacred in 491 (according to the *Anglo-Saxon Chronicle*[42]) indicates that at least one of these fortresses was still an occupied and crucial strategic site eighty years after the end of Roman rule. One candidate for Arthur's battle of 'Glein' in the later fifth-century is Glynde, near Pevensey (as used by the writer Henry Treece).

The post-Roman political situation: Britain and Europe in the fifth century

In 406, in the reign of Theodosius' weak younger son Honorius under the regency of the Germanic general Stilicho, a large body of Germanic tribesmen crossed the frozen Rhine and poured into Gaul. This was not the first such incursion, others having occurred in the mid-270s and 350s, but on this occasion there was no quick despatch of an Imperial army to drive them out. Left to their own devices, the leaderless provinces of Gaul were ravaged and the army in Britain revolted, elevating two ephemeral 'Emperors' (Marcus and Gratian) in quick succession and then removing them. In 407 a more successful commander in Britain, Constantine III, set up a longer-lasting regime and crossed to Gaul to tackle the invaders. The Roman sources say that he took the army with him. In 410, as his regime crumbled with one of his generals (Gerontius) in revolt and the

Germans unchecked, Britain returned to the allegiance of Honorius whose own troubles prevented aid being sent north. (This was the year of the Goths' sack of Rome itself, with their army at large in Italy and the Emperor holed up in the marsh-protected city of Ravenna.) The British authorities who had written to the Emperor are supposed to have been told to look to their own defences, according to the contemporary Italian historian Zosimus.[43]

In 435/6 Armorica – traditionally regarded as a 'federate' settlement of British troops dating from Maximus' time – broke away from the Empire during Gallic disturbances involving a peasant revolt. The *Gallic Chronicle* presents a picture of a large-scale rising of the peasant brigand 'bacaudae' which Western Roman commander-in-chief Aetius put down.[44] The lands of Armorica were supposed to have been vacant when refugee Britons moved in, having fled their homeland in the Saxon revolt of the 440s; it has been suggested that a collapse of the rural economy produced this situation and that Aetius invited 'pro-Roman' landholders from ravaged Britain to help restore order. The 'appeal to Agitius/Aetius' from Britain around 446, testified to by Gildas and the *Anglo-Saxon Chronicle*,[45] would thus have been followed by a reply by Aetius, regretting that he would not intervene but inviting his correspondents to move to Armorica to aid the Western Imperial government. (Gildas typically muddles events up, calling Aetius 'thrice consul', ie dating the event after his third consulship in 446, but then implying it was before the arrival of the first Saxon mercenaries c. 428.) The names of two of the three new later fifth-century kingdoms in Armorica – Dumnonee and Cornouaille – would indicate that their ruling classes came from Dumnonia and Cornwall, the nearest British tribal regions. The supposed founder of Dumnonee was known as Riwal 'the Great', possibly from his Latin name 'Pomponius Regalis'.[46]

Following Constantius III's death in 421 and a revolt at Ravenna against his infant son Valentinian III's succession to Honorius in 423, central Roman power was weakened again. A usurper seized power in Ravenna, but was deposed in 425 by an Eastern army sent to reinstate Valentinian by his cousin Theodosius II; the new ruler's mother Galla Placidia ruled as regent with a power-struggle developing over the military command between the generals Aetius and Boniface. In the process, Gaiseric and his Vandals (who had crossed the Pyrenees into Spain during the war between Constantine III and Honorius in 410–11) invaded North Africa.

Eventually, stable rule in ravaged Gaul was restored by the campaigning of new commander-in-chief Aetius in the 430s. Violence however continued from bands of Germans and revolting, landless peasants (the enigmatic 'bacaudae') throughout the 430s and 440s. It is not known if the latter had any equivalent in Britain, though the greater size and wealth of the Gallo-Roman 'villa' estates may suggest that social inequality and resulting discontent was less in Britain. The polemics against excessive riches and a heartless, godless aristocracy by British Christian zealots such as Pelagius the heretic and the 'Sicilian Briton' (and the Rhineland historian Salvian c.440)[47] may refer only to conditions on the Continent which were more unequal than in Britain.

There is no evidence of large-scale peasant revolt in Britain. The evidence of a homily addressed to a young widow by a British bishop called Fastidius c.410 would seem to show that unjust and corrupt magistrates had recently suffered appropriate Divine retribution and had left homeless and ruined widows and children.[48] But this may have been due to raiders instead of peasant revolts, and not even refer to events in Britain.

(iv) Politics and War: a British over-kingship after 410?

This is the picture of the 'state' of which Arthur assumed leadership in the works of Geoffrey of Monmouth. But how historical is it?

The independent tribal polities and surviving towns are supposed in later literature to have owed allegiance to a supreme ruler of Britain, who Geoffrey refers to as a 'High King'. (The name 'king' is Anglo-Saxon, but there were pre-Roman warlords dominating several kingdoms in Britain eg Cassivellaunus, Caesar's foe in 55–4 BC.) The absence of functioning coinage naming rulers and of contemporary documentation means that the authenticity of later legends cannot be proved, though it would appear from the vague account of Gildas over a century later that the local authorities – civic or tribal – were able to organise a successful defeat of the initial Saxon raids. The contemporary historian Zosimus and the *Gallic Chronicle* confirm this. Gildas' complaint is that the victorious British then abandoned themselves to luxury and sloth:

> 'the island grew affluent.The abundance of commodities outstripped the memory of any earlier age. But with prosperity grew luxury.. and all the vices natural to man… hatred of truth… and love of lies'.[49]

This is probably rhetorical exaggeration, seeking to explain their subsequent sufferings at Saxon hands as Divine punishment with a hint of Jeremiah's polemics about sinful Judah before Nebuchadnezzar invaded, rather than strictly factual; Gildas seems to have seen himself in the role of a British Jeremiah predicting disaster for his godless countrymen. However if it is correct that the 'proud tyrant', the 'over-king' Vortigern, had to call in German 'federates' within a couple of decades this implies that the local civic and tribal leaders could or would not raise and train enough troops to meet the needs of defence. Logically, the civic authorities in the towns could raise and pay for a local militia and 'tribal' aristocrats in the rural areas could call on their tenants and kinsmen as armies were raised to drive back the raiders. The continuing military threat would then make such temporary measures permanent and give successful commanders authority as protectors of the civilian population. In tribal areas, the bonds of kinship and the prestige of lineage would give men claiming descent from traditional – or pre-Roman – rulers added weight, and the Welsh genealogies show that the names of a few pre-Roman rulers like Caratacus were remembered and placed in the new kings' genealogies. If Gildas' abuse about 'usurpers' is not merely literary polemic, some new rulers lacked traditional links to the local societies and could be opposed as such. Given the crises of the fifth-century, capable military leadership was the obvious way for such men to emerge as local 'protectors' with their war-bands and then formalise their authority – so was 'Arthur' (later known as a war-band leader in Welsh poetry) one of these men?

The titles used for such rulers are unclear, but would logically be those of Late Roman civil and military authority. Geoffrey's 'anachronistic' use of twelfth-century titles for his rulers were not that incorrect in some cases although their meaning had shifted from their Roman origins by the time that he wrote. He makes Arthur's kingly vassals include 'Dukes', most notably of Cornwall, and the word derives from the Late Roman title for military governor of a province ' *dux*'). It would be a logical title for a local ruler, in origin a military defender (or oppressor) of the local populace, to use – as was the next 'rung' down the twelfth-century titular ladder, 'Count' (the French version of the English/Scandinavian 'Earl'), which was a Late Roman title given to wide-ranging military commanders. The original Latin word, 'Comes', meant 'Companion' and was a honorific title given to courtiers – including officers – in attendance on the Emperor, then being used for military commanders on the frontiers. In Britain, the supreme military commander across the five Diocletianic provinces in the fourth-century appears to have been the 'Count of Britain'; there was also a coastal commander called 'Count', possibly the 'Count of the Saxon Shore', who is referred to in Ammianus' account of the invasions. Hence a military ruler commanding, or a general serving, a group of local kings against a foreign invader – as 'Nennius' portrayed Arthur doing – could have used the title of 'Count'.

The legends of 'High Kings' may reflect the emergence of a supreme military authority, as Robin Collingwood speculated in the 1930s based on a German theory of the 1890s. He guessed that the logical centre of authority would be the 'Count of Britain', the overall military commander of the island in the fourth-century as seen by Ammianus' account[50] – though it is uncertain if this office was still in existence by the 400s. The Welsh title 'Gwledic' given by subsequent writers to major British commanders in the fifth-century, e.g. Ambrosius Aurelianus ('Emrys Wledig') and the Votadini prince and founder of Gwynedd, Cunedda, may reflect some sub-Roman military title that they took up – possibly 'Count' or 'Duke'. The title was applied, in retrospect in some cases, to the greatest military commanders such as Maximus, 'Macsen Weldig', and king Ceretic of Strathclyde, greatest ruler in the North around 450–70 – and also to men who cannot be definitely named as kings, such as the shadowy 'Amlawdd Wledic' (according to mediaeval Welsh genealogy, father of Arthur's mother Ygyr/Igraine). It therefore has a primarily military rather than royal connotation. The civilian equivalent would seem to be the equally obscure title of '*Pendragon*' – again, probably given in retrospect by later Dark Ages tradition as much as reflecting a real contemporary fifth-century title. The holders of that title could be kings – and thus war-leaders and overlords of their neighbours – such as Maelgwyn of Gwynedd (ruled c.520–47/9), Vortigern, Coel 'Hen' of Northern Britain (fl. 420–40?), and Aedan mac Gabhran of Dal Riada (fl. 560–80). They were however not as renowned for military triumphs as the men known as 'Gwledic', from which it has been inferred that the difference in terminology used to refer to them was deliberate.[51] The word 'Pendragon' used of Arthur's supposed father Uther may well have come from the useage of a dragon standard by such kings, as this flag had been borne into battle before Late Roman commanders – especially Emperors – by the later fourth-century. The mediaeval literary notion that it was first used of 'Uther Pendragon', due to the appearance of a comet – a 'Dragon Star' – at his accession appears in Geoffrey of Monmouth's story c.1135,[52] and was probably his invention. Elsewhere in Welsh literature the title is used of rulers before his time, of which he seems to have been unaware.

Religious sources for fifth-century literary evidence and what they have to say: *Pelagius, Germanus, Patrick, and the British Church*

In reality, despite the many later 'histories' of events in mainland Britain in the fifth-century the only reliable evidence is in religious sources, namely material dealing with the careers of St Germanus and St Patrick – as textual expert David Dumville warned when savaging John Morris' reliance on later works in his 1973 study '*The Age of Arthur*'. The only major contemporary source to deal in any detail with Britain is the later fifth-century hagiography (by the monk Constantius) of St Germanus of Auxerre, Bishop of that North-Central Gallic town. He visited Britain to preach against the 'Pelagian' heresy in 429(?) as a result of a Gallic clerical initiative (indicating the apparent prevalence of the British(?) Pelagius' unorthodox theology in his homeland and the local clergy's failure to combat it). According to Constantius, the local 'Pelagians' were rich and powerful – implying that they were an important faction of secular landowners or townsmen, including civic authorities? He dealt with civic officials at a site presumed to be Verulamium (St Albans), without writing of the identity of the current authorities in Britain. As an ex-army officer used to command, Germanus was a tough character capable of standing up to them. The cause of his mission, the theological controversialist Pelagius, apparently a student in Rome in the later fourth-century (possibly in law), was also involved in British society, as he was evidently British (or possibly Irish) according to his orthodox foe St Augustine of Hippo and the historians Orosius and Prosper. Concerned with the demands of natural justice ('aequitas') for Christians, he turned against the oppressive and unjust secular order of society and denounced the selfish greed of the rich in *De Divitiis* after early work on the letters of St Paul.[53] He denounced the sin of avarice and resultant oppression, and urged a return to the absolute virtue of poverty demanded by Christ rather than continuing the equivocations of past Church writers who had been prepared to excuse wealth if properly 'stewarded'. This was in line with the renunciation of worldly goods carried out by personal example by recent holy exemplars like St Martin or urged on the rich by the uncompromising Patriarch John 'Chrysostom' of Constantinople (in office 397–404). Pelagius also mounted a theological challenge to orthodoxy which opened his views to easier attack. He inaugurated an early fifth-century 'heresy' that sought to deny the necessity of Divine Grace for salvation and promote the idea that Man could achieve his own perfection and conquer sin ('impeccantia'). He thus undermined the role of the clergy as intercessors with God, which led to a major confrontation with orthodox thinkers in the 400s; his flight from Rome at the time of the sack by Alaric in 410 brought him to Africa where he entered into debate with St Augustine of Hippo. Initially he escaped personal condemnation despite Augustine's suspicions. But by 415 Pelagius, now teaching in Palestine as the diaspora of intellectual refugees from Rome spread East, came under attack from St Jerome in Bethlehem and two bishops from Gaul arrived to demand a local synod investigate his 'heresies'.

Pope Innocent's condemnation of Pelagius in 416 followed, but was briefly reversed by his successor Zosimus. Intensive lobbying won over Emperor Honorius in Ravenna and persuaded Zosimus to bow to pressure. A Western Imperial order of 30 April 418 demanded the expulsion of the Pelagian ringleaders from Rome and seizure of their property. In the west, Pelagian sympathisers continued to be pursued and driven out of the Church during the 420s; in the East hopes were raised of the unorthodox new Patriarch Nestorius (founder of his own 'heresy') but the condemnation was renewed at the Council of Ephesus in 431. We do not know what became of Pelagius, who seems to have died in obscurity, but after a major orthodox offensive in Gaul in 425 (led by Bishop Prosper of Aquitaine) the Catholics' attention turned to heretics in Britain. The heresy had taken root in Britain, with a bishop called Agricola involved, and the rest of the local church lacked the will or ability to combat it. Its opponents called on the Gallic bishops for help according to the Gallic chronicler Prosper. They recommended Germanus, as a former military commander ordained as Bishop of Auxerre in 418. His mission was allegedly successful as portrayed by his hagiographer Constantius (c.480). Notably, the latter's book did not mention any aid for Germanus from the principal contemporary secular authority in Britain, the elusive 'Vortigern' who later tradition regarded as the ruler of southern Britain by c.430 – the man who a visiting missionary would normally call on for support. Does this mean that 'Vortigern', or other 420s rulers in Southern Britain, were Pelagian sympathisers so Constantius 'wrote him out' of the story as a 'heretic', or just that Germanus did not encounter him? Despite Germanus' supposed success in 429 he had to return again in the early 440s, and 'Pelagian' ideas survived in St David's south-west Wales well into the sixth-century. The austerity and renunciation of comfort of 'Dewi Sant' himself, a man who wore skins and only drank water, may owe something to this influence, though our main surviving evidence is the late eleventh-century life of him by Rhygyfach.[54] The fact that David was vigorously austere and allegedly only ate grass and drank water was a contrast to the worldly ex-estate monasteries of most of South Wales, to which he clearly set himself up in opposition. But was his inspiration British or Irish, and did it trace its pedigree back to Pelagius? A dim memory of the importance of austere holy hermits in fifth-century British culture – arguably traceable to both Pelagius and St Martin – survived into mediaeval Arthurian literature, where mysterious hermits crop up from time to time advising travelling knights on their moral duties.

Germanus dealt with post-Roman authorities at a town with a shrine – probably Verulamium as he apparently visited the shrine of St Alban – but they lacked a military commander to tackle the Saxon and Pictish invaders. They had to call on the experienced Saint to rally their army and lead it against an army of raiders, though the location of the clash in hilly country must have been a long way from lowland Verulamium. Perhaps it was eastern Powys near Llangollen as suggested by mediaeval Welsh legend. The later fifth-century hagiography refers to an ambush of the raiders arranged by Germanus in hilly country.[55] Germanus' biographer is supposed to have spoken to the Saint's companion Bishop Lupus, who would have been one of the attendant bishops at the battle, so there is a reliable source for it. The battle was known as the 'Alleluia' victory from the British bishops' rallying – call which apparently put the enemy to flight.[56] It can be assumed that if the local civic leadership had to call on the Saint, a foreigner albeit one with military experience, there was currently no capable commander available in that area of Britain; therefore presumably the pre-410 Roman provinces of lowland southern Britain ('Flavia Caesarensis' and 'Maxima Caesarensis') had not any adequate commanders in residence by c. 429.

The second source of literary information for this period is the career of St Patrick who was crucially from a relatively well-off, literate and 'Romanised' rural family somewhere in western Britain. His hagiography and subsequent 'official' Irish accounts of his career such as the *Annals of Ulster* may have contained some myths and played up his role as leader of the conversion of Ireland, given that a tradition venerating him grew up at his new see of Armagh. Nor are his dates definitive due to a muddle over when he was active or if there were two Patricks not one – but his basic story can be trusted. If he was the man who started his evangelization c. 431, around c.410–30 he returned to his apparently peaceful home in western Britain, some fifteen or so years after being carried off aged sixteen as a slave by Irish raiders, probably to Leinster. (The alternate dating of him later in the fifth-century would make this later, but if so it extends the peaceful conditions of his home region in Britain even later after the end of Roman rule in 410.) This raiding has been linked by some to the Irish myths of the wide-ranging freebooter 'High King' Niall, founder of the 'Ui Niall' (O'Neill) dynasty that monopolised the Irish high kingship for six hundred years, who died around 407 – but he was king of Midhe not Leinster. Patrick subsequently decided to join the church and take the Gospel to his former captors; later biographers seeking to show his links to the prestigious leaders of the Gallic Church connected his training to Germanus of Auxerre, who logically as an ex-soldier would see the value of taming the Irish raiders. Patrick's return home cannot be dated as precisely as the first visit by Germanus, as Patrick's dates are disputed. He was active in Ireland for about thirty years (one version said sixty to fit in with an apparent date of death c. 493) and his mission followed the less successful one c. 431 by Palladius, the Papal adviser who had recommended Germanus for the British mission. The account of Patrick's mission given in Gallic sources by the writer Prosper of Aquitaine, dating it around 431, is near-contemporary and probably accurate apart from patriotic pro-Roman 'playing up' the involvement of the Papacy.

Patrick's kidnapping around twenty years earlier would thus seem to be dateable around 405–410. The kidnapping logically took place somewhere within easy reach of the West- facing coasts which Irish raiders were troubling at the time. The '*Book of Ulster*' and early hagiographers claimed that he lived to Moses' age, i.e. 120.[57] But this is clearly based on Old Testament parallels and trying to extend his career to c.430–90. English mediaeval monastic writers also referred to a link with Glastonbury that may have been suggested by the presence of someone of a similar name in their records – or been invented. He was probably based at his new episcopal see of Armagh – usefully close to the Ulster royal fortress of Navan. It was probably Patrick who had the idea of adapting the administrative system of the church within the urbanised Roman Empire (and Britain) to the rural society of tribal Irish kingdoms. The bishops were to be based at Royal courts, not at (non-existent) urban centres as was the 'norm' of the Roman world. This new system also appeared in the rural tribal kingdoms of north and western Britain, with the new bishops of kingdoms like Dyfed. In sixth-century Ireland the great centres of Church wealth and influence were to be the monasteries under great abbots of royal blood like Columba/Columbcille of Derry, not the bishoprics. That was also true of the sixth-century Church in the British kingdoms, with their isolated island monasteries like that of Piro at Caldey Island in Dyfed (where St Samson was trained) and that of St Cadfan at Bardsey off Gwynedd. The idea of island monasteries was however Roman, the first one having been at Lerins near Marseilles in the early fifth-century. Even on land, the most notable monasteries were to be established far from the temptations of Royal courts, in the 'wilderness', as at Glastonbury in the Somerset marshes (extant before the Saxon conquest in 658). This followed the original tradition of monasticism as it had emerged from Egypt, where the institution had been created in the desert safe from Roman authority at the time of the 'Great Persecution' c.300. What had been necessity at the time of the first great monastic founder, St Anthony, became a positive virtue in renouncing secular society. An alternative form of monasticism used former secular estates, like Llanilltud Fawr and Llancarfan in Siluria. St Illtud, founder of Llanilltud, had formerly been living in retreat in the 'wilderness' at Merthyr Mawr; he, Samson, and St Cadoc of Llancarfan were all from the local landed gentry in the manner of Irish princely monastic abbots. Dyfrig/ Dubricius, abbot of Moccas in Ewyas/Gwent but also bishop of the kingdom of the Silures and supposedly first bishop of Llandaff, was of local royal blood. Another group of saints, including Cadfan of Bardsey, were linked to an Armorican dynasty; there were others from the dynasty of Breichiniog and St David was connected to the Dyfed dynasty.[58] It is possible that the Church was staffed by landed aristocrats across Britain, as was the norm in post-Roman Italy and Gaul, Tradition gave post-Roman Britain three monastic centres where a 'perpetual harmony' of monks chanted prayers around the clock. This was a genuine fifth-century monastic practice in use around Constantinople. The sites of these monasteries are unclear, one being 'Bangor Wydrin' (meaning 'enclosure of the monks'), another 'the island of Avallach' (a possible original for the later myth of Glastonbury as 'Avalon'), and the third 'Caer Caradoc'.[59]

The evidence of contemporary writers Constantius and Gildas; the possibilities of 'Old King Cole' – 'Coel Hen' – as a fifth-century North British warlord and equivalent of 'Arthur'

Germanus' biographer Constantius refers to some high officials based in surviving Roman towns. There is no mention of a a local 'king', either there or in the hillier country where he fought the invaders, but that may be because the ruler was hostile to him. There were also bishops, if ineffective ones, as late as the Saint's second visit c.445, and a secular official called Elafius hastened to greet him as he arrived.[60] There were presumably 'kings' as well by the 420s to 440s, mostly in the more rural 'tribal' areas of the north and west where the mediaeval genealogies make it clear that the pre-Roman kingdoms were revived in the early fifth-century, if not who ruled them. The territorial units which emerged in the fifth-century were usually those of the pre-Roman Celtic kingdoms, which certainly survived as the basis of local administrative districts in Gaul (e.g. the Treveri and Parisii) so the same plan was probably followed in Britain. Thus on the ending of central control by civilian governors ('*praesides*') and military commanders ('*duces*') of the five British provinces the less 'Romanised' areas, lacking towns and town-councils, would fall into the control of local landed nobles – or of newcomers claiming their role.

De Excidio Britanniae written by Gildas a century later, our main but problematic source for events in fifth-century Britain, is fond of abusing fifth-century and sixth-century British kings as 'tyrants' and magistrates as corrupt and oppressive, ruling an immoral people who deserved Divine wrath.[61] But this picture implies that there was a formal government structure in the 'kingdoms', which was now misused by its holders in contrast with their virtuous forebears. The names of some fifth-century rulers in the later genealogies, such as 'Triphun' – 'Tribune' – of Demetia/ Dyfed, suggest that they held power by virtue of some Roman office, or at least sought to justify their rule by assuming a regular title to cover their usurpation. Recently, Christopher Snyder[62] has suggested that Gildas' term 'tyrannus' for these fifth- and sixth-century rulers reflects the contemporary uncertainty over what legal term to use for these 'new men', rulers who lacked the legitimacy of Roman administrative titles and ruled by virtue of self-assumed authority (aided by military force) rather than by traditional right.

Logically, the obscure Coel 'Hen' ruling in Northern Britain near Hadrian's Wall – the 'original' of 'Old King Cole' – could have been connected to the fierce Brigantes tribe, who had lived between the Humber and the Wall, or else have taken over the local militia defending the Wall as his private army. This sort of independent action is logical enough for a trained officer or local noble stepping into a military vacuum under threat of external attack, as seen by the career of ex-senior Roman officer Aegidius in northern Gaul after Roman rule there collapsed after 455. Gildas writes of the Picts and Irish overunning the far north beyond Hadrian's Wall and the British having to abandon their walls and cities to fight back from hills, moorland, woods, and caves, suggesting a memory of some military disaster soon after the Roman army left in 407 and a subsequent revival which the local military settlers ('limitanei') and tribal aristocrats would have led. Does this imply that Gildas had personal knowledge from his youth in Strathcylde, or that he met sons or grandsons of survivors?

John Morris and others suggest that Coel's remembered eminence, and his position as the founding ancestor of a major dynasty of the 'Men of the North', arose from his inheriting a local military command on the Wall after the Roman troops left in 407. He would then have acted as the protector of the area against the 'Picts' to the North who were the major source of raiding in the early fifth-century. The 'Notitia' names a Roman military 'dux' as commanding at York – was this Coel's office during the 407–10 period, when the main army left for Gaul? In archaeological terms, it appears that some Roman forts on the Wall (e.g. Birdoswald) were still occupied well into the fifth-century, albeit less as defensive strongpoints than as farming-settlements with building-work in wood not stone as in Roman times.[63] Their occupants, presumably descendants of the late fourth-century soldiery as there is no obvious break in settlement, would have been under the authority of some local ruler to ensure political stability, logically a man who could claim power through the overwhelming local military supremacy of a commander of the Wall's garrisons. The idea of a 'kingdom of the North', whose founder's supposed descendants ruled at the Late Roman military headquarters of Eburacum/York and Luguvallium/Carlisle, is possible as much from the military situation of c.410 as from anachronistic later legend.

In the mediaeval English literary legends 'Arthur' himself is linked to a kingdom with its court at Carlisle and a nearby site near Penrith came to be called 'Pendragon Castle'. A modern theory of Arthur as a local king has emerged. This is also linkable to the modern scholarly theory that the amount of 'Arthurian' references in sources linked to the North British realms of the post-Roman period, eg the 'Gododdin' poem commemorating an attack on the Angles of Bernicia c. 600, implies that the 'original' was a warlord from this region celebrated by its bards. He need not have been a ruler of Rheged or in the Pennines, ie linked to Coel's dynasty – instead he might have been a ruler or commander from Lothian. This 'Northern origin' theory was first suggested by the Scots scholar W F Skene, who analysed the possible local origin for the elusive 'Twelve Battles of Arthur' named by 'Nennius' c. 829 and who published a major collection of the Old Welsh Arthurian texts in 1868, and has been taken up in recent decades by Rachel Bromwich. An alternative theory links him to the 'Artuir' who was a son of the (ethnically Irish 'Scots') king Aedan mac Gabhran of Dalriada in Argyll and fought wars against the Picts around the Antonine Wall near Glasgow in the early 580s.

'The' Arthur does not appear in the early mediaeval genealogies of the 'Men of the North' as a ruler of Coel's dynasty, the family (or political grouping rationalised in dynastic terms) ruling the area. There are several names like 'Arthur' in the dynastic lists, but of uncertain date (probably sixth-century) and only minor rulers at that – probably in Yorkshire and the Peaks, with one, the mid-sixth-century son of king Pabo, linked to the dynasty of Elmet around Leeds.[64] At most, visible proof of ancient Roman military remains in the area (e.g. the Wall) and oral stories of Arthur's local battles may have given the idea for this association. Merlin was partly based on the 'Myrddin' known to have been connected to the battle of Arderydd/Arthuret, near Carlisle, c.573, and the 'Lailoken' who lived in the Ettrick Forest. Arthur's brother-in-law 'Lot of Lothian' was clearly meant to be a local king, and was probably based on the Votadini ruler Llew.

The creation by one warlord holding senior military rank of a post-Roman 'kingdom' in a frontier region, based on his personal prowess, has a close Gallic parallel for this exact period. Aegidius, a senior officer of the western commander-in-chief Aetius who had restored Roman power in Gaul, created a personal domain in Northern Gaul after the collapse of Roman authority there on Emperor Valentinian III's murder in 455, based on the province of 'Belgica' (from modern Normandy and Paris to Artois); it lasted until his son Syagrius was overthrown by Clovis the Frank in 486. Creating a similar British kingdom based on Eboracum/York and the Wall was a logical move for local defence against the tribes north of the ex-Roman frontier (the Pictish kingdom in particular) and raiding Irish and Saxons. And the concept of a supersession of legally-appointed Roman officials by 'ad hoc' warlordism by the region's most effective defenders gives a hint as to what an 'Arthur' could have done in similar circumstances in the South.

Chapter 2

Arthur's Predecessors? Vortigern and Ambrosius

Lacking any other contemporary source, our earliest literary account of the mid-fifth-century is that of the historian generally known as 'Nennius' in the 820s – or whoever later amended his surviving manuscripts. He was writing in Gwynedd, the Northernmost of the three major Welsh states which had survived the 'Anglo-Saxon' political and military takeover of southern and lowland Britain, at a time of crisis 300 years after the 'Arthurian' era and 400 after the end of Roman rule. This is a long time for any oral memories to have survived except as garbled legends, or for written documents to have been preserved safe from civil wars and invasions. Indeed, the only known repositories of records were monasteries, which had their own – religious – priorities and outlooks; there were no secular libraries or towns in ninth-century Wales. The few literate people were usually Churchmen, and their interests were in their own religious heritage not in secular politics – most of the so-called '*Cambrian Annals*' recorded in tenth-century Dyfed, for example, were of events connected to saints and bishops. Gwynedd, formerly the isolated region of 'Venedotia' in the military zone of Roman Wales, had survived Anglian military attack and partial occupation under King Edwin of Northumbria in the 620s. Under its ferocious king Cadwallon, Edwin's killer in battle in 633/4, it served as the leader of the final British attempt to push the Angles out of northern Britain in the early 630s. But by 'Nennius' time its military greatness was long gone, it was under heavy attack by the Midlands kingdom of Mercia, and it had recently been taken over by a new dynasty under 'Nennius' sovereign, King Merfyn 'the Freckled' – who as we shall see had his own reasons for using an inspiring legend of a past British fight-back against the Anglo-Saxons.

'Nennius', writing the *Historia Brittonum* in the 'fourth year of king Merfyn' ie. c. 829, has a large section on 'Arthur' – following on direct from 'Vortigern', the over-king who invited the first Germanic settlers to Britain as mercenary soldiers – in contrast to Gildas. But he hardly mentions Gildas' hero Ambrosius Aurelianus, 'last of the Romans', except as Vortigern's 'great' successor.[1] His work was originally thought of by modern Arthurian enthusiasts as an invaluable near-contemporary record, but his reliability has been savaged in recent years by David Dumville and others – which endangers his account of military affairs regarding the 'British vs Saxons' wars. His account of Arthur, indeed, is that of a 'miraculous' hero who with God's help defeats the invaders with near-impossible feats, not a sober account of a battle-campaign – and until the Nennian text was surveyed in detail in its literary context nobody thought of worrying why his battle-list had four battles not one at 'Dubglass'. After 'Nennius' we come to sparse records even further distant in time from c. 500 – the later ninth-century *Anglo-Saxon Chronicle* and the tenth-century Welsh *Cambrian Annals* and genealogies. All were written long enough after the fifth-century for major errors to have emerged. Both these chronicles, one 'English' and one Welsh, had a paramount political aim, as glorifying their patrons – King Alfred's Wessex and King Hywel's Dyfed – and omitted politically irrelevant details. The Anglo-Saxon 'record' – written in Wessex – omitted almost all reference to such minor kingdoms as Essex and East Anglia, and much about Wessex's foe Mercia. The Annals' sixth-century account had more detail about Irish and North British dates than those in Wales and in the South of Britain, so it is assumed it incorporated what other records the compilers (?monks at St David's) had to hand. The analysis of the Annals by Kathleen Hughes in 1973 showed that it used one Irish source (the 'General Chronicle') and one North British one for material before the St David's local chronicle began in 796 – the material was not even Welsh for events pre-796.[2] Then David Dumville identified some North British (Strathclyde) material as being interpolated in the Welsh annal as late as 870, and the Irish source used as a particular version of their chronicle from Clonmacnois covering events to as late as 941. The compilation of the annals' 'early' material was thus post-940. (The latest suggestion is 977.) At the time, the Welsh under national unifier King Hywel of Dyfed were in danger of conquest by the aggressive new kingdom of England and their propagandist *'Armes Prydein'* prophecies were calling for a war to defeat the latter – so was the Arthurian detail in the Annals part of this?

Nor did authors such as 'Nennius' have a clear and accurate picture of post-Roman Britain, as can be inferred from those errors that crept in for the Roman period where we possess other sources to check them against. Like Gildas, their view of Roman rule is at odds with that in contemporary Roman sources and anachronistic references are made to kings and events which never existed. This shows that whatever 'histories' had been written between c.400 and 545 – or oral memories preserved by bards – were concerned with literary stories rather than accurate facts. Nor did much of a dateable account of fifth- and sixth-century British history survive in Ireland. Had such records existed in Irish church libraries such as Clonmacnois, we can presume the St David's chroniclers would have incorporated them. But the monks had other, non-secular priorities.

The rulers of the ninth- and tenth-century had their own political reasons for seeking to magnify the achievements of a coherent 'over-kingship' in the fifth-century so that they could claim to be its heirs – on which grounds Nicholas Higham and other recent analysts have declared their accounts to be unreliable.[3] Alfred in Wessex and Hywel in Dyfed were more similar than might at first appear – with Hywel, a contemporary and reluctant vassal of Alfred's grandson Athelstan, possibly acting as Alfred's copier. (Alfred's biographer Bishop Asser, d. 909, had come from Dyfed.) Both national revivers and unifiers, the two kings had a political 'narrative' for their chroniclers to assert, with Hywel as the leader of a coalition of kings like Arthur – though not one inclined for war as he meekly turned up at his English overlord King Athelstan's court to witness charters rather than aiding the Scots and Dublin Vikings in attacking him in 937. The chronicles were carefully constructed political documents, not objective histories written solely for scholars.

The catastrophic Anglo-Saxon revolt of the early 440s(?) was traced to the contemporary British ruler Vortigern's disastrous policy of calling in the Germanic marauders as 'federates', mercenaries to fight the more dangerous Picts and Irish. This story also had a political purpose in 820s Gwynedd and 940s Dyfed – namely that 'collaborating' with the treacherous Saxons brought disaster. The name 'Vortigern' actually means 'High King', so it is a title not a name; he is presumably the man who Gildas (c. 540) calls the 'superbus tyrannus', ie 'proud tyrant', with an echo of the last Roman king Tarquinius Superbus in Livy's first-century AD Roman history. As he had authority in Kent he presumably led the kingdoms or provinces of southern Britain, but is given the title of king of Powys (mid- Wales) in the eighth-century 'Pillar of Eliseg' inscription in the Vale of Llangollen. (This was transcribed by the antiquarian Edward Lluyd in 1695 and now cannot be read.) Either Powys was his own kingdom, providing him with the warriors to take over in the lowlands too, or he was annexed as the local 'founder king' in later legend due to the alleged descent of the rulers of a region of south-eastern Powys, 'Gwerthyrnion', by his descendants. The genealogy on the Pillar alleges that he married the daughter of Macsen 'Wledig' (ie 380s Emperor Maximus), Severa, and the tales taken up by Geoffrey of Monmouth had him treacherously seizing power from a British 'High King' called Constantine or his son Constans – Vortigern's brother-in-law and son-in-law, and possibly descended from Macsen. He thus usurped the throne from Constantine's younger son, Ambrosius, who fled into exile. He initially called in three shiploads of Germanic mercenaries, and allowed himself to be talked into recruiting more and more of them by their leader 'Hengest' (a name meaning 'Stallion'/ 'Gelding', from which modern commentators have denied his historicity). In due course they broke into revolt, ravaging the country.[4] This was one of the great stories of post-Roman history in subsequent centuries, with Vortigern portrayed as the epitome of arrogant and short-sighted folly, but that does not mean that it was inaccurate. Logically, it would make sense for a ruler of the former Roman lands in Britain – short of troops since the end of a formal military presence in 407/10 – to rely on external mercenaries. Indeed, if Vortigern had usurped control of the former kingdom of Constantine by regicide he might have preferred to use his own hirelings to the tenantry of Constantine's former nobles.The gamble failed to pay off in that case, and it made a deep impression on subsequent literary myth. The question of 'Hengest' the mercenary leader craftily using his daughter Rowena to ensnare the lecherous king into marriage is more likely to be a literary addition from some saga. David Dumville argues that the entire 'Nennian' account comes from the Jutish/ Saxon 'foundation myth' of Kent, a saga composed to promote the legendary Hengest – and certainly the Welsh account of the wars that resulted seems to use Germanic place-names translated into Welsh.[5]

It was Vortigern's son (by his first marriage) Vortimer, not him, who led the British campaign against the rebel Saxons in 'Nennius' history. Does this imply that he probably deposed, or at least eclipsed, his disgraced father? Vortigern was recalled after Vortimer's successful campaign and subsequent death, recalled Hengest whose daughter Rowena he had married, and was captured and forced to surrender Kent by Hengest whose men massacred Vortigern's councillors at a truce-meeting. This infamous 'Massacre of the Long Knives' was similar to other stories in Germanic legend, but this does not mean that it was entirely invented as some scholars have loftily assumed. The site of it is unknown, but by Geoffrey of Monmouth's time c. 1135 it was linked to the stone circle at Stonehenge in Wiltshire – presumably as the latter was the most impressive stone monument in southern Britain and Geoffrey or his source had Ambrosius erect a large monument to the victims. Vortigern then fled to Wales as his enemy Ambrosius returned from exile, made his base at a hillfort (supposed to be Dinas Emrys in Snowdonia), and was killed in a fire during a siege at this or another hillfort. The site of the latter was on the lower Wye at Doward near Symonds Yat, in Powys, or at 'Nant Gwerthyrn' in the Lleyn Peninsula. The final confrontation may have involved prayers for Vortigern's destruction by his enemy St Germanus, leading to the fire as a sign of Divine wrath against the tyrant, but other versions name Germanus' foe in this incident as king 'Benlli'.[6] The latter's grave is traditionally sited at 'Moel Fenlli' on the Berwyn Mountians in eastern Powys, but he is not placed in the Powys genealogy. Germanus then selected a new, humbly-born king for Powys – Cadell, son of a swineherd. Given the genealogical link of Vortigern to the rulers of Powys in the 'Pillar of Eliseg' inscription, it was presumably assumed that the king who Germanus replaced by Cadell was Vortigern. The date would have been c.445 if Germanus was involved, as that was when Germanus was in Britain for his second visit according to Gallic sources. Notably, it is before Bede's date for Hengest's arrival in England (449–50)[7] – so is the latter inaccurate?

Given the distance in time between his assumed 'reign' and the main strand of the Arthurian story, Vortigern has always been a peripheral figure in the Arthurian literary 'canon' within England and is largely absent from that in France. His role loomed larger in Welsh legend as the arch-traitor who had allowed the Anglo-Saxons into England and was responsible for the woes which followed. He played a significant role in Geoffrey of Monmouth's story, as the foe of Ambrosius, and Geoffrey's version expanded on and Normanised the basic tale told in Gildas' and 'Nennius' books of his folly and punishment (with Merlin replacing St Germanus in the role of the prophet of his ruin). From then on his role shrank, and he vanished altogether from Malory who began his story with Uther. The post-Galfridian English and French writers had no reason to make him a pivotal figure, as he was a reminder that the 'real' Arthur and the original Britons had been Welsh not Anglo-Norman.

According to the literary tradition in the *Historia Brittonum* of 'Nennius', Vortimer led his father's troops to defeat the first Saxon assault. The four main battles are cited as taking place at sites that have been tentatively placed in Kent, advancing from the River Darenth to Aylesford and then a battle on the Channel shore, thus presuming a campaign based in London to drive the invaders back to their bridgehead in Thanet which was supposedly thrice besieged. But it has also been suggested that the 'Derguentid', the Celtic name for one battle in 'Nennius' which seems to be connected to the word for 'oak', might be a river Derwent in Yorkshire (or a linguistic connection to the Roman town of 'Derventio' in Lancashire?), and that 'Aeglesthrop', the name in the *Anglo-Saxon Chronicle* for another, need not be Aylesford.[8] 'Nennius' has the invaders besieged thrice by Vortimer on their island base, presumed to be Thanet, and temporarily expelled. An unnamed battle that followed may have been a British defeat that saved Hengest's invaders, possibly the battle at 'Creganford' (Crayford?) cited as a victory of Hengest's in 457 in the *Anglo-Saxon Chronicle*. Vortimer died soon after his victory, possibly poisoned by his Jutish stepmother Rowena on her father Hengest's behalf, leading to his father's recall. He requested to be buried on the seashore as some sort of 'talisman' against the invader – a probable pagan British practice, as seen in the legend of the head of Bran 'the Blessed'. Given the dramatic nature of the tangled story of Vortigern, Vortimer, and Rowena, it is quite possible that some Dark Ages British heroic poem or a Saxon saga were used by the compilers of the legend that 'Nennius' in the ninth-century and later Geoffrey of Monmouth used. The infamous 'Massacre of the Long Knives', where Hengest's men pulled knives out of their long sleeves at a truce-meeting with Vortigern's unarmed councillors and killed them, recalls a strategm used in other Germanic myths and may be unhistorical.[9]

But this is not to say that no powerful fifth-century British king was ever treacherously kidnapped and/or forced to cede lands by a rebellious Germanic officer in his army; the incident if not the exaggerated details are logical. The story would have entered Welsh literary culture, and the idea of Ambrosius erecting a large stone circle as a monument to the victims was taken up and potential sites for this identified. Would this story have impressed itself so deeply on Welsh mythology had it merely been imported in the ninth-century from a Kentish saga, as sceptics have claimed?

Ambrosius, king of Britain after Vortigern, was known as 'the last of the Romans' following Gildas' account. The only extant early Anglo-Saxon historian of this period, the Northumbrian monk Bede in the 730s, also refers to him; he probably used Gildas' account. But he did not dwell much on Ambrosius' career, presumably as this British leader was of little interest to the descendants of Ambrosius' foes for whom Bede was writing. Nor was Ambrosius of any didactic use to Bede, who marginalised the role of 'native' Christian Britons in his book so as to play up the role of the Rome-derived Catholic missionaries from 597 in converting the island to Christianity. His account was a history of the triumph of the Catholic missions to the Angles and Saxons after 597 and of 'holy' Catholic English kings, not of the Catholic Britons/ Welsh. (By the same reasoning, he had no reason to mention any post-Ambrosius British warlords like 'Arthur' even if he had heard of them; he does not mention the definitely historical later sixth-century North British leader Urien of Rheged.) As seen by Gildas and Nennius, Ambrosius was the successful leader of British resistance to the Anglo-Saxons, probably in the 460s to 480s as he started the successful war which led eventually to the victory of Mount Badon. In Gildas' epic account of the fight-back:

> 'After a time, when the cruel plunderers had gone home, God gave strength to the survivors. Wretched people fled to them from all directions, as eagerly as bees to a bee-hive when the storm threatens, and begged whole-heartedly that they should not be altogether destroyed. Their leader was Ambrosius Aurelianus, a gentleman who, perhaps alone of the Romans, had survived the shock of this notable storm; his parents, who had certainly worn the purple, had been slain in it. Under him our people regained their strength, and

challenged the victors to battle. The Lord assented, and thc battle went our way. From then on, victory went now to our countrymen, now to their enemies, so that in this struggle the Lord could make trial of this latter-day Israel to see whether it loved him or not. This lasted right up to the year of the siege of Badon Hill…'[10]

Gildas refers to him as of aristocratic birth and to his parents having worn (Imperial?) purple and been killed in the Saxon assault. This may refer obliquely to the stories which survived to Geoffrey of Monmouth's time, where his father Constantine was the post-Roman ruler before Vortigern and the son of Emperor Maximus or of a Breton ruler. This man may be the king 'Custennin Bendigaid', ' Constantine the Blessed', of mediaeval Welsh myths, though that man is also named as a king of the Dumnonii in Devon (or of Gwent?) rather than of all Britain. Alternatively, the 'purple' may not be a royal robe but the purple stripe on the toga of a Roman consul – except that a British noble of the post-410 era would not have held a consulship in Rome itself and the title would have had to be a local British rank given to senior magistrates. Gildas is notable for his lack of specific details.

Mediaeval Welsh legend called Ambrosius 'Emrys Wledig', and placed him as Emperor Maximus' grandson or his wife's brother's grandson. The title 'Wledig' implied an overlord of other kings, like Maximus and the Gwynedd dynastic founder Cunedda. Constantius, biographer of St Germanus, a near-contemporary, called him the great king who succeeded Vortigern.[11] It is Geoffrey of Monmouth who brings in the Breton link so it cannot be traced back beyond the early twelfth-century. Another member of the Aurelius/Aurelianus family was father to the early sixth-century Silurian holy man, St Paul Aurelian, who seems to have come from Dumnonia,[12] and a relative called Aurelius Cynan/Conan was ruling Gloucester in Gildas'time c.545. Gildas indicates that the current descendants of Ambrosius had fallen off from his good qualities, so did they still have royal political power?[13] They may well have suffered the takeover of their kingdom by the Saxons and lost power as the dynasty does not appear in mediaeval Welsh genealogies. The kingdom must therefore have been in Southern Britain, not unconquered Wales.

'Nennius' dated the 'conflict between Vortigern and Ambrosius' to twelve years after Vortigern's accession, that is, presumably Vortigern's assumption of the 'High Kingship' in succession to Constans which is dated in the consulship of emperors Theodosius II and Valentinian III – 425.[14] This conflict is linked to the battle between Ambrosius and 'Vitalinus' – taken by some commentators as Vortigern's real name – at 'Guoloph' (possibly Wallop, near Andover, Hampshire?). The possible location of the battle-site in a settled, 'Romanised' region of prosperous farming-estates near the south coast may indicate that Ambrosius drew his support from the local aristocracy, who maintained links with Gaul and resented the rule of an 'alien' dynastic usurper. It is assumed that due to his family background Ambrosius represented a 'Roman party', probably of southern British landowners with contacts to the Gallic nobility and the Roman authorities there, who asked Aetius for help against the 'hill-country' dynast Vortigern. As 437 is far too early for Vortigern's overthrow – the Saxon revolt against him was in 441/2 according to the Gallic records – were the 'Roman party' defeated at Guoloph? The appeal to the Roman authorities in Gaul for aid in 443, recorded in the *Anglo-Saxon Chronicle*,[15] would have followed this defeat. Possibly the threat of Rome invading was such as to drive Vortigern to bring in 'Hengest' and his Germanic mercenaries as a loyal military force, and Thanet would be a logical place to station them against a Roman force crossing from the major port of Gesoriacum (Boulogne).[16]

Geoffrey placed Ambrosius' death as within a few years of his return, during Merlin's mission to Ireland to bring over the stones from Killara (untraceable) to form the 'Giant's Dance' (Stonehenge) as a monument to Vortigern's slain councillors.[17] But this is problematic; this brief a reign would not have been likely to make the major impact on Welsh memory that Ambrosius did – nor is it clear whence Geoffrey acquired his story of a Saxon agent poisoning Ambrosius. The comet which appeared at the death of Ambrosius and accession of his brother Uther might be a record of the comet of 467 (if this was visible in Europe), but it could just be a mistaken etymological link of Uther's 'Pendragon' sobriquet with a 'Dragon Star'. The long(ish) reign of the successful victor over the Saxons in Geoffrey's story, of around fifteen years, should be attributed to Ambrosius rather than the obscure 'Uther Pendragon' given that Geoffrey ascribes the longish Saxon war to this commander. Geoffrey says that Ambrosius had to fight a war with Vortigern's son Pascent, a historical figure of early Welsh tradition recorded as ruler of the Builth area in Southern Powys, and his Irish ally 'Gilloman'.[18] The latter name is not found in any Irish records; nor is that of his successor, Arthur's ally 'King Anguish' (Angus?).

The fortified towns of Bath, Cirencester, and Gloucester in the Cotwolds only fell to the Saxons in 577; it was possible that Ambrosius, linked by Welsh tradition with local Woodchester, could have raised a fighting-force there. The mediaeval story that Ambrosius erected Stonehenge as a monument to the British nobles killed by Hengest in the 'Massacre of the Long Knives' at the suggestion of Merlin, who brought the stones from Kilara Mountain in Ireland, is clearly fictional. Some scholars have argued that it is a garbled descendant of a genuine record of his erecting a monument, near a place called Caer Caradoc according to the Welsh *Brut Tyssilio* that Geoffrey may have used as a source.[19] Various sites have been suggested for this place, e.g the stones on 'Mynydd y Gaer' above Pencoed in Glamorgan (by Baram Blackett and Alan Wilson) using the identification of the site's founder as 'Ambrius' in the *Llandaff Charters*. Alternatively there are the stones at Cerrigydrudion ('Stones of the Heroes') near Llangollen in Powys (preferred by Steve Blake and Scott Lloyd).[20] The site was apparently one of the 'Three Perpetual Choirs' of Britain, 'Cor Emrys'; Geoffrey of Monmouth places the memorial stones set up to the murdered councillors at the 'Cloister of Ambrius'.[21] The attributions of these sites as the place where the murdered nobles were buried may owe more to mediaeval guesswork than reality, as with 'Arthurian sites'.

It should be noted that one recent theory – by Frank Reno – suggests that Ambrosius was both 'Arthur' and the mysterious British ruler 'Riothamus' of the late 460s. According to this, the latter two names both derive from Brittonic words for 'High King' – there was only one such ruler in the later fifth-century, but later writers were confused over his name. Following this, Thomas Green suggests that Nennius or unknown eighth-century/ninth-century mythographers decided to abandon Ambrosius as their chosen military prototype for a Welsh 'fight-back' commander as he was definitively 'Roman', so unsuitable for a British hero. They thus chose a mythical 'Arthur' instead.[22] But would not the 'Roman' link have been usefully prestigious and suitable for playing up? The greatest contemporary ruler, Charlemagne in Francia, was claiming to revive the Roman Empire, and was crowned as Emperor in Rome in 800. Thus, would it not have been logical for a Gwynedd Christian propagandist of the 820s to play up Ambrosius and/or Arthur's 'Roman' connections?

Ambrosius' Heir or an Invention? Uther Pendragon

Uther was the father of Arthur in mediaeval Welsh poems and hence in English literary romance – but he has a shaky basis in reality. It is uncertain if he ever ruled or was the brother of Ambrosius, which the Welsh poems do not state. It is certainly extremely unlikely that he could have ruled for a full fifteen years or so as 'High King' as claimed in the work of Geoffrey of Monmouth (and his elusive Welsh or Breton source?)[23] without leaving some trace on recorded history, even in the obscure political situation of the 490s. Geoffrey has him as a vigorous defender of his people against the Saxons in a series of battles, none of them traceable back to Welsh literature – though interestingly one takes place at St Albans, a Romano-British town and possible 'sub-kingdom capital' not conquered by the Saxons until 571. This is certainly a logical place for a major British/Saxon battle, with the latter advancing from the Thames towards a British enclave. The sick Uther is carried to his final battle in a litter, presenting him as a candidate for the role of the 'maimed king' of mediaeval Grail mythology whose physical condition is symbolic of his kingdom, the 'Waste Land'.[24] The young and unknown Arthur coming to the rescue of the leaderless kingdom is thus the forerunner of the 'Grail-seeker' Sir Galahad.

But the two nearest historical sources to the fifth-century – Gildas and Nennius – do not mention any successor to Ambrosius and the reign of Uther first appears in Geoffrey's work. The name might be a mistranslation of a Brittonic honorific, 'the awe-inspiring Head Dragon', this being Baram Blackett and Alan Wilson's solution to the problem of his identity.[25] 'Uther' thus could have been a title of a man with another name. The title 'Pendragon' was one of a number given to post-Roman rulers who held authority over various junior rulers, such as Maelgwyn of Gwynedd in the 540s – though it was not given to all 'over-kings', e.g. Ambrosius, or 'Arthur'. It probably derives from the Late Roman use of a dragon on the standard of military commanders. Whether it was formally or informally used in the fifth-century to refer to commanders is another matter.

'Uthr' is a Celticization of the Latin name Victor, which was that of Magnus Maximus' eldest son (executed in 388). Logically, the name could have been passed on within the family and so support the idea of 'Uther' as connected to this dynasty. The main references to a character in early Welsh literature are when Mabon is called the 'servant of Uther Pendragon' in 'Pa Gur' ('Who is the Gatekeeper?'), a poem set at Arthur's court, and when Uther is stated in the *Triads* ('The Three Great Enchantments') as an enchanter who taught a certain Menw.[26] Both are probably tenth-century at the earliest, and neither is clear evidence of Uther as a person. But it is significant that Uther appears in these Arthurian stories as an apparently non-royal protagonist, 'magician' or not, rather than the king who precedes Arthur as ruler of all Britain. Was Uther originally thought of as an 'outsider', an enchanter not a king – and is this the origin of the story that Merlin magically transformed King Uther into the likeness of his inamorata Ygraine's husband? Was he ever Ambrosius' brother outside Geoffrey of Monmouth's imagination? Recently J.D. Koch as even suggested that the epithet 'Pen Dragon' refers not to his being 'Head Ruler/Dragon' but a 'Wonderful/ Wonder-Working Head' – the head in question being that of Bran 'the Blessed', severed in battle in Ireland but then presiding over the late King's companions' feasting on the island of Gwales for seven years. In his view, Uther was originally Bran, and thus was a god not a man.[27] But this is unlikely, as the Bran story is not linked to the post-Roman 'Arthurian' period. The myth of Bran as the great 'lost leader' of the distant past whose death in a ruinous battle ended the 'golden age' may however have contributed to that of Arthur's death at Camlann.

Patrick Sims-Williams has suggested that a reference in the early mediaeval 'Mawrnad Uthr' to 'Uther' saying that the world owed its existence to his offspring may imply that Arthur is his son. In the twelfth-century 'Ymddiddan Arthur a'r Eryr', 'The Dialogue of Arthur and the Eagle', the eponymous 'Eagle' is the magically transformed 'Eliwlod', Uther's grandson, and Arthur says that Eliwlod is his nephew[28] – so is Uther his father? This would suggest that 'Uther' was seen as Arthur's father in some Welsh stories, but there is no indication that Uther is a king or that he is connected to Ambrosius. If Nennius was hinting at Arthur's paternal line in his statement that many kings who served under Arthur were 'more noble than he', this implies that by the 820s Arthur's father was not seen as a king (unless Arthur was the illegitimate son of one).

Geoffrey's story of Uther's reign gives no clue as to its origins, and the foes who Uther fights are not identified with his career by earlier writers. Pascent, son of Vortigern, is a contemporary client of Ambrosius in 'Nennius', and Octha (son of Hengest) and Eosa (possibly 'Eoppa', the father of Ida who traditionally took Bamburgh in Bernicia in 547) are nowhere linked to wars with Uther. At the most Octha, supposed by 'Nennius' to have been sent to command Saxons in the north-east, and Eosa/Eoppa are placed in the right geographical location for the war that Geoffrey makes them fight against Uther in Northern Britain.[29]

If the dynasty of Ambrosius ruled in the Severn valley and the Cotswolds, as implied by the apparent location of his royal relative Aurelius Cynan/'Caninus' in Gildas' time, the extinction of the kingdom by the Saxons would explain why no trace of Uthr survived into mediaeval Welsh genealogies or history. Efforts have been made to link him and his title with a 'Dragon's Head' comet visible in the 490s, but this seems to derive from Geoffrey's story of the comet which marked his accession and it is not clear where Geoffrey acquired that information. The only useful records of the fifth-century comets are Chinese with only one of their comets dateable to this era, in 467 – and these phenomena may not have been seen in Britain. Moreover, the untraceable story that Geoffrey narrates of the sick Uther being carried on his final campaign in a litter has overtones of the maimed 'Fisher King' and his wasted kingdom that awaits redemption by a saviour, which was to form part of the 'Grail' legend. Geoffrey's story is the account of Uther's reign which Mary Stewart used in her '*The Crystal Cave*' and '*The Hollow Hills*'.

Arthur in SW Britain? Dumnonia and the Battle of Llongborth

The alternative mediaeval legends of Arthur's location linked him to another identifiable post-Roman kingdom, within modern England but an independent Brittonic land to the ninth- or tenth-century. This was the originally pre-Roman tribal territory of the 'Dumnonii' was modern Devon and Cornwall, which was conquered by Rome some time in the 40s or 50s AD with the fortified town of Isca Dumnoniorum ('Waters of the Dumnonii'), ie Exeter, being founded as a Roman military base to control the region. What we now call 'Cornwall' did not acquire its name until part of the Midlands tribe of the 'Cornovii' were moved there some time in the early to mid-fifth century to evict Irish settlers, and various rulers of Cornwall are recorded independently of contemporary Dumnonian kings. The Dumnonian dynasty was allegedly descended from Emperor Maximus, with the first King Erbin as a son of the British 'High King' of the early fifth-century, Maximus' son Constantine 'the Blessed'. Its main dynastic line is recorded in the Welsh pedigrees, but this omits a number of kings who are recorded as ruling in Cornwall in the late fifth- and sixth-century. These were presumably sub-rulers, with the lack of survival of their states meaning that their dynastic predigrees were not preserved by later kings (and written down) as in Wales. We have no idea who ruled even at the major archaeological site of Tintagel, though it is significant that mediaeval legend correctly identified it as a post-Roman site.

That there was the survival of a hazy tradition about 'King Mark' in south-east Cornwall is probably due to his connection with the Tristram story which poets embellished. But logic would suggest that if 'the' Arthur had ruled a Cornish kingdom the fact would have survived into Dark Ages legend, rather than him being connected with a nebulous 'Logres' and South Wales hagiography. But some stories do give Arthur a tentative Dumnonian connection, such as the hagiography of St Carantog which places him as ruling at Dindaithov (Dunster) with the Dumnonian king Cador[30] and the Melwas story in Gildas' hagiography which brings him to Glastonbury. Both can be explained as indicating that his domains included the Bristol Channel lands – but were not restricted to their Southern shores. The early Welsh poem 'The Dialogue of Arthur and the Eagle' called him 'chief of the battalions of Cornwall' (or Cerniw in South-East Wales?).[31]

The names of the early kings are unclear, though there is a link in one genealogy to Eudaf 'Hen' – the ubiquitous ruler of Ergyng in South Wales and father-in-law of Emperor Magnus Maximus.[32] This link may have been introduced to emphasize the dynasty's connections to the prestigious Welsh dynasties claiming descent from the Emperor. Eudaf, living c.380 if not invented, could not have ruled an independent kingdom under Roman rule and would thus have been a personal ancestor not a political predecessor of the fifth-century kings. The first agreed fifth-century king is 'Erbin', father of Gereint and possibly son of 'Kynaor' or 'Cynfor'. Some versions of the pedigrees also mention a brother of his called Custennin (Constantine) 'Fendigaid', 'the Blessed', who is given as Erbin's father in the *Peniarth Manuscripts* no. 24. He may have been the same man as – or mixed up with – the 'over-king' Constantine of Geoffrey's work.

Geraint, son and successor of Erbin, was known to Welsh legends by c.1100 as a contemporary of Arthur and was probably the man subsequently remembered in Welsh tradition (the *Triads*) as 'Llyngesog', the 'Fleet-owner'. His headquarters was probably at the fortress at Trewithian South-East of Truro subsequently known as 'Dingerein'. In the tenth-century Welsh genealogy *Penarth Manuscripts* no. 24 he is husband to Gwyar the daughter of Amlawdd 'Wledig' (and aunt of King Arthur).[33] By the time the tales of the Mabinogi were composed (the twelfth-century?) he was regarded as Arthur's first cousin. According to a poem attributed to Llywarch 'Hen', a princely poet of Coel 'Hen's dynasty active in the last decades of the sixth-century, he was probably killed at the battle of Llongborth, the 'Port of Ships'. The poem refers to:

> In Llongborth, I saw Arthur's Heroes who cut with steel
> The emperor/commander, ruler of our labour
> In Llongborth, Gereint was slain Heroes of the land of Dyfnaint
> And before they were slain, they slew.[34]

Gereint has been suggested as the important British prince killed at Portchester (?) around 500 by the Saxons Bieda and Maglos in the *Anglo-Saxon Chronicle* (890s?), presumably while opposing their landing and seizure of the local Late Roman 'Saxon Shore' fortress. John Morris argues that the fortress at Portchester and the adjacent harbour make the site an ideal one for a 'port of ships' of strategic interest to Dumnonia; the area's British rulers are unrecorded apart from the possibly Pictish'Natanleod' of the Totton-Netley area who Cerdic of Wessex killed around 508.[35] But is this man's name just a later rationalisation of a place-name as referring to a resident, not a geographical feature? Saxon and British traditions are confused about the details of the battle of Llongborth and its outcome. The later Welsh *Tale of Geraint ap Erbin* (preserved in its present form in the thirteenth-century *Black Book of Carmarthen*) refers to the king and his men of 'Dyfneint', aided by the heroes of 'Arthur the emperor', being defeated[36] – but it is not clear that Gereint was killed. There is no clue as to where Llongborth was, with various English and Welsh locations being suggested – the name would indicate a harbour then in use as a port. Portchester is only a guess. If Gereint was accurately recalled as a fleet-commander, it would probably be a port in his domains where he kept ships. Recently Chris Barber has suggested Cardiff Bay, which has traces of pre-mediaeval structures and thus could have been shared by the Dumnonii and Silures to defend the Bristol Channel;[37] a site in Cardigan Bay has also been suggested.

Chapter 3

King Arthur in Mediaeval Culture. An Anachronistic Picture

Arthur: the historians, the sceptics, and the mediaeval romances

The 'real King Arthur' is problematic as he has been successively re-interpreted by each century in its own terms, building up layers of myth which cannot be regarded as applicable to the real figure of a post-Roman warlord. We now see Arthur in the terminology of a mediaeval king and patron of chivalry rather than that of a warlord in the fifth-century who may have borne a kingly title (probably a post-Roman one using Latin or British terminology – the word 'king' is Anglo-Saxon) or just been a successful general. During the twentieth-century successive efforts were made to portray Arthur in realistic fifth-century or early sixth-century terms, a development that at least made him plausible as a real ruler. Some writers had always seen Arthur as a historical figure distinct from the hero-king, leader of chivalrous knights, and international conqueror created by fabulists, with William of Malmesbury in the early twelfth-century already expressing irritation at the unlikely nature of the current stories which did the real King a disservice.[1] He already seems to have been aware that the literary stories of Arthur must be inaccurate. Edward Gibbon, following eighteenth-century Welsh historians, regarded him as a historical figure – and as the King of the Silures. The Welsh writers he used were 'Romantic' enthusiasts keen to lay claim to the King as a local hero and thus to use every possible favourable interpretation, this being the great era of national cultural revival. The contemporary enthusiasm for 'Celtic' traditions was centred on Welsh expatriate literary circles in London, and was to lead to the foundation of the Eisteddford on Primrose Hill, London by 'Iolo Morgannwg' (Edward Williams) in 1792. Ambitious enthusiasts even speculated about a twelfth-century Welsh prince, Madoc, sailing to America and spent a fortune on explorations of the Mid-West looking for lost 'Welsh Indians'. But the eighteenth-century historians cannot just be written off as unscientific fabulists, although the most has been made of Iolo's drug-taking and inventions of 'ancient' bardic rituals. Many were respectable clerical scholars who made painstaking investigations of old documents, although they like – recent enthusiasts for the accuracy of early mediaeval writings – seem to have been unaware of the possibility of manipulating stories for political purposes. They may have had access to early records that are no longer extant. They should not be written off as hopeless amateurs unfit to be taken seriously by modern scholars.

The Arthur of literature – from Geoffrey of Monmouth onwards

(i) Geoffrey

The mediaeval literary Arthur that was enshrined in Malory's *Morte d'Arthur* is essentially a creation of the twelfth-century romancers' reinterpretation of and additions to earlier Welsh legends to suit a courtly audience in Anglo-Norman England and northern France. Geoffrey of Monmouth, claiming to be using an earlier British (or Breton?) work that has never been traced conclusively and which Archdeacon Walter of Oxford gave him, created the story of the chivalric warrior-king who united Britain and then invaded Gaul and other neighbours in *The History of the Kings of Britain*, written around 1135. The work was immensely popular, as shown by the scores of early manuscripts of it which have survived, and inspired a whole succession of histories and chronicles of Britain during the twelfth-century and thirteenth-century. His dating of British royal history from the mythical Trojan hero Brutus indeed led to many being called 'Bruts'. Less is known of him than about his work, as he only appears as witness to a series of charters in Oxford from c.1129 to 1151 and in the latter year became Bishop-elect of the North Welsh see of St. Asaph. (He may never have actually set foot there, due to the denial of English secular or religious authority there by its ruler Owain of Gwynedd.) Given his French name and constant references to Brittany in his book, he was possibly of Breton origin; he was presumably but not definitely from Monmouth, currently held by Breton lords. His principal patron Robert, Earl of Gloucester (d. 1148), illegitimate son of Henry I, was the current lord of South Wales (and was married to a descendant of the Welsh kings of Glamorgan including 'Arthwys') and was shortly to gain fame as the principal support of his half-sister Matilda in the long-running civil war that followed Henry's death. Indeed, he was married to the daughter of the first Norman lord of Glamorgan, Robert Fitz Hamon, and of the heiress of the last Welsh king Iestyn ap Gwrgan. As the latter was dynastically connected to the line of the ancient kings back to Arthwys and Mouric, Robert had a motive for playing up the reign of his wife's heroic ancestor so he could claim kinship – though in Geoffrey's book Arthur, while ruling from a capital within Robert's lands (at Caerleon), is not linked to the kings of Glamorgan as opposed to all 'Britain'.

The chaos in late 1130s England made the picture of a peaceful Arthurian empire stretching across Europe particularly appealing – with the failures of King Stephen, who had usurped the English throne from Matilda in December 1135, as a warning against weak and 'illegitimate' rulers to a literary protégé of Earl Robert. Stephen faced repeated challenges as Arthur did, but was unable to suppress his rebels by decisive action – was he the real-life antithesis to Geoffrey's imaginary successful warlord? The inclusion of French lands in the post-Conquest Norman royal family's domains after 1066 was reflected in the assigning of French conquests to Arthur. Arthur's overseas domains were a congenial topic for an audience of knights and barons who had family connections there. Arthur's knights could be given provinces in France to govern which existed in the twelfth-century but not in the fifth- or sixth-century. From Henry I's deposition of his brother Duke Robert in 1106 England had been united with Normandy, although this was to be interrupted during the civil wars of 1136–53 as Matilda's family sought to evict Stephen's officials. Thus there was every reason for Geoffrey to play up Arthur's Continental links and to show him as a ruler of Normandy – taken from Stephen's loyalists during the 1140s by Matilda's and Earl Robert's faction – and of Anjou, Matilda's husband's county.

Geoffrey may have relied on earlier works, which have been suggested as including early Welsh chronicles. The differences between his story and that in the main twelfth-century Welsh version of it, the *Brut Tyssilio*, have led to suggestions that the latter (of uncertain date) was not the straightforward translation of it that used to be assumed, but a derivation from a Welsh 'original' that it had in common with Geoffrey. The one element of the Arthur story that Geoffrey definitely did take from Welsh legends was the Royal hero's role as a giant-killer – he has Arthur kill the giant Retho, who has a cloak made of the beards of kings he has slain, and the giant of Mont-St Michel in Normandy. 'Retho' is the giant 'Rita Gawr' of Mount Eryri (Snowdon) in Arfon who Arthur kills in single combat in the *Brut y Brenhinedd*. Whether or not Geoffrey did use early Welsh books for his 'military' events, he introduced or extended key elements of the story to a wider audience and led to these being used for future versions. Most crucially, it was Geoffrey who placed Arthur in his accepted dynastic context as the son of 'Uther Pendragon', nephew of Ambrosius, and grandson of Constantine; earlier writers like 'Nennius' had not referred to his ancestry and the Welsh genealogies had only given sketchy details. Arthur's mother Ygyr/Ygerna was easier-located than his elusive father in this highly status- conscious network of references, giving him links back to Cunedda of Gwynedd and giving him Gereint of Dumnonia and St Illtud as his cousins. This might indicate uncertainty over his birth as well as his paternal dynastic connections – or even that he was already thought of as an illegitimate 'outsider'.

But now Geoffrey placed Arthur firmly in the fifth-century line of 'High Kings' and back through their ancestors to the pre-Roman dynasty that had been overthrown by Julius Caesar and Claudius. He stressed the survival of a concept of one British kingdom from the earliest times to give it prestigious antiquity – and presumably to outrank the 'parvenu' rival French royal house, new to the throne in 987 and at best dynastically traceable to the sixth-century. He went as far as to link the British royal line to the historical sack of Rome by 'Gauls' in 390/386 BC testified to by Livy, and duly gave the first ruling dynasty a connection to the exiled royal line of Troy (led by Aeneas) in pre-Roman Latium mentioned by Vergil. Geoffrey may have had access to details that the contemporary or earlier Welsh writers lacked, presumably Breton, and he certainly did not invent 'Brutus' who appears in 'Nennius' as a pre-Roman ruler (possibly the eponymous ancestor-king of the British, due to the similarity of his name to 'Britain'). But infuriatingly his accuracy for dynastic details is only sporadic – he gives the sixth-century genealogy of Gwynedd correctly but creates all sorts of spurious details for the Roman period. He is totally unaware of many of the real-life royal dynasties of sixth-century Britain, Coel's line in the North included, and thus had at best partial access to Welsh sources. He does not even know of the local rulers of the area around his native Monmouth, e.g. Pebiau of Ergyng – though he does know of the local late fifth-century bishop, Dyfrig/Dubricius.

The unhistorical stories he used, like that of Arviragus' marital alliance with Claudius, and the problematical early church mission to 'King Lucius' in the second-century, suggest that a major source was Welsh material – particularly 'Nennius' – with a greater awareness of Roman histories than theirs. Livy and Vergil are clearly in evidence for the Roman period, with such important 'cross-references' as the 'Celtic' sack of Rome c.387 BC. But Geoffrey takes the Welsh claims of a continuing royal British line in power through the Roman period at face value. This owes more to Welsh patriotism than to reality – the Romans made a point of suppressing native dynasts within their Empire, as seen by the annexation of the Iceni territory on the death of Prasutagus in AD 60 which sparked off Boudicca's revolt and the ending of the loyal allied kingdom of Togidumnus/Cogidubnus of the Regni (around Chichester) in the 60s or 70s. Indeed, to Geoffrey the Romans appear as an embarrassing irritation to the notion of British independence, and are as marginalised as is possible – at variance with all the Roman histories of this period. The pre-Roman 'kingdom of Britain' is shown as reappearing quickly after the Romans left; in fact there had never been such a kingdom and the 'all-Britain' dynasts who faced Caesar (Cassivellaunus) and Claudius (Caratacus) had ruled only the kingdom of the Catuvellauni in the Home Counties. If the 'king' who returned from Brittany to assume authority after 410, Constantine, had royal lineage it was not 'all-British', and any lordship that he created was based on the five Late Roman provinces of Britain – of which Geoffrey is unaware.

Geoffrey then gives the 'standard' account of the usurpation of Vortigern, invitation to the Saxons, and treachery and revolt of Hengest, as in 'Nennius'. It is unlikely that Ambrosius really died as soon after his reconquest of Britain as Geoffrey states as then he would not have made the major impact as war-leader which Gildas and 'Nennius' ascribe to him; the briefness of Ambrosius' and length of Uther's reigns are not found in any extant pre-Geoffrey source. The title of '*Pendragon*', which Geoffrey says was given to Uther due to the comet appearing at his accession, has no etymological link to a 'dragon' star – the 'dragon' is probably the honorific standard borne before Late Roman rulers and their successors in battle. Geoffrey was evidently guessing or using earlier Welsh/Breton guesswork about the meaning of the term.

Geoffrey's coherent story of Arthur's life formed the basis of future writings. His new elements of it included: Arthur's paternity as the son of Uther and Ygerna (Igraine); the peculiar nature of his conception owing to Uther's tryst with his wife-to-be disguised as her current husband Gorlois of Cornwall; his conception and birth at Tintagel; his coronation at the age of fifteen by Dubricius; his conflict with the kings who denied his right to rule; and his conflict with the Roman Empire in Gaul in the reign of Leo. (The 'hidden years' of Arthur's youth as the ward of one of Uther's vassals may have already existed in Welsh tradition; we cannot tell how old is the identification of Lake Bala/Vrynwy as the place where he was fostered at Caer Gai.) The 'time-line' used by Geoffrey led up to Arthur's final battle, here placed at AD 542; it may have been based on an extended version of the *Annales Cambriae*, or other Welsh documents, no longer extant. The existing Anglo-Saxon records give us contradictory clues as to his scheme of dating – Hengest, who Geoffrey has being killed by Ambrosius before Arthur's birth, supposedly died in 488 and Aesc/Oesc, supposedly killed in battle by Arthur's father Uther shortly before Arthur's accession, died in 512(?). The plan of Arthur's campaigns against the Saxons, in which he is helped by his Breton ally Hoel, involve both some names from the 'Nennius battle-list' (e.g. Dubglass, the wood of Celidon, and Badon/Bath) and some existing twelfth-century towns which did exist in Roman times.

Arthur, aided by 'Duke' Cador of Cornwall, fights an early battle at York, and a later one at a place named in garbled Celtic as 'Kaerliudoeit', which is probably 'Caer Luit Coed' ('Fortress of the Grey Wood'?) i.e. Leicester though this battle is not referred to by 'Nennius'. The defeated Saxons break a pledge to go home and invade the south-west instead, and the siege and battle of Bath (Badon) follow. It is after the crushing victory that Arthur wins over the invaders there – 21 years before his final battle in the *Annales Cambriae*, so by Geoffrey's time-scale c. 521 – that he can move on to overrun neighbouring countries, starting with a war in Scotland against the Picts and Scots and their Irish ally Gilmaurius. He restores Loth (Llew) to the kingdom of Lothian, and his sibling Urien (in real life later sixth-century) receives Moray (Rheged, his real-life kingdom which was far to the south, in the *Brut Tyssilio*). In Welsh genealogy, Llew and Arawn are the sons of an elusive 'Cynfarch', a descendant of Coel 'Hen' of Northern Britain and of suitable royal blood to rule there.

Having married the beautiful Guenhumara (Guinevere), of Roman descent, Arthur builds a fleet and invades Ireland to defeat Gilmaurius. He extends his empire to include Iceland (ruled by Malvasius, possibly a garbled version of the Welsh 'Melwas'), Norway – which is unhistorically given to Loth – Gothland (which in Dark Ages parlance meant the land of the Geats, i.e. southern Sweden), and northern France. His victories are celebrated with a grand coronation at Caerleon, but this is interrupted by a demand for tribute from the Roman consul 'Lucius' and Arthur's resulting Continental campaign. The latter ends in a decisive victory, but before Arthur can march on Rome he receives news that his nephew Modred has revolted in Britain and has to return to his homeland. The final series of battles against the rebel, moving west from Kent to Salisbury Plain and ending with Camlann, follows.

Analysing Geoffrey's picture of Arthur and his dynasty

The nature of certain episodes, e.g. the interruption of Arthur's Gallic war for his combat with the giant of Mont St Michel in Normandy, suggested a deliberate attempt to bring in current French (Breton?) as well as earlier Welsh stories about Arthur. 'Guenhumara' is the Welsh 'Gwenhwyfar', i.e. 'White Shadow/Enchantress'. There is no indication of where (apart from his imagination) Geoffrey acquired the unlikely stories about Arthur conquering Scandinavia and holding court for his vassals from all over Europe; perhaps he was meant to be surpassing the French hero-king Charlemagne. The concept of Arthur's coronation as king of the British also owes more to the twelfth-century than to any real-life events involving a fifth-century ruler, though the rite of coronation by an eminent Churchman had been introduced for the Eastern Roman Emperors in 457 and could have been used in Britain. The crowner Dubricius, i.e. the Welsh 'St Dyfrig', was placed in the later fifth-century by current hagiographies. He was also the first bishop of Llandaff, at least as recalled by the later eleventh-century and in the *Llandaff Charters* – the cathedral at the present site near Cardiff was a later foundation but he would have been the territorial bishop of the kingdom of Glevisseg. He is supposed to have founded a monastery at Moccas near Hereford and been related to king Peibiau – a logical choice for first 'bishop' of the Gwent see. As a native of Monmouth in Gwent, Geoffrey would have known of the Llandaff traditions.

By giving Arthur the role of restoring 'Loth' to his ancestral lands, did Geoffrey use the story of the sixth-century Arthur restoring his relative-by-marriage Llew ap Arawn to a kingdom of the Northern Britons in Lothian? Interestingly, in Welsh genealogies Llew ap Arawn was the son-in-law of King Meurig of Siluria, whose realm extended close to Monmouth, and thus Meurig was the 'original' of Uther Pendragon in this respect – but Geoffrey was unaware of this. Notably, Geoffrey's 'Uther' is not given Meurig's wife (Onobrawst) or father (Tewdrig). The sources for his details of Arthur's campaigns are unknown, with sites across Britain and Saxon names (e.g. Colgrim and Badulf, the principal invading commanders) which have no clear early Welsh precedents. The latter's colleague is 'Cheldric', which sounds like a garbled version of Cerdic – except that in the Saxon records Cerdic dies in 534, rather later than the approximate date in Geoffrey's account, and there is no record of him fighting outside Hampshire or encountering Arthur at all. 'Lucius Hiberius' the Roman consul is unknown to history, though Mike Ashley suggests that he might be a derivation of the current Frankish warlord Clovis (died 511) who ruled Northern Gaul. Nor is there any indication where the wars between Arthur's father Uther and the Saxons came from. Only the Arthurian battles of the Wood of Celidon and Badon/Bath can be traced to the list of twelve given in 'Nennius', though it is possible that Geoffrey's details of the 'Irish' aiding the Saxons in the Scottish Lowlands derive from a real alliance of Irish raiders or the Irish-descended kingdom of Dalriada in Argyll against 'Arthur'.

The site of Arthur's court, Caerleon, came from Welsh tradition along with his queen Guenhumara (Gwenhwyfar), the senior British officers Bedivere (Bedwyr) the cup-bearer and Kay (Cai) the seneschal, Arthur's loyal nephew Gawain (Gwalchmai) and treacherous nephew Mordred (Medraut), Arthur's brother-in-law Loth of Lothian (Llew ap Cynfarch), and Archbishops Dubricius (St Dyfrig) and Samson. Among Arthur's sub-rulers in Britain – of Cornwall, Albany (Scotland), Demetia (Dyfed),and Venedotia (Gwynedd) – Cador of Cornwall came from Welsh tradition and Auguselus of Albany is probably the historical Arawn, father of Llew/Loth. Some, like king Stater of Dyfed (a garbled version of a Roman title?), are as unidentifiable as some of the names of Arthur's Continental vassals and those of his Roman enemies, tribune Frollo of Gaul (possibly derived from a genuine fifth-century Romano-Gallic family, the Ferreoli, one of whom acted as a tribune in the 450s) and the consul Lucius Hiberius. As will be seen later, there is some evidence that Arthur's Gallic campaign was based on a genuine Breton work, the *Life of St Goeznovius*, rather than being an invention – appealing to a writer of the 1130s when the Anglo-Norman kings had domains in northern France.

Geoffrey's recent sovereign Henry I was Duke of Normandy, which Arthur conquers and gives to Bedivere; Geoffrey's patron Duke Robert of Gloucester's half-sister the Empress Matilda had married the Count of Anjou, which Arthur conquers and gives to Kay. The neighbouring state of Poitou/Aquitaine (conquered by Hoel on Arthur's behalf) was ruled by Duke William X, patron of troubadours and father of Matilda's son Henry II's later wife Eleanor. It has also been suggested that Geoffrey could have used an early version of the extant but later *Brut y Brenhinedd*, a Welsh history of the legendary kings from 'Brutus the Trojan' c. 1000 BC to Cadwaladr of Gwynedd in the 630s which is similar to Geoffrey's work but has enough differences not to be a direct, later translation of it.

There are many different texts of this, usually placed into six distinct basic versions; the dates are unclear but most scholars would put them all thirteenth- or fourteenth-century, with the earliest and closest in content to Geoffrey's text being 'Llanstephan Mss 1'. (One of the main but not earliest versions of this, the 'Brut Tyssilio', was ascribed to a prince of Powys, Tysslio, who seems to have lived around 600.) The copy in Jesus College Oxford (c. 1500) has a note ascribing the original to a translation from the Welsh by Walter, Archdeacon of Oxford, the 'source' used by Geoffrey – but this could be a later deliberate attempt to present the Brut as Geoffrey's source. There is still no agreement among scholars that any of it evolved independently of Geoffrey's work.

Patriotic embellishment – and creating a British rival to French and Roman legends?

Geoffrey may have used – and embellished – a genuine early source. But his talent for invention was apparent, even to scornful near-contemporaries such as William of Newburgh. He shamelessly contradicted all the Roman historians in minimalising the impact of the Roman conquest of Britain and presenting the British rulers of the time as often independent and victorious over Roman armies. Even if he used erroneous Welsh tradition for this, he made no attempt to counter-check it with Roman sources (e.g. Tacitus) which would have made the mistakes clear. He minimised the consequences of the Claudian conquest, and was totally confused about incidents such as the reconquest of rebel-held Britain by Constantius and Asclepiodotus in 296. Geoffrey's imagination ran riot with pre-Roman history, as he patriotically invented a long line of kings back to the time of the fall of Troy. This was probably to give the British royal line as ancient a lineage as the legendary Franks, ancestors of his patrons' Capetian rivals, who also claimed to be of Trojan descent. There had been notable literary attempts on the Continent to aid the prestige of the post-Roman 'newcomers' to monarchic power by grafting their ancestry onto well-known Roman legends. The new German 'ruling class' thus established a literary ancestry to match the literary culture of their Roman subjects. Long-lasting and heroic royal ancestry had been created for the Goths, new lords of Italy, by Jordanes in the sixth-century. In the seventh-century it was the turn of the Franks, initially in the work of Fredegar which was later embellished. Geoffrey now went one better and linked the British to the family of the hero Aeneas, subject of Vergil's Aeneid. The tribal Celtic leader 'Brennus' – from 'brenin', 'king' – who sacked Rome was made a British ruler, thus linking his achievement to Arthur's later war against Rome, and the god Belinus was made his brother.

All this has damaged Geoffrey's reputation ever since, though it does not preclude that his famous 'ancient book' of British history (British/Welsh or Breton?) – cited as given him by Archdeacon Walter of Oxford[2] – did exist and was merely embellished. Walter himself was real; he appears in the foundation-charter of Oseney Abbey near Oxford c. 1129 as a witness with Geoffrey, who is called 'Galfridus Artur' so Geoffrey's second name was seemingly Arthur – possibly the main stimulus to his Arthurian interests. The mention by Geoffrey of 'Brutus' as ancestor of the British people first appears in an Irish chronicle of the seventh-century and again in 'Nennius', so Geoffrey did not invent that even if he was the first to attempt to link Brutus with the events in the *Aeneid*. The notion of the leadership of his people coming to the British Isles from overseas to replace a semi-divine race was also originally Irish, as their legends refer to the mysterious 'Sons of Mil' arriving in Ireland from Spain c. 1000 BC to drive out the divine 'Tuatha de Danaan' (gods not giants as in Geoffrey's story). Was he trying to make sense of references that he did not understand at points in his narrative?

After Geoffrey: propaganda for the Angevin dynasty

Geoffrey's work provided Anglo-Norman England with its own response to the current French legends accumulating around the figure of Charlemagne, founder of the French 'empire' and progenitor of the current royal family. The real-life Frankish King Charles had become the mythical head of a court of chivalric paladins who fought the heathen, most notably in the late eleventh-century '*Song of Roland*', and now a British ruler could be represented as creating a similar court and empire long before him. Geoffrey's work became the centre of a new mythology, and was translated into Anglo-Norman (first by Geoffrey Gaimar in the 1140s), Latin, and French and worked on by other twelfth-century authors. Robert Wace, a Channel Islander educated at Caen in Normandy and in the 1170s a canon of Bayeux cathedral, created the world of the courtly 'Knights of the Round Table' with their quests in the *Roman de Brut* around 1154.[3] Thereafter the knightly quests – with an increasingly other worldy dimension – took centre stage and were the staple of mainly French writers who had minimal interest in British politics. The Arthurian stories from now on tended to open with the conception of the king, rather than venturing into the history of his family. Thus Ambrosius became sidelined, and the much less historical 'Uther Pendragon' occupied the opening section of the narrative. The lead in creation of the 'Round Table' chivalric romance in the mid-twelfth-century was taken by French writers, not English ones – and thus it reflected their contemporary ideal knightly culture, not the rough inter-dynastic feuds of sixth-century Wales. The only contemporary new English version of the Arthurian story, by the 1190s West Midlands priest Layamon, was to be far less 'polished' if more authentically British. The Anglo-Norman and Angevin courts spoke French, not English, and were attuned to contemporary pan-European knightly culture, not to the traditions of their 'Celtic' neighbours; thus the English courtly writers and minstrels did not have much interest in the Welsh legends of Arthur.

A protégé of Henry II and his wife Eleanor of Aquitaine who presented his work to Eleanor in 1155, Wace may well have modelled the Arthurian court on theirs. The increasingly independent-minded and formidable figure of Guinevere in the mid-later twelfth-century seems to owe something to the example set by Eleanor, sovereign in her own right of the Duchy of Aquitaine from 1137 and adventurous enough to go on Crusade with her first husband Louis VII of France in 1147–8. Notably, Eleanor was also surrounded by sporadic rumours about adultery – there had been stories of her unseemly relationship with her uncle Raymond of Poitou, lord of Antioch, on the Crusade, Louis forcibly dragged her away from Antioch to accompany him onwards to Jerusalem, and she and the conventionally pious Louis proved incompatible. Having divorced him, she almost immediately married his principal rival for domination of France, the much younger Count Henry of Anjou and Maine, Duke of Normandy and soon to become King of England, in 1152. Later in life, she was to turn against Henry and cause their elder sons to join her in rebellion against him in 1173–4; he held her in secure custody for the final fifteen years of his reign. Once he had died, she served as regent of England for her favourite son Richard I in his absence on Crusade after helping to halt the attempted usurpation of her youngst son, John, and was still active in politics when she died in 1204 aged either 80 or 82. The spirited and talented Eleanor – head of her own court and surrounded by devoted knights like William Marshal – was very much an exemplar for the literary Guinevere, a woman now shown as capable of conducting a long-term affair behind Arthur's back and ending up disgraced as Eleanor was in 1173. Wace also started off the concept of Arthur not dining on a holy feast-day until he had heard of some marvellous deed, and claimed that the Welsh believed that he would return from 'Avalon'. The stories had spread far enough afield for a representation of one scene to appear in carvings on Milan Cathedral in the mid-twelfth-century. The likeliest connection with Italy was the movement of Normans to and from their other major conquest of the later eleventh-century, the kingdom of Naples – which had English chief ministers in the mid-twelfth-century.

(ii) The later twelfth-century and thirteenth-century

The 'historical' chronicles.

The 'saga' epic, without courtly quests and otherworldly figures, was extended by Layamon, priest of Areley Regis in Worcestershire, in his *Brut* in English around 1190. His name, the Scandinavian term for the office of 'Lawman' and more common on the Isle of Man than in England, suggest that he was of Viking heritage. He kept some of Geoffrey's and Wace's elements of the fabulous such as the King's combat with the giant of Mont-St.Michel, having the wounded Arthur carried off to Avalon by the elf-queen Argante after his last battle, but played down the chivalry – presumably as appropriate for a local audience of less sophistication than Wace's courtly patrons. His story is more in the 'secular' Saxon tradition of warrior stories like *Beowulf*, and his concentration on the 'historical' and military rather than the courtly side of the legend was a tradition that lost out in subsequent tellings. This aspect of Arthurian storytelling was continued in Robert Mannyng's re-telling and elaboration of Wace, *The Story of England* (1328), and in John Hardyng's *Chronicle* (1461) which – like Malory – drew on the current feuding of York and Lancaster. This version of the Arthurian story presented it in a sober 'chronicle' form not as outright romance, ie it was meant to be seen as 'real' history.

The patriotic concept of Arthur ruling most of northern Europe was particularly suitable for the time of the Angevin 'empire', when Henry II, Richard, and John (to 1204) ruled more of France than the French king did. Arthur was a particularly apt figure to write about in the 1190s, following the 'discovery' of his grave – with a marker-cross naming him and Guinevere as the occupants – by monks at Glastonbury Abbey in 1190/1, recorded by Giraldus Cambrensis.[4] The recent devastating fire at the Abbey in 1184 and need to find funds to rebuild it suggests a reason for the discovery – and Arthur's alleged sword 'Excalibur' had been given by someone to King Richard I by 1190 when he took it on Crusade and presented it as a gift to his ally King Tancred of Sicily.[5] Giraldus specifically named Glastonbury – in its capacity as the 'Island of Apples' – as the wounded Arthur's destination after Camlann, which Geoffrey had not done. Richard I's nephew and putative heir – son of Duchess Constance of Brittany – was named 'Arthur' in 1187. There had been legends of Arthur in Brittany for many generations, but no use of the name in its Ducal family until then – the impetus presumably came from Arthur's father Geoffrey, son of Henry II and Eleanor. Arthur was beaten to the English throne by his uncle John in 1199, captured in a later attempt to seize Normandy and Anjou, and disappeared at Rouen in suspicious circumstances in spring 1203. The name was however used again for later, reigning Dukes after the late thirteenth-century; and ironically Duke Francis' brother Arthur of Richemont was a leading general of the Valois kings of France against the English Kings in the struggle for France after 1415. The cult of the king was taken up by the

English monarchy, particularly by the aggressive Edward I who sought to rebuild an 'Arthurian' empire across Britain. Edward I organised a royally-sponsored reburial of 'Arthur' and 'Guinevere' in Glastonbury Abbey in 1278[6] – though the event also reminded the king's Welsh enemies that their hero was dead and would not return to save them. As conqueror of the last independent kingdom in Wales (Gwynedd, ruled by Maelgwyn's descendants) in 1283, Edward duly carried off assorted pieces of 'Arthurian' memorabilia to adorn his treasury to emphasize that he, not the dynasts he had suppressed, was Arthur's heir. His attempted conquest of Scotland, of which he was already overlord like Arthur had been, from 1296 was in the Arthurian tradition of creating an 'empire' of all Britain. He would have seen himself, the ultimate warrior-king, as Arthur's natural heir, and there are Arthurian echoes in contemporary 'staged' incidents like the siege of Caerlaverock Castle and the vow which he forced on his son and his knights to reconquer Scotland after Robert Bruce's revolt in 1306.

Edward III created the 'Order of the Garter' using an Arthurian model, and held 'Round Table' chivalric events at Windsor Castle (the probable site of which was dug up by Channel Four's *Time Team* in 2006). He also called his second surviving son Lionel, Duke of Clarence, after one of the new Round Table figures to emerge in contemporary, post-Chretien romances – Lancelot's cousin, a Gallic prince and brother of the worthy Grail-quester Sir Bors. Edward IV and his brother-in-law Lord Rivers sponsored enthusiasm for 'Arthuriana' at the time of Malory's Arthurian Romances, and Edward could claim to be a descendant of the ancient Welsh kings via his Mortimer ancestors – as was used to obtain Welsh backing for his coup in spring 1461.[7] Henry VII, who made much of his royal Welsh descent to link himself to Geoffrey's final Welsh 'High King' Cadwaladr, called his eldest son Arthur and had his birth take place at Malory's choice for the site of Camelot, Winchester.

Henry VIII apparently had his own likeness painted on the imitation 'Round Table' displayed at Winchester Castle, and it is arguable that his aggressive concept of himself as an 'Emperor' of the British Isles – which bolstered his self-esteem in dealing with the 'real' Emperor Charles V after 1519 – was helped by the literary legends of his illustrious forebear's conquests. Arthur had conquered the 'Celtic fringes' and been crowned Emperor according to Malory, and Henry was to formally annex Wales and proclaim himself 'King of Ireland' and attempt to be elected Holy Roman Emperor in 1519. Henry's vast conceit needed little prompting, but as a young King he operated very much in an 'Arthurian' world of knightly chivalry, taking part in tournaments himself and invading France in 1513, and once he had decided on a religious breach with Rome the alleged precedent of Arthur defying Roman authority could give him spurious legal justification.

Certainly the alleged independence of the 'Apostolic era' Church in Britain, whether dateable to Joseph of Arimathea or to 'King Lucius' c.160, was used as a politico-religious weapon by Thomas Cromwell in breaking off dependence on the Papal Curia. Henry made much of the rights of the King of England as an 'Emperor', sovereign within his island, and the literary Arthur was the obvious source of this claim.

The main Arthurian tradition – the chivalric court

But the main route from a fairly plausible hero-king – albeit reworked in a twelfth-century context to resemble the current ruler of England and much of France, Henry II – to an idealised fantasy world of knightly quests involving the supernatural was developed from the 1170s by the Northern French romancers rather than by English writers. They centred around the court circles of Henry II's Queen Eleanor and her daughter Marie of Champagne. In this international world, the political concept of Arthur the warrior and empire-builder began to fade into the background as the elaborate world of his knights and their ladies was developed, and the famous 'love triangle' of Arthur, Guinevere, and Lancelot emerged. The adulterous behaviour of Queen Eleanor may have been a model for the equally independent-minded and unreliable Guinevere. Henry II faced revolt from an ungrateful younger generation as Arthur did, and later Richard I put the idealistic Christian quest to reconquer Jerusalem – ruled by his Angevin relatives – from the Infidel above his duties in his own kingdom. Marie has been equated with the mysterious mid-twelfth-century romantic author 'Marie de France', author of *Lanval*, but this is now thought unlikely – the latter may be Henry's illegitimate half-sister the Abbess of Shaftesbury.

Chretien of Troyes was the first to downplay Arthur's personal role and to create a series of long tales of knightly heroes, including the new leading hero Lancelot 'of the Lake', in his *Chevalier de la Charette*, *Erec et Enide*, *Cliges*, *Yvain: Le Chevalier au Lion*, and *Le Conte du Grail* (about Perceval). The first, a courtly re-working of Guinevere's abduction by King Melwas from the 'Life of St Gildas' – here the king is 'Meleagaunt' – for the twelfth-century and the first romance to mention Lancelot, was commissioned by Marie of Champagne and may owe something to the current works about Tristan's forbidden love for his king's wife; the 'Conte du Grail' was commissioned by Count Philip of Flanders, later himself a Crusader. The 'Grail' was of particular interest in Chretien's home – town of Troyes, with its links to the Order of Knights Templar and to the cult of Mary Magdalene (see below). Having started off his career translating the love-poetry of Ovid, Chretien came to the Arthurian 'cycle' from a different, literary romantic angle and was not that interested in Arthur's military career. As a Northern Frenchman not an English 'historical' writer, with an 'internationalist' chivalric perspective, his interest lay in the courtly culture, not in politics. Arthur's lineage and ancestral progenitors were of no importance and were sidelined.

Chretien and his immediate followers created the names of most of the knights as they were known by Sir Thomas Malory's 'finalised' version of the romances around 1470, and the familiar legends about Lancelot and Guinevere as the doomed lovers at the heart of Arthur's circle, Merlin the 'magician' with his otherworldly father and human mother, Morgan Le Fay the enchantress (who ultimately became the enemy of the king and his knights), and the 'Ladies of the Lake' Nimue and Viviane. (Morgan had already been named as Arthur's kinswoman and the lady of 'Avalon' by Geoffrey in his work on Merlin.) The abduction of Guinevere was already present in Welsh legends, but the form that it now took – involving Launcelot's rescue – seems to have definite parallels to a notorious incident in 1168 when Eleanor was ambushed by a disgruntled Poitevin baron, Guy of Lusignan (later the incompetent King of Jerusalem who lost his kingdom to Saladin), and William Marshal held off the attackers. For some reason Chretien did not complete either the Lancelot story (which was finished by Geoffrey de Leigny) or the Grail romance; the latter was extended by four continuators between c.1190 and 1220, the second being Gautier de Denain, the third by Manessier, and the fourth by Gerbert de Montreiul. By the time of the last two, the work was being influenced by the new version of the Grail story by Robert de Boron.

The tales of Lancelot became linked to the symbolic family of the mysterious King Pelles and his daughter Elaine, by whom Lancelot had his son the 'perfect knight' Galahad, and links to the 'Grail dynasty' descended from Joseph of Arimathea began to be elaborated. The central role of Gawain as the leading Arthurian knight in Geoffrey's work began to be eclipsed, as Chretien brought in his more spiritually-accomplished rival Perceval (achiever of the Holy Grail) and the chivalric Lancelot. Gawain was already being presented as an imperfect character by Chretien, namely as an impulsive lecher, and this flaw in his character became more pronounced in future French (though not English) romances. It was notable that the later linkage of Lancelot to the Grail quest, both personally and as the father of the eventual Grail-achiever Galahad, and his relationship with the 'Grail dynasty' descendant Elaine were *not* present in Chretien's version – these developed later. This suggests that they were new literary inventions, not extant mid-twelfth-century tales – if they had been in existence by this date, it is probable that Chretien would have used them and built up Lancelot not Perceval as the 'Grail hero'. Given that Perceval was based on the Welsh hero Peredur, as seen in the tales of the 'Mabinogi', Chretien seems to have had access to contemporary Welsh literature – possibly to romances recited by travelling (Breton?) bards. But, as with Geoffrey of Monmouth and the *Brut Tysilio*, we cannot say if any extant Welsh versions of the story of Peredur developed out of or independently of Chretien's work or if he used them as a source.

Following Chretien's work, the subsidiary tales of Erec and Yvain were adapted into German by Hartmann von Aue in *Erek* (1180s) and *Iwein* (c. 1202). They also appeared in altered versions as *Geraint ab Erbin* and *Owain* in the Welsh collection later known as the 'Mabinogion', with Erec being linked to the Dumnonian king Gereint of around 500. It is unclear if this literary development was solely a direct derivation from Chretien, or had independent Welsh sources. Gereint being a Dumnonian king known to heroic Welsh poetry, the latter could have been the source of most of the twelfth-century tales about him. But some inconsistencies and departures from the 'accepted' behaviour of twelfth-century courtly knighthood in the tale of Erec may suggest that Chretien was using a 'Celtic' source. A whole cycle of complicated stories of quests, known as the *Vulgate* after comparisons with the similarly definitive

Bible translation of St Jerome, was in place in the early thirteenth-century and gives us the essential core of the story which was reworked by Sir Thomas Malory in the fifteenth-century and later by Tennyson and T.H. White. This massive trilogy of around 18,000 words divided the Arthurian story into three sections – the first on the adventures of Lancelot; the second on the quest of the Holy Grail, here achieved by Galahad, his son by Elaine; and the third on the plot of Arthur's nephews Agravaine and Modred which leads to the fracturing of the brotherhood of the Round Table and Arthur's death in Modred's rebellion. Lancelot's adventures became extended with a mixture of straightforward chivalric heroics and the complications of his relationships with Guinevere and Elaine. Interestingly the writers did not think it unapt to present this knightly paragon as a figure capable of suffering nervous breakdowns and losing his memory, with one story in the c.1215 'Prose Lancelot' having him running away from Camelot insane after the pressures of his guilty passion for the Queen became too much to bear. Caught trying to seduce the visiting Elaine after the jealous Guinevere set a trap, Lancelot jumps out of a window and spends two years roaming Britain insane until he is located as an amnesiac 'fool' at King Pelles' court. The equally imperfect Gawain was increasingly written off as a thug and was credited with unknightly blood-feuds, killing Sir Lamorak who he found in bed with his mother Queen Morgause; Lancelot remained a hero despite his failings and was portrayed with a degree of psychological depth.

The 'human' Lancelot was bound to appear as more interesting to the audience than the 'perfect' and flawless Galahad, although in both cases their deeds were written up with a large degree of symbolic 'sub-text' about the meaning behind the nature of their challenges and opponents. Assorted mysterious ladies setting tasks, 'Black' and 'Red' Knights challenging the heroes to duels, warriors hiding their true identities (easier from the fourteenth-century once fully – concealing helmet and full armour were developed), and castles full of temptations littered the tales, and were elaborated to the point of confusion – but not yet parody. In the process any connections between the mysterious lands through which the questing knights travelled and 'real' Britain – either contemporary mediaeval or ancient post-Roman – was lost, in which the French nationality of many of the writers helped. There was no contemporary effort to identify sites, though the interest of the English monarchs in

Arthur as their progenitor provided opportunities for playing up what little was guessed about the 'reality' – the identification of Arthur's burial-site with Glastonbury since the excavations of 1190/1 being useful. As Glastonbury expert Geoffrey Ashe has admitted, any topographical 'clues' in the romances are early thirteenth-century at the earliest e.g. the probable identification of the chapels on and near Glastonbury Tor in 'Perlesvaus' c.1210. The identification has been challenged by Baram Blackett and Alan Wilson, who prefer to argue that the approach to the site of Arthur's resting-place described in 'Perlsevaus' is that from Nash Point, Glamorgan, to the church of St.Peter on Mynydd y Gaer near Pencoed – but this is very much a minority viewpoint.

Following the claims in the text, the *Vulgate* trilogy was supposed to have been composed by Walter Map, a canon of St Paul's Cathedral, London (born in the Welsh Marches) who died around 1209 and is known to have been interested in 'Arthuriana' and romances. Most scholars apart from Noel Currer-Briggs now discount this, the literary language in the three books being sufficiently different to suggest three different authors. At best the overall scheme may have been designed by one writer, and the existence of a nearly-exact earlier version of the Lancelot story (incomplete) may have been this person's 'original' version of one of the three books. Map's writings contain a probable 'original' for the Breton romance of Sir Orfeo, and it is thought that he may have composed a poem on Lancelot – possibly the 'original' *Lancelot du Lac* which the *Vulgate* section on Lancelot drew on. The *Vulgate*'s threefold division of the tales into the knightly deeds of Lancelot, the quest of the Holy Grail, and the downfall of Arthur meant that in the process the youthful rise to power and battles of Arthur were pushed into a minor role. The main wars covered were not those where Arthur defeated his British or Continental rivals, but the later war between Arthur and King 'Galehault', ruler of the 'Remote Isles', in which Lancelot defeats the invader and wins his adherence and friendship. (The similarity of the names of Galehault and Galahad has led to speculation that they came from one 'original'.) The Arthurian Grail quest in the earlier versions had earlier concentrated on the deeds of Perceval and/or Gawain; it was now 'fixed' as covering the search by Lancelot, his son Galahad the rightful occupant of the 'Siege Perilous', Perceval, and Lancelot's cousin Bors. Gawain's deeds only served to show where and why a 'secular-minded' knight was bound to fail. Lancelot failed to achieve the Grail due to his adulterous love for Guinevere but was granted a partial redemption with a brief, imperfect vision of it; Galahad the pure-hearted succeeded, Perceval retired to a hermitage, and Bors returned to Camelot to tell the story after Galahad's death. The landscape of the Middle East in which Galahad's group made the final stages of their quest was definitely thirteenth-century, with pagan 'Saracen' rulers not real-life fifth- or sixth-century Romans, and daringly Galahad was allowed to heal the sick like Christ.

No major additions were to be made to that collection, once the *Vulgate* trilogy itself had been extended with two more books – the *Estoire du Saint Graal* and *Estoire de Merlin*. The former updated the story of Robert de Boron concerning the 'Grail dynasty' from Joseph of Arimathea to the time of Lancelot's grandfather. The latter retold Robert de Boron's version of the Merlin story until Arthur's accession, and then went on to describe Merlin's role at Arthur's court and his downfall at the hands of the enchantress Vivian. It introduced the idea of Arthur deliberately passing himself off as his brother-in-law King Lot to seduce his half-sister, resulting in Modred's birth, and of Merlin being imprisoned in the Forest of Broceliande (in a tower not an oak-tree). After this, new additions consisted of elaborations to existing tales not major new ones, and the role of the Arthur-Guinevere-Lancelot 'triangle' became the centre of attention in place of the King's rule.

The *Vulgate* was revised by the 1230s into a new *Roman du Graal*, usually known as the '*Post-Vulgate Cycle*'. This made no major additions in content, though there were a few symbolic new elements such as the 'Questing Beast' and its hunter Sir Pellinore (who were humorously updated by T.H. White in the 1930s) and the alteration of the nature of the 'Dolorous Stroke' which created the 'Waste Land'. This was now attributed to the 'rogue knight' Sir Balin, and has been claimed as being meant to symbolise the fall of Jerusalem to the Muslims in 1187. A bizarre new development had Arthur seeking to kill all the newborn babies in his kingdom in order to prevent the survival of his incestuous bastard Modred, equating Arthur with Herod; it has been speculated that this was a satire aimed at the current Holy Roman Emperor Frederick II. Meanwhile tales of Arthur's court and its chivalric environment even travelled as far as the remoter regions of Scandinavia, though in that region it appears that a more 'matter of fact' politico-military approach like that of Layamon's 'Brut' was more popular than the imaginative excesses of contemporary French courtly literature. More or less faithful translations of some of the major tales appeared in Old Norse in the central third of the thirteenth-century, and were apparently commissioned at the court of the greatest warlord of the era, King Haakon IV 'The Good' (ruled 1217–63). This restorer of Norwegian stability and regional influence after an era of coups, who voyaged to the Hebrides and invaded Scotland in 1263 in a bid to restore Norway's overseas 'empire' of the eleventh-century, was an appropriate admirer and emulator of Arthur like his contemporary Edward I of England, and the Scandinavian tradition of 'sagas' of great leaders was adapted for the Arthurian stories. The main ones commissioned were the 'Tristrams saga', the 'Ivens saga' (a version of the tale of Yvain), the 'Mottuls saga' (adapted from the Breton French 'Lai du cort mantel'), and the 'Parcevals saga' (the story of Perceval and the Holy Grail). These mostly came from the basic texts by Chretien de Troyes, and were identified by Arthurian scholar Henry Leach in the 1920s as a systematic 'programme' of creating a local courtly version of Arthurian legends by Haakon from 1226. In due course the tale of Yvain was translated into Swedish too, in the saga of 'Ivan Legonriddars', by the wishes of Queen Euphemia, wife of Haakon's grandson King Haakon of Sweden. The tales were also adapted into Icelandic in a (republican) country famous for its tradition of heroic literature featuring bold adventurers, and parts of Geoffrey of Monmouth's 'historical' tales and 'Merlin's prophecies' were adapted at an Icelandic monastery by Gunnlaugr Leifsson (d. 1218) as 'Breta sogur' and 'Merlinus spa'. Most scholars agree that the original Arthurian impetus in Scandinavia for the '*riddarasogur*', '*Tales of the Knights*', came from the Norse court though it diffused to a lower social level later – as did the later mediaeval English provincial Arthurian creations (eg '*Sir Gawain and the Green Knight*').

(iii) Malory

After this, the next major mediaeval collection – and updating – of the central story was in Sir Thomas Malory's *Morte d'Arthur* in the 1460s. The confusion over Malory's identity was worse than that over Map's authorship (or not) of the *Vulgate* cycle, given the anonymous nature of the author and the number of men of that name alive at the time. P. J. C. Field, in *The Life and Times of Sir Thomas Malory* (1993), seems to have solved the controversy in favour of the Thomas Malory of Newbold Revel, Warwickshire, who died in Newgate, London in March 1471. This Malory was a possible protégé of Edward IV's brother-in-law Anthony Woodville, Lord Scales and (1469) Earl Rivers, a chivalrous enthusiast and tournament-competitor with a mystic streak who wore a hairshirt and ended as a victim of Richard III. Rivers was a possible inspiration of his work which was completed in the ninth year of Edward's reign (1469/70), and the current enthusiasm for 'Arthuriana' at the young King's court provided an appropriate context. (The royal Gwynedd descent of Edward, via the Mortimers, had been used for propaganda at his usurpation in 1461, making him appear as the 'son of prophecy' who would restore Welsh pride and power.) Malory was arrested and imprisoned in Newgate Prison in 1468–70, completing his text in the ninth year of Edward's reign i.e. in March 1469 – March 1470. He presumably wrote the work while he had enforced leisure in gaol, though he may have been working on it earlier. This arrest could be explained as due to his involvement in the Lancastrian plot of 1468 against Edward in which London's Lord Mayor Thomas Cook was implicated.

Malory had been a protégé of Edward's cousin and chief adviser, Richard Neville ('the Kingmaker'), Earl of Warwick, the local magnate for his Warwickshire estates, who he had fought under for the Yorkists in 1460–2 and who was married to the daughter of Malory's former military patron in France, Richard Beauchamp, Earl of Warwick (d. 1439). By this time the earl was becoming estranged from the King, and Malory's alienation from the Court could be linked to this. Knighted around 1440, he had served for a number of years in France (he may even be the Thomas Malory who had been in the Calais garrison soon after Agincourt) and had been an MP – thus a leading local figure trusted by the gentry to represent their opinions in London – in the turbulent later 1440s. He was probably one of the MPs who were highly critical of the concentration of patronage in the hands of a few unpopular magnates close to the easily-influenced King Henry VI, and thus graduated to support for the reforms proposed by the King's cousin Richard, Duke of York in the early 1450s. Logically the emphasis placed on the destructive family 'factions' and blood-feuds at King Arthur's court in the *Morte d'Arthur* can be interpreted as a commentary on the feuding of the great nobles and royal kin in the chaotic England of the 1450s. In particular, the bloodbath at Towton Moor in 1461 as the usurper Edward IV destroyed the Lancastrian army of Queen Margaret of Anjou – which Malory probably participated in as a member of Warwick's retinue – has been suggested as an inspiration for his account of the day-long slaughter at Camlann. Malory also took part in the Yorkist siege of Bamburgh Castle, then identified as the probable site of Lancelot's 'Joyous Guard' stronghold, in 1462 and so could have used his experience in constructing the story of Arthur's siege of Lancelot there. Conceivably, his repeated affirmation of the importance of a knight's loyalty to his patron despite political conflict (e.g. Lancelot's to Arthur) might be reflected in his politically dangerous decision to plot against the established king in favour of his old patron Henry VI in 1468. But unfortunately for Malory's reputation his earlier gaolings in 1452–60 were linked to multiple allegations of attempted murder, rape, and robbery over a number of years. One of a number of miscreant knights who had fought for the English cause in France and then taken part in the semi-anarchy of the 1450s, he had been ambitious or foolhardy enough to attempt to kidnap a leading and very wealthy nobleman with Royal blood, Humphrey Stafford, the Duke of Buckingham, in 1450. Given Buckingham's local estates, this could have been part of a land-dispute and the Duke may have exaggerated the charge out of spite. Malory was accused of raping the same woman (a Mistress Smith) twice – though in current legal terms this might mean no more than a cuckolded husband seeking revenge with the aid of Malory's enemies like Buckingham. He had conducted a vendetta against Combe Abbey (Warwickshire) involving armed robbery. He may have had powerful enemies keen to charge him and was vulnerable to prosecution, and the Combe Abbey incident be linked to a land-dispute.[8]

Nor were his activities uncommon for the turbulent local politics of the period powerful families across various counties, including the Pastons and their rivals the Mowbrays in Norfolk, fought out their differences under a weak government. But Malory went further than most such aggressive local notables, twice breaking out of prison, and the number and variety of the accusations over a long period indicate that he was not exactly blameless. He was clearly guilty of some brigand-like activities, unusual for a respectable author of moral tales about the great deeds of virtuous kings and knights, and had made the most of the endemic disorder and weak law-enforcement of the 1450s. Some commentators have argued that he reformed his violent and unscrupulous character with age, others that there must be a mistake and 'the' Sir Thomas Malory has not been located yet. This Malory died in spring 1471, within months of his final release from prison; it is not known what part he played in the warfare of that time when his ex-patron Warwick fought against the deposed Edward's return to power.

But whatever Malory's failings, he created a magnificent and comprehensive collection of the Arthurian stories, covering the entire 'cycle' from the affair between Uther and Ygraine to the final battle between Arthur and Modred. He followed the traditional pattern in starting with the conception of Arthur (though he omitted the story of Merlin's origins) and then proceeding on the basic lines of Geoffrey's story through Arthur's wars against the rival kings of Britain and Continental conquests – which could now be linked to Henry V's triumphs. But he went further than usual in having Arthur take Rome and be crowned Emperor. This war, in the first section of the book, also took place earlier in Arthur's reign than it had previously been placed – the war with Rome comes immediately before Modred's rebellion in Geoffrey's version. The best-known of the tales of the principal Knights of the Round Table followed, starting with Gawain and Yvain and leading up to the collection of Lancelot's adventures which were based on the *Vulgate* version, concentrating on Lancelot's chivalric prowess and leaving the tale of his adultery with Guinevere until later. (Thus the adventure of the 'Knight in the Cart', the 'Chevalier du Charette', derived from Chretien's story, had to come with the section on the love-affair later as it deals with the knight and the Queen's relationship.) Showing his sympathy for Lancelot, Malory allowed him a consolation for missing out on achieving the Grail – he was not spiritual enough to be the 'perfect knight' but he could heal the (deeply symbolic) wounds of a visiting knight who had been told that only the best knight in the world could aid him. This 'laying-on of hands', probably linked to the new fourteenth–fifteenth-century ceremony of 'touching for the King's evil' where the English King could heal scrofula, provided a more satisfying conclusion for the story of Lancelot than leaving him bereft of the Grail and his son. It was retained as the climax of Lancelot's story in T.H. White's *Once and Future King*.

A new and long section of the work described the adventures of Gawain's brother Sir Gareth of Orkney in his knightly training, following his anonymous arrival at Camelot. The exploits of a humble squire of unknown origins who put up with the hostility of his superiors as he learned to become a knightly paragon, together with his backing by a mysterious patroness – the 'Bel Inconnu' story – was a variant on Lancelot's early adventures and a staple of mediaeval chivalric tales. The villain of the story was made Sir Kay, now transformed from Arthur's foster-brother and close companion into a bullying steward at Camelot. The Gareth story mainly derived from that of Yvain in Chretien of Troyes' trilogy, via its Welsh version ('*Owain or the Lady of the Fountain*'). The Tristram tales formed another substantial section of Malory's text, with him now firmly connected to the Round Table as a friend of Lancelot and his guest at the 'Joyous Guard', and was followed by the quest of the Grail and then the story of Arthur's downfall at the hands of Modred. The story of Lancelot and Guinevere's affair now led into the plot by Modred and Agravaine to expose it, the sentencing and rescue of the queen, and the war between Arthur and Lancelot. The basic storylines were not much altered from the 'canon' established by the *Vulgate*, except for the date and outcome of the Roman war; but there were a few additional characters (particularly Gareth) and minor plots brought in from lesser-known mediaeval Arthurian stories. Presumably Arthur was given the extra years of triumphant European sovereignty after his defeat of Lucius to 'play up' his – and by transferrance Edward IV's England's – glory and make him seem a paradigm of peaceful rule to a divided England and divided Europe in the 1460s. He may also have been a reflection of Henry V, the epitome of British military triumphs on the Continent in the fifteenth century who was looked back to with nostalgia in the 1450s and 1460s.

Like a magpie, Malory seems to have connected all the Arthurian tales being told or written in fifteenth-century England; his rationalisation and ordering of the sequence of knightly deeds now became as definitive for the following centuries as had Geoffrey's version of Arthur's wars. The main sources for the sections of the book were:

1. 'The Tale of King Arthur – the 'Suite de Merlin', minus the story of Merlin's supernatural origins.

2. 'The Tale of King Arthur and Emperor Lucius' – as developed in the thirteenth-century from Geoffrey of Monmouth's story, but now placed earlier in the Arthurian timescale.
3. 'A Noble Tale of Sir Launcelot du Lac' – from the *Vulgate* 'Prose Lancelot'.
4. 'The Tale of Sir Gareth of Orkney' – probably from a lost English adaptation of Chretien de Troyes' story of Yvain.
5. 'The book of Sir Tristram de Lyones' – from the 'Prose Tristan'.
6. 'The tale of the Sankgreal' – the 'Prose Lancelot' story of Sir Galahad's origins and thence the *Vulgate* 'Quest del Saint Graal'.
7. 'The Book of Sir Launcelot and Queen Guinevere' – the *Vulgate* 'Quest del Saint Graal' and the 'Mort Artu'.
8. 'The Most Piteous Tale of the Morte Arthur' – the 'Mort Artu' and the English stanzaic 'Morte Arthur', its probably late fourteenth-century translation.

There were also new ideas specifically connected to contemporary culture, such as the Grail as a receptacle for the blood of Christ (which has been connected to the cult of the 'Holy Blood' at Hailes Abbey near Malory's Warwickshire home). As with Geoffrey's work, this retelling reflected contemporary politics in that the paragons of knightly virtue were meant as an inspiration to aspiring 'courtly' figures such as Earl Rivers, Edward IV's wife's brother, and were a reproach to the mindless violence and brigandage of assorted unruly English knights in the turbulence that followed the defeat in France. The anarchy and disorder which Arthur suppressed reflected the anarchy of the 1450s under the weak rule of the mentally ill Henry VI and his feuding factions of great lords, thus implicitly linking Arthur with the stronger rule of Edward IV, and the renewal of faction at Camelot thanks to Modred's party and the resultant bloodbath at Camlann were a warning of the fears for new disorder as the Yorkist regime fell into factional disputes in the late 1460s. This contemporary relevance was carried through into Malory's 1930s re-telling, the T. H. White *Once and Future King* trilogy, where it is the use of cannon by Modred that symbolises the end of the chivalric Arthurian era.

The Arthurian parallel of the then current political distemper and chaos in England in Malory's time was also made by and possibly inspired the chronicler John Hardying, whose matter-of-fact version of the story was first published in 1457 – in an interval between two rounds of the 'Yorkist vs Lancastrian' feuding at Henry VI's court. This made a comparison between the 'Waste Land' of the Grail kingdom under its sick king and politically unstable England under the mentally afflicted Henry VI. This may have lined him up politically with the party of Duke Richard of York that was seeking a new and strong government under a more capable ruler, and this point was more openly made in the chronicle's revised version in 1464 by which time York's son Edward IV had replaced Henry. Two more collections of alleged prophecies from Arthur's time, now supposedly foretelling Henry's reign, were published around 1461–5 – the dating suggesting that this was 'Yorkist' propaganda presenting Edward IV as Arthur who had rescued his people from chaos.

Malory's work was then printed by Caxton in 1483–5, the book's printing having been suggested by Edward IV (ie before he died in April 1483) and being completed on 31 July 1485 as Henry Tudor was sailing to invade England. Caxton was right up to date for events, as he changed Malory's version of Arthur's dream as he invades Gaul from him as the 'dragon' doing battle with a 'bear' to the 'boar' ie Richard III's heraldic emblem. Caxton imposed his own title, the *Morte d'Arthur*, instead of Malory's more wordy *The Whole Book of King Arthur and His Noble Knights of the Round Table*, and created the divisions of the stories into eleven sections. The crucial link between him and Malory would seem to have been Earl Rivers, their joint patron, who may have inherited the manuscript of Malory's book in 1471 and seems to have presented it to his wife's brother Edward IV. The new technology brought the Arthurian world to a far larger audience, with the new Tudor dynasty claiming dynastic links to the sixth-century Celtic British sovereigns and Henry VII naming his eldest son, born at the significant site of Winchester as chosen for the 'lying-in' of Queen Elizabeth by Henry in 1486, 'Arthur'. The latter unfortunately died young at Ludlow during an epidemic of the 'sweating sickness' in April 1502. Arthurian chivalry was still the vogue at the court of the young Henry VIII, who invaded France in 1513 and seems to have commissioned the painting of the 'Round Table' at Winchester Castle with his own features being used for Arthur's. (The occasion for this may have been the state visit of Emperor Charles V in 1521.)

Chapter 4

Decline and Revival. Arthur after Malory. More Anachronisms

As historical enquiries into Britain's past began to appear, the record of 'Arthurian' topography across the country was investigated by William of Worcester (c.1480) and more extensively by the indefatiguable John Leland in the 1530s. The latter, commissioned by Henry VIII to gather records of the now defunct monastic libraries, believed in Arthur's historicity as a real king and duly recorded the beliefs of the locals in the Cadbury Castle hillfort being Camelot. (This is not serious evidence of its factual basis; the villagers may have heard about Arthur from visiting literary enthusiasts and equated him with the unknown king – more likely from the name being Cador of Dumnonia – who had lived there.) Already some sceptical chroniclers, most notably Polydore Vergil in the 1490s, regarded Arthur as a literary creation. More topographical evidence was collected by the patriotic William Drayton in *Polyolbion* (1612), and the enterprising 'magician' Dr. John Dee used Geoffrey's stories of Arthur's wide-ranging empire as a useful historical justification for the planned Elizabethan colonial empire. Arthur, ruler of the Northern isles as far as Orkney and Iceland, could point the way to Elizabeth's 'sea-dogs' ventures to America, assisted by the even more dubious Welsh legend of Prince Madoc's voyage c.1170. The firmly Catholic nature of Arthurian imperial and knightly myths was 'down-played' by the newly Protestant state. Significantly, the 'Glastonbury Thorn' of Joseph of Arimathea was vandalised by a 'Puritan' protester as part of the attacks on all 'Popish' relics. The decline of the knightly 'milieu' in which Arthurian tales flourished then brought an end to major interest in the world of the 'Round Table' for some four centuries until the Victorian revival in enthusiasm for knightly chivalry, barring occasional Tudor royal tournaments.

The Arthurian story continued to produce 'spin-offs' such as Spenser's *Faerie Queen* (1590) and John Dryden's Arthurian opera. Spenser, a participant in the new Protestant imperial mission as a settler in Ireland (Munster), used a mysterious 'Artegall' as his hero rather than Arthur, probably deriving the name from Geoffrey of Monmouth's king Archgallo, but with Arthurian overtones and an Arthurian empire including Ireland. A rare Arthurian venture into the world of the Elizabethan theatre saw Thomas Hughes and various collaborators, including the young (Sir) Francis Bacon, write and put on 'The Misfortunes of Arthur' (based on Malory's tale of the break-up of the Round Table but with a few changes) before the queen in February 1587. Florid verse romances and novels full of imaginative but unlikely quests then went out of vogue across Europe, helped by the merciless satire of their pomposity and implausibility by Miguel de Cervantes in 'Don Quixote'. But there was still room for a 'political' Arthur – in the 1690s Richard Blackmore produced major poems on Prince Arthur and King Arthur, equating him with William of Orange as a valiant champion against tyranny – and 'Rome' i.e the Catholic Church and its Jacobite allies. In 1691 John Dryden wrote and Henry Purcell composed the music for 'King Arthur, or the British Worthy', a first Arthurian opera – though more of a vague romantic extravaganza featuring Arthur and a Saxon warlord fighting for the hand of a Cornish princess than an adaptation of any past work. Major new contributions were however lacking until the burgeoning of Romantic poetry, with the Arthurian story 'definitive' after Malory's exhaustive work and no political motive for a re-telling. The Catholic religion became equated with the national enemy, and the Arthurian 'cult' was reduced to a useful source of patriotism for Tudor and Stuart monarchs and a template for a British overseas empire.

The later seventeenth- and eighteenth-century were a low point in interest in 'Arthuriana', whose mediaeval aristocratic culture and religious overtones served no useful role for contemporary authors and seemed to have no resonance with the literary public. William Ireland's retelling of Geoffrey of Monmouth in his play 'Vortigern' (supposedly a 'lost' work by Shakespeare) was booed into oblivion by the Drury Lane audience at its first night in 1796. But then the fashion for 'sensibility' and Gothic tales brought a new audience, as the occasional appearance of new buildings built in 'mediaeval' style became more widespread after 1800. The 'Gothic' rebuilding of castles such as Windsor and Arundel in what was assumed to be the authentic mediaeval style was accompanied by new interest in mediaeval courtly values and in England's past, and the aristocracy and the new aspirant middle-classes began to 'buy into' mediaeval culture. Robert Southey produced a major new edition of Malory's work in 1817, and Sir Walter Scott started a fashion for mediaeval chivalry with his works including a new edition of the Tristram story (as told by the thirteenth-century Scots Borders poet Thomas 'the Rhymer' of Ercildoune) in 1804 and 'Lyulph's Tale' in his verse romance 'The Bride of Triermain' in 1813 (featuring the revenge of a forgotten illegitimate daughter of Arthur by a witch who ends up cast under a sleeping-spell by Merlin). His re-creation of Richard I's reign in *Ivanhoe* indirectly did a lot to inspire a general revival of enthusiasm for the mediaeval world and hence Arthurian Britian. Those inspired by Scott included William Morris, a passionate admirer of allegedly 'uncorrupted' idealistic mediaeval virtues (e.g. in crafts), who was a keen reader of Southey's edition of Malory at Oxford in 1853–5. He tackled the Arthurian story as told by Malory in his 'Defence of Guinevere And Other Poems' (1858). The bohemian Morris was far less antagonistic to the adulterous Queen than were 'respectable' writers such as Tennyson, and sought to explain and be sympathetic to her adultery with Lancelot which she confesses to the uncomfortable Gawain as she is about to be burnt at the stake. He then showed Guinevere and Lancelot admitting and being tormented by their guilt at the disaster which their forbidden love has caused to Arthur and the Round Table as they meet after the king's death in 'King Arthur's Tomb'. He did not excuse but he did understand their 'grand passion', unlike the virtuously shocked Tennyson's approach. Indeed, his own marriage ended up as an uncomfortable trio in the manner of Arthur, Guinevere and Lancelot with his wife Jane Burden entangled with his colleague Dante Gabriel Rosetti. His portrayal of Galahad and his helpers achieving the Grail Quest stressed the importance of a band of loyal comrades to the success, and so gave a hint that the questers were the model for his own 'Pre-Raphaelite Brotherhood'.

The mediaeval revivalist enthusiasm inspired Tennyson's *Idylls of the King*, of which the first Arthurian poems were published in 1842 and the first main collection in 1858. 'The Lady of Shalott' was originally written in 1832, based on a minor incident in the thirteenth-century French *Mort Artu* featuring the doomed love of the 'Demoiselle d'Escalot' for Sir Lancelot which was expanded in the Italian novella *La Donna di Scalotta*;

Elaine of Astolat could be confused with King Pelles' daughter Elaine of Corbenic, mother of Galahad. (One of the most quotable lines in the poem was then used as the title for Agatha Christie's Miss Marple mystery *The Mirror Crack'd*.) Tennyson began his selection of twelve Arthurian stories with 'The Coming of Arthur', in which he saves Guinevere's father Leodegran and marries her, and included ancient Welsh stories such as 'Geraint and Enid' (from the 'Mabinogion') and ones that only appear in Malory (such as 'Gareth and Lynette', the adaptation from 'La Belle Inconnu'). Indeed, the 'Mabinogion' itself was rediscovered as far as the English literary elite were concerned, with a new translation by local South Wales enthusiast Lady Charlotte Guest. Malory's knights had owed more to the fifteenth-century than to Geoffrey of Monmouth's world, let alone the sixth-century, and now Tennyson presented his heroes as the paradigms of Victorian gentlemen. The picture given of Arthur and the Grail-seekers owed more to conceptions of the role assumed by Prince Albert than to realistic reconstructions of the Dark Ages, although there was coverage of the tensions and impossible demands produced by idealism as well as propaganda for the Victorian monarchy. Tennyson was predictably hard on the adulterous Guinevere, as befitted Victorian morality, and had her flee to a convent after being caught with Lancelot rather than being sentenced to execution (piety replacing outmoded mediaeval punishments?). The spiritual struggles of the Grail-questers Galahad, Bors and Percivale reflected the intense piety of the leaders of the 'High Church' movement. Following on from Tennyson, Matthew Arnold produced a new poetic version of Tristram's story, 'Tristram and Iseult', in 1862; a more mystical version was Algernon Swinburne's 'Tristram of Lyonesse' in 1882.

The contemporary craze for 'Arthuriana' and Camelot – the Middle Ages as they should have been – was reflected in events such as the 'Eglinton Tournament' in 1839. Queen Victoria and Prince Albert, patrons of Tennyson, dressed up as the fourteenth-century Arthurian patrons Edward III and Queen Philippa at a famous fancy-dress ball and christened their third son 'Arthur' (partly after his godfather the Duke of Wellington) in 1850. The romantic Gothicised 'Camelot' appearance of Windsor Castle was however pre-Victorian, the renovations having been done by Sir Jeffrey Wyatville for George IV after 1815. The Arthurian stories provided a crucial inspiration and reference-point for the 'Pre-

Raphaelite Brotherhood', who by their choice of name were desiring to get back to pre-Renaissance idealism and religiosity, and they took Sir Galahad as their lodestar and the Round Table as their paradigm. Following their use of Arthurian subjects for their first major commission, the Oxford Union murals in 1857, Camelot provided a number of suitable subjects for the tapestries and poems of William Morris and the paintings of Dante Gabriel Rosetti, William Holman Hunt, and the Brotherhood drew on the imaginary chivalric world of the knights as a 'golden age' to be emulated. Morris was particularly interested in the Arthurian world, as representing an idealised pre-capitalist mediaeval order ruled by conscientious and chivalric lords; and his idealised version of women came to be linked with this world's heroines. The 'Pre-Raphaelite ' artists' illustrations of the 1857 edition of Tennyson's Arthurian poems provided some of the most influential and accessible imagery of the era. Burne-Jones' most famous paintings included 'Merlin and Nimue' (1861) and 'The Beguiling of Merlin' (1872–7), a favourite subject since Tennyson included the episode in '*Idylls of the King*' and a condemnation of inappropriate sex-based relationships between different age-groups. His works also included 'Morgan Le Fay' (1862) and 'King Mark and La Belle Iseult' (1862), but the most famous Victorian Arthurian painting was probably the non-Pre-Raphaelite Brotherhood (PRB) John Waterhouse's 'Lady of Shallott' (1888). The credits of memorable Arthurian art now extended to illustrations for editions of both Malory – such as Aubrey Beardsley for the Dent edition of 1893–4 and Arthur Rackham for the Macmillan edition of 1917 – and Tennyson's 'Idylls' – such as Gustav Dore's work for the 1868 edition.

As the Brotherhood wanted to revive the idealism of Christian mediaeval craftsmen yet used modern 'mass-produced' methods of industry at the works of Morris & Co., so a new fashion of architecture emerged to create Victorian country houses in the imagined style of the fifteenth-century. Vast baronial piles were built, like Eaton Hall in Cheshire for the Dukes of Westminster, where the nobility and those with 'new money' aspiring to that status could live in what they fondly imagined to be the manner of hospitable and chivalric mediaeval lords. The 'Gothic' style of architecture also significantly extended into education for the newly popular mid-Victorian public schools, those of the Woodard Foundation (including Lancing, Hurstpierpoint, and Ardingly) for example. William

Dyce produced inspiring – if ludicrously unhistorical – propagandist Arthurian murals for the new Palace of Westminster from 1849. The mediaeval chivalric ideal, ultimately derived from Malory in its literary inspiration via the medium of Sir Walter Scott, made 'Arthurian England' the exemplar for much of high culture in the period from c.1850 to 1914 – forgetting the irony of a 'Celtic' Briton who had fought the Saxons serving as a patron for an empire which was explicitly led by the 'Anglo-Saxon peoples'. Dyce eventually turned Catholic, and there was a problem over the contemporary High Church 'Catholicising' implications of Malory's orthodox Catholic theology in his writings on the Holy Grail – which Tennyson skated over carefully. His idealistic Arthurian knights had to be Anglican to avoid claims of propaganda for Cardinal Newman-style unpatriotic 'Romanising', a 'live' issue in the 1850s.

Modern Arthurian culture

In Germany, Wagner produced Arthurian grand operas – *Tristan und Isolde* in 1865 and *Parsifal* in 1882 (though with little actual connection to Camelot or the main Arthurian storyline). His version of the Arthurian story sought to go back 'beyond' the orthodox Catholic Christian version of Arthur's world in the mediaeval romances, to an 'authentic' earlier spirituality that had 'pagan' overtones – a Germanic version of the late Victorian interest in mystical 'alternative religion' seen in the work of mythographer such as Sir James Frazer. Gottfried von Strassburg's version of the Tristram story was his main source. He developed the mediaeval German telling of the 'Perceval' legends further in another opera on the story of Perceval's supposed son Lohengrin, the 'Swan Knight' (unknown to British sources), first performed in 1850. This mingled the Arthurian world with the unrelated traditional Low Countries tales of the 'Swan Knights' as mysterious protectors of embattled kingdoms and their heiresses, though its notion of an order of chivalric protector knights fitted in with the Round Table. Wagner's version was taken up by his eccentric admirer King Ludwig II of Bavaria (ruled 1864–86) as the centrepiece of his Arthurian fantasy-world, with the King an extravagant and psychologically unstable mediaeval revivalist obsessive seeking to make up for his Wittelsbach dynasty's and his kingdom's humiliating eclipse by the new German Empire. Unable to confront the unwelcome new

Empire with its Prussian-led armies, he saw himself as a new Lohengrin and constructed an appropriate fantasy grotto at Herrenschiemsee where he could sail around on a replica of Lohengrin's boat. The chivalric ethos created by the spendthrift Ludwig at Neuschwanstein Castle in Bavaria (the name a reference to the 'Swan Knights') owed more to Wagner than to Wolfram, a little to the symbolic quests and characters created by Chretien, and nothing to the 'political' twelfth-century world given to Arthur by Geoffrey and Layamon. This was an Arthur set within a romantic mediaeval Germanic context of soulful troubadour 'meistersingers' rather than an Anglo-Welsh king.

This nineteenth-century German romantic and supernatural reinterpretation of the Arthurian world – derived ultimately from Wolfram via Malory – had more interest in the mythical implications and interpretation of the romances than their geographical setting, and no more than a hazy sense of its historical background. It led in due course to the Nazis' interest in the Grail and other 'cult objects', now regarded as pagan Germanic talismans which had been usurped by the church. The notion of an 'Arthurian' order of virtuous and heroic knights – via the medium of the Templar Order – had an indirect influence on Himmler and his rituals for the SS, whose Prussian castle headquarters had its own version of the 'Round Table'. (The locally-based Teutonic Knights, whose Order had ruled East Prussia until the Reformation, had been a sort of 'Arthurian' knightly elite, created in the image of the twelfth-century Templars and Hospitallers.) Rudolf Hess was among the occult enthusiasts involved in this 'revival' within a Germanicised context; it implied a degree of brotherhood with the English as racially suitable 'Aryans' and the home of Arthurian chivalry. The concept of an order of warrior-heroes extended to the new German air-force, and its Wagnerian racial development into 'Germanic' brotherhood may have had some influence on the efforts to prevent a second Anglo-German war in 1939 and thence the mysterious flight of Hess to Scotland in 1941.

Britain – Tolkien et al

In Britain, more harmless reinterpretations included Glastonbury enthusiast (and local festival-founder) Rutland Boughton presenting socialistic folk-operas about Arthur in the 1920s. Boughton took the personal development of William Morris' ideal of mediaeval crafts-brotherhoods into communistic Socialism a stage further, together with trying to turn Glastonbury into an Arthurian Bayreuth with himself as the Wagnerian impresario. His opera 'The Queen of Cornwall', based on Thomas Hardy's poetic version of the tale of Tristram and Isolde, did not achieve success though his cultural efforts had the backing of Elgar and George Bernard Shaw. He staged a nativity play featuring Christ as a miner's child and ended his Arthurian saga with a workers' revolt in Marxist fashion, but this antithesis of usually conservative and royalist Arthurian culture did not lead far and put off sponsors. On a more mystical plane, the Christian – and pagan – religious symbolism of the myths inspired individualistic poets such as John Cowper Powys with his *Glastonbury Romance* (1932). To Powys, the mythography of Glastonbury and the world of the 'Grail' transcended Christianity and could provide the basis for a 'superior' pre-Christian spirituality, with the Somerset town as a British version of Jerusalem, Mecca, or Lhasa. This duly led to Katherine Maltwood and her search for the 'Glastonbury Zodiac' plus the feminist neo-pagan admirers of a local order of priestesses based at the Tor.

J.R.R. Tolkien was an Anglo-Saxon not a 'Celtic', literary expert, specializing in 'Beowulf', but was well-read in mediaeval Welsh literature too. His names, e.g. Frodo, Gandalf, and Thorin, were mostly taken from Old Norse. His warrior-king Aragorn in *The Lord of the Rings* owed much to Arthur, as the wizard Gandalf did to Merlin. (It has been suggested that Tolkien was influenced by the PRB paintings he had seen as a boy in a Birmingham art-gallery.) Aragorn emerged from obscurity as the 'hidden heir' to a great but declining kingdom like Uther's, namely Gondor, after being fostered by a mystical mentor (the elven lord Elrond) and 'proved' his right by possession of a sword (Anduril). Merlin had led Arthur to Excalibur in the lake; Elrond had kept the broken shards of Aragorn's ancestor's sword Anduril ready for use by his chosen heir. Aragorn also had Otherworldly backers, namely the 'High Elves' under Elrond whose daughter Arwen he married; like an Arthurian hero, he had to 'prove' himself to Elrond before he was granted Arwen's hand. Aragorn secured his new kingdom by defeating its enemies at a time of maximum danger. Arthur materialised from obscurity to rescue Britain after Uther died during the Saxon war; Aragorn, a minor warrior seen as a mysterious 'outsider' living in the wilderness at his first appearance to the hobbits, brought his 'Rangers' (plus the supernatural 'Army of the Dead') to rescue Gondor's capital as the Dark Lord's forces were storming it. The nearest equivalent to the knights' Otherworldly female patronesses was the Elves' Lady Galadriel, who received the 'Fellowship of the Ring' in her magical realm of Lothlorien (where normal time did not apply, as in Avalon?) and gave them gifts though the Catholic Tolkien probably used 'Our Lady', the Virgin Mary, not the *Ladies* of the Lake as a direct influence. After this Quest was over the wounded hero Frodo Baggins left by sea for the Elves' realm, in the manner of Arthur leaving Britain for Avalon with Galadriel and Elrond on board the 'magical' vessel. The great towered city of Minas Tirith bore obvious resemblances to Camelot, and the knights of Gondor were duly shown in 'Arthurian' suits of armour in the 2000s film-adaptation of the trilogy by Peter Jackson.

It was the humble like Frodo (until the final test) and Sam Gamgee who showed they could resist worldly temptation, like Galahad. The worldly and arrogant like Boromir failed in their tasks, as did Gawain in the Grail story. Gandalf was the inspiration for the Quest and the teller of the 'back story' to its participants, in the manner of Merlin; he disappeared from the story due to 'enemy action' before the final conflict, as Merlin did in the Arthur story (and the wizard headmaster Dumbledore did in the Harry Potter books) – though he reappeared later. Tolkien notably restored the Elves to their proper size and role as a parallel race to humanity as in the earliest 'Celtic' legends, not an under-sized source of good or malign magic as seen since the sixteenth-century (for which Shakespeare bears a lot of responsibility).

Tolkien's fellow-'Inklings' made their own contribution in the 1940s and 1950s, with elements of 'Arthuriana' entering C.S. Lewis' world of Narnia. The 'Waste Land' had an echo in the condition of Narnia ruled by the White Witch, before it was redeemed by Aslan and under-age (like Arthur) new human sovereigns. The Pevensie children go on a 'quest' to link up with the 'Talking Beasts' resistance to the invading White Witch and her army of 'baddies' from mythology, some of whom seem a little out-of-place for a semi-English or 'Northern' Scandinavian/ 'Celtic' world – as Tolkien, who disliked the book, pointed out. 'High King' Peter is presented with a sword to lead his army – oddly, by Father Christmas. The Witch (an unscrupulous, power-hungry temptress like the Arthurian

Morgause and Morgan) and her army, like the invading Saxons and the unruly British kings who resist Arthur from Geoffrey's work to Malory's, seem a daunting foe but are duly overcome against all odds. Lewis, a specialist in mediaeval allegory, also presented Prince Caspian in his second Narnian book as a dispossessed rightful heir needing to secure his throne by battle, like Arthur. In 'The Voyage of the Dawn Treader' a mixture of a 'quest' and constant Christian allegory was dominant in the story. Those who reached Aslan's land, such as the mouse knight errant Reepicheep, could not return to Narnia – as Galahad could not return to Britain. The Narnian 'capital', the grandiose castle of Caer Paravel, was obviously based on Camelot. Another 'quest', for a missing heir abducted by an Otherworldly 'Lady', appeared in 'The Silver Chair'. The final book, describing the revolt of power-hungry fraudsters against the rightful king and the catastrophic 'Last Battle', had echoes of Camlann as well as of the Book of Revelation' – and a word should also be put in for the evocative 'Arthurian' mediaeval illustrations of the Narnian books by Pauline Baynes, who had illustrated for Tolkien as well.

Tolkien and Lewis' colleague Charles Williams made a more specifically Arthurian contribution, utilizing sixth-century Welsh poetry. Unusually for a literary interpretor, he made Taliesin the central figure in his highly symbolic (and obscure) new version of the myths in *Taliessin Through Logres* (1938) and *The Region of the Summer Stars* (1944). (Interest in the Welsh legends had revived, but been a 'specialist' not mainstream pursuit, since Lady Charlotte Guest translated the '*Mabinogion*' – her term – in 1839.) This version of Arthurian Britain was firmly set in the sixth-century and went back to the Welsh legends, ignoring all the mediaeval accretions – an increasingly popular twentieth-century practice. Williams himself was a member of an offshoot of one of the Late Victorian 'neo-pagan' spiritual brotherhoods which had been inspired by the revived interest in 'Celtic' myths; the Irish poet W.B. Yeats belonged to another secret society, the Order of the Golden Dawn. The later Victorian interest in the origins of myths, most exhaustively by Sir James Frazer in *The Golden Bough* (1890), also provided a new avenue to approach the 'established' version of the Arthurian legends. Investigating the background of the pagan myths behind the Grail legend, Jessie Weston analysed the original centrality of the 'Waste Land' and the 'Fisher King' as opposed to the Grail itself in *From Ritual to Romance* (1920). This explanation and re-ordering of the symbolism was then used by T.S. Eliot in 'The Waste Land'. Romantic reactions to Eliot's 'arid' and modernist interpretation included those of the early twentieth-century novelists Arthur Machen and Mary Butts.

In the latest literary inspiration from the Arthurian story, it can be argued that some elements of it are present in the Harry Potter saga; Harry was left with ordinary foster-parents by a wizard (Dumbledore) and only recalled to face his destiny as an adolescent, though the bullying suburban Dursleys were a good deal less useful to him than Sir Ector and Kay were to Arthur. The oafish Dudley Dursley perhaps owed something to the traditional literary portrayal of Arthur's self-important foster-brother Kay. Some of the teachers at Hogwarts were reminiscent of T.H. White's Merlyn, in transformations into wildlife in particular. The pupils at Hogwarts and the 'Order of the Phoenix' recall the Knights of the Round Table – with Ron Weasley in the 'Lancelot' role and Lucius Malfoy as the jealous, bitter 'Mordred' figure? The 'good witch' role of Nimue as the King/ hero's resourceful protectress is taken by Hermione Granger, and Harry and his friends end up on a quest to retrieve the missing 'horcruxes' containing the scattered parts of the 'dark lord' Voldemort's soul to prevent him regaining his old power. A grand battle between good and evil ends the quest, as with Tolkien's battle at the Black Gate of Mordor and Arthur's battle at Camlann. The talking owls probably come from Merlyn's pet owl Archimedes in T.H. White's 'Sword in the Stone', and Hogwarts itself comes from Camelot as well as from Victorian boarding-school stories and its architecture in the films shows the influence of Neuchwanstein. The interiors were filmed at grandiose fourteenth-century Alnwick Castle, also used for the BBC's Late Mediaeval 'spoof' in the first series of 'Blackadder'.

Reactions to nineteenth-century 'revivalist' chivalry – cynicism and a search for a more 'accurate' picture of a 'Dark Ages' king

Once the chivalric world of Arthur fell out of vogue again after 1914 the literary use made of it turned more to satire. The excesses and bombast of idealised chivalry at Tennyson-style Camelot had already inspired Mark Twain to write *A Connecticut Yankee At the Court of King Arthur* in 1889, with the practical worldly commonsense of its American hero presented as superior to the code of the knights. The First World War also presented a blow to the enthusiastic militarism and associated piety of the Victorian knights, showing up the Victorians' naivety about what happened in 'real' war and decimating the upper-class 'gentlemen' who flocked to the colours. The public-school headmasters and militant clergy who had cheered on their charges into joining up were attacked for callousness, and the ideal of mediaeval chivalry went out of fashion – as did its architecture. In the 1930s Evelyn Waugh parodied the excesses of Victorian Gothic 'Arthuriana' in his creation of Hetton Court with its Arthurian-named bedrooms in *A Handful of Dust*, with a naïve young Arthurian enthusiast as the easily-deceived hero.The adulterous anti-heroine naturally has the bedroom named after Guinevere, and her lover is not a knightly paragon but a parasitic young 'lounge-lizard'. Indeed, this cold-hearted and scheming adulteress, an object of devotion from both the naïve Tony and the feckless young Mr Beaver (whose bossy mother, the equivalent of Lancelot's guardian the 'Lady of the Lake', is a tasteless interior decorator) is memorably shown as being relieved that a reported fatal accident involves her brattish young son, not her lover. The hero's 'quest' ends up with him trapped in the South American jungle reading Dickens to a madman. The next literary revival of 'Arthuriana' centred on a 'realistic' portrayal of a historic Arthur, stripped of mediaeval accretions, as explored above.

The imaginary and unhistorical world of Arthur's chivalric knights, as seen by Malory and Tennyson, was left to the quirky genius of T. H. White, a mediaeval enthusiast (and expert at the chivalric sport of falconry) who re-told Malory's version of events in four books collected as *The Once and Future King* in the 1930s. The first section, *The Sword in the Stone*, was the most 'original' – and popular – with its creation of Arthur's education by an individualistic Merlin (born backwards in time so he could tell his pupil about the 1930s) and magical transformation into animals. Merlin (Merlyn in this version) was seemingly based on the author, whose passion for falconry was utilised. This story was followed by one book on the Celtic youth of King Lot's children (Gawain, Agravaine, Gareth, Gaheris, and Modred) which explained their 'clannish' nature and the blood-feud which destroyed the Round Table; a third on the relationship between Lancelot (here talented but ugly) and Guinevere; and a fourth on the downfall of Arthur. The last two were taken almost verbatim from Malory, though with more psychological background and some up-dating; the 'Grail Quest' was virtually omitted. White gave up any attempt to make the 'too-perfect' Galahad understandable for modern readers, impossible due to the weight of the much-parodied Tennysonian poems, and concentrated on Lancelot; Arthur receded into the background after *The Sword in the Stone* but was shown as an essentially decent person who put up with his wife's and best friend's affair sooner than lose them.

White's own pacifist interpretations of the reasons for knightly aggression and war produced some oddities, most especially in his (only posthumously published) final section *The Book of Merlyn* where Merlyn explained to Arthur where he had gone wrong on the eve of the final battle of Camlann. The most memorable addition to the story was Merlyn's transformation of Arthur into a variety of birds and beasts to gain an insight into the world; it was the magicians, e.g. Merlin's prototype Gwydion/Taliesin, who were the sole 'shape-shifters' in Welsh myths. In the process of his unique creation White was able to provide both comedy, with ferocious but brainless giants, and chilling satire with his picture of the totalitarian world of the ant-colony. White made a major contribution in his addition of Arthurian humour. The absent-minded Merlyn, the eccentric King Pellinore, and 'Blimpish' military buffers like Sir Grummore Grummursum were particularly memorable. The antithesis of a chivalrous knight, the Flashman-like bully and cheat Sir Bruce Sans Pitie, was described in 1930s terms as a 'cad', and White had the idea of introducing Robin Hood to Arthur's guardian Sir Ector's hunting-party and being treated as a social embarrassment like a 1930s Communist. Not surprisingly the first part of the book, *The Sword in the Stone*, was taken up as a Disney film (1967), albeit with Americanisations disliked by purists. Then a Broadway musical (*Camelot*) was created out of the section on Lancelot and Guinevere, being filmed in 1967 with Richard Harris (Arthur), Vanessa Redgrave (Guinevere), and Franco Nero (Lancelot). The Lerner and Loewe stage-production of the early 1960s luckily coincided with the self-proclaimed youthful idealism of the Kennedy White House and so provided a new connection for 'Camelot' – with its hero being unjustly cut down by traitors just like Arthur. The prime literary backer of the Kennedy/Arthur analogy was John Steinbeck. The swashbuckling potential of the Arthurian era was also transferred to a new medium, with the *Prince Valiant* comic strip of the late 1930s. Created by Hal Foster for

William Randolph Hearst's newspaper syndicate and the longest-running cartoon adventure strip of the era, this presented a visualling stunning and hugely popular version of the basic 'Lancelot' story, with the invented 'Valiant' as the son of a deposed and exiled king who seeks help from Arthur and becomes a trainee knight at Camelot. In this version our hero's father is the king of 'Thule' (a mysterious invented Northern realm of mediaeval myth bordering on the Arctic which the Nazis later claimed to be a real ancient homeland of the 'master-race') not of 'Benwick', and he starts his swashbuckling career as a page to Sir Gawain who is a well-meaning but careless and hot-tempered womaniser as in later mediaeval stories. 'Val' becomes a Knight of the Round Table and then regains his father's kingdom and tours the world as a knight errant exporting the noble values of Camelot – including both wars with the real mid-fifth-century Germanic invaders of the Roman Empire (eg the Huns) and quests across the world to the Middle East and the Americas.

Arthur in the new twentieth-century media

The first film with an 'Arthurian' theme had been an attempt to film *Parsifal* in 1904, and from 1920 the American cinema made a number of variations of the Mark Twain *Connecticut Yankee* story (the most famous with Bing Crosby in 1949). Surprisingly, the first serious attempt to make a serious version of Malory's story on film had to wait until *The Knights of the Round Table* (MGM) in 1953. *The Black Knight* (Warwick/Columbia, 1954), with a new 'low-born' hero but the traditionally malevolent King Mark of Cornwall, foe of Sir Tristram, as the villain, was the most successful of the adventure-films which followed. The creation of comedy out of the Arthurian story had to wait until the Monty Python team's 1975 film on the quest for the Grail, with its memorably bizarre 'take' on horseless knights using coconut-shells to simulate hooves, the 'Knights who say 'Ni', and a 'Black Knight' who refuses to surrender despite having his limbs chopped off one by one. The classic answer to the excesses of obscure mediaeval allusiveness (written partly by a student of mediaeval history, Terry Jones), the film had the ultimate reply of an unimpressed castellan when asked if his lord would like to join the quest for the Holy Grail 'No thanks, he's already got one'. The initial film has now led to a second stage version in the hugely popular *Spamalot*.

'Arthuriana' is as popular as ever in the new millennium, but it remains to be seen whether it was the 'unhistorical' mediaeval King or the 'real' Dark Age warlord who will attract the most new interpretations. The mediaeval version of Arthur's court was retained for the first American TV version, centring around the adventures of Galahad, in 1950. The first – sanitised for family viewing – British TV version was '*The Adventures of Sir Lancelot*' in 1956–7, starring William Russell (who re-surfaced thirty years later in *Coronation Street*), Ronald Leigh-Hunt, and Jane Hylton. This version centred around Lancelot and his (unknown to traditional literature) squire Brian, with Merlin to give advice and plotting Morgan le Fay – but also Roman survivors and Vikings – among the villains. It had no inconvenient dalliance between the knight and his queen, but the literary 'baddie' Meleagraunce (as 'king Meliot' of Somerset) and others appeared. A 'realistic' Dark Ages setting was used for '*Arthur of the Britons*' (hampered by its low budget) in 1975–6, with Brian Blessed among the stars and plenty of skirmishes in the mud, but failed to take off. This version owed more to Rosemary Sutcliff, with fur-clad warlords living in wooden halls. Further TV 'spin-offs' on an Arthurian theme included an episode of 'The Goodies' in 1973, set at late fourteenth-century Bodiam Castle, with the three protagonists trying to open an Arthurian 'theme-park' at Tim Brooke-Taylor's eccentric upper-class uncle's castle.

In 2008 the BBC used the current Harry Potter phenomenon to film a new TV series on the 'early years' of Arthur and Merlin (here made his exact contemporary in defiance of all literary tradition), with the Potter-like 'boy wizard' Merlin endeavouring to protect the teenage Arthur from assorted villains and to hide his own powers from the intolerant King Uther Pendragon. In no other version of the story had Arthur been shown as living at Court in his teens, rather than being an adopted ward of a minor noble unaware of his real identity. The young but already scheming Morgan Le Fay and Guinevere were introduced – the latter, bizarrely, as a servant-girl not a neighbouring princess – and a teenage Lancelot also made an appearance. Morgan was made a complex mixture of good and bad, with her unscrupulous half-sister Morgause bringing out the worst in her but Merlin relatively sympathetic to her problems. The idea of Uther banning magic and the use of a resident dragon living under Camelot were peculiar to this interpretation – the dragon, played by John Hurt (best known as Caligula in 'I, Claudius'), may have been inspired by that in 'Beowulf' or by Smaug in Tolkien's *The Hobbit.* The use of dragons, malevolent magicians, and supernatural creatures as foes for the teenage Arthur and his friends and kingdom seemed to muddle up elements from Tolkien, Lewis, J.K. Rowling, and video-games, though it had a precedent in the equally fantastic 'quests' of the later mediaeval romances. The portrayal of a teenage Merlin owed much to the Potter films, no doubt in a blatant attempt to interest their fans, with sensible and helpful servant-girl Gwen (aka the later Guinevere) as the equivalent of Hermione Grainger, and was supposed to have been inspired by the portrayal of a young 'super-hero' with magical powers learning to use them wisely in the American TV series about the early years of Superman, 'Smallville'. (Both heroes had superhuman powers and came from an Otherworldly origin, but why did the script-writers rely so heavily on exclusively American culture?) The portrayal of Arthur as an initially boorish 'Hooray Henry' presumably owed much to the perceived personas of royal princes. As in Geoffrey of Monmouth, the warlike but naïve Uther ended up poisoned (though by different foes), and the assortment of scheming Royal advisers with their own agenda included one of the villains in Malory and T.H. White, Agravaine (here made Uther's brother-in-law). A chance to be original was quirkily reinterpreted, with much altered from most previous versions for no obvious reason except a desire to do something new. Had the writers actually read the Malory and T.H. White stories, or were some names picked up and re-used without much knowledge of their 'originals'? The end result was probably unsatisfactory to most viewers aged over twelve or so.

A realistically 'gritty', semi-pagan Dark Ages world appropriate for the sixth-century rather than the fifteenth-century was created in the first 'realistic' film of the Arthurian story, *Excalibur* in 1981 – with a Merlin more like the wild sixth-century Druidic 'shaman' than the usual mediaeval figure. John Boorman directed, with Nicol Williamson as Merlin, Helen Mirren as Morgan(a), and Cheri Lunghi as Guinevere. In 1995 another cinematic version of the mediaeval story updated the Melegaunce abduction of Guinevere in *First Knight*, filmed in Gwynedd and starring Richard Gere as Lancelot with Sean Connery as Arthur and Julia Ormond as Guinevere. This went back to the use of fifteenth-century armour and knightly chivalry with which America was more familiar, but compressed the whole saga of Lancelot and Guinevere into one short period and missed most of the traditional story-line (presumably to prevent American audiences becoming bored). The costumes and militaria were taken from Malory's time not from the fifth- or sixth-century. In 2004 another 'realistic' film 'King Arthur' starring Clive Owen, portrayed the AD 180s general – updated to the 460s to fit in with the fall of Rome – Lucius Artorius Castus as 'the' Arthur, using Sarmatian mercenaries against the Saxons on the Roman Northern frontier. The costumes and warfare were realistic, but the story mixed up 'real' fifth-century figures like St Germanus (here portrayed as the combined political and religious regional commander for the collapsing Western Roman Empire and Arthur's superior) with mediaeval introductions such as Lancelot and various other Arthurian knights. Keira Knightly (best known for her Jane Austen film roles) played Guinevere as the sword-swinging tomboy daughter of the initially anti-Roman rebel British warlord Merlyn, a leading Druid.

Arthur as a historical figure for serious historians

The first serious effort to consider Arthur as a historical warlord in the context of late fifth-century or early sixth-century post-Roman politics was made by Joseph Ritson in his *Life of King Arthur* (written in the 1800s, published in 1825). This was the heyday of the Welsh and 'Celtic' cultural revival, with the creation of the 'Gorsedd' and the romantic fabulations of Edward Williams, 'Iolo Morgannwg', the Glamorgan stonemason and amateur scholar who held the first modern 'eisteddfodd' on Primrose Hill in London in 1792. The post-Roman, pre-Anglo-Saxon warlord Arthur was a suitable figure to act as the standard-bearer of national pride in the 'Romantic' era, though Williams' concern for reviving the traditions and culture of the Druids as allegedly centred on his own homeland of Glamorgan was more pre-Roman than post-Roman in tone. Arthur appeared as a key part of the 'narrative' of early Welsh history, a figure about whom much more had been written than the shadowy post-Roman kings of Wales (of whom most were unknown, Maelgwyn of Gwynedd excepted) or the pre-Roman 'independence fighter' Caratacus. It was not necessary to be a specialist in Welsh myth to know about him, whereas Maelgwyn had only appeared in the legends of his presumed contemporary Taliesin (and then not in a 'respectable' Christian context but as a patron of pagan Druids). Caratacus was only known via a brief notice in Tacitus' *Annals*, but Arthur had been in 'mainstream' British culture for centuries as a paragon of Christian kingship. He was a national war-leader for an age of scholars researching 'racial' origins for the Welsh as a riposte to English Victorian enthusiasm for the Saxons. The main favourite 'Early Britain' figures for nineteenth-century British cultural nationalists were the virtuous Christian kingly 'resistance leader' Alfred the Great (d 899), defeater of the great Scandinavian invasions, who was made much of as 'founder' of the Royal Navy and of Oxford University; the pioneering historical novelist Charles Kingsley's favourite subject was Hereward 'the Wake', leader of the anti-Norman resistance in the early 1070s.

This presentation of Arthur was annexed by the Victorians to make him a 'British' rather than a Welsh king, a suitable forerunner for Victoria and Albert. But the need to present a historical figure in keeping with the conditions of the post-Roman period, and a non-historical knightly patron with a 'Round Table', accelerated as the grandiose chivalric creation of Sir Thomas Malory became unfashionable and subject to parody and scepticism along with its contemporary Victorian revival. In the early twentieth-century the post-Roman military captain came more into vogue as the layers of mediaeval romance exemplified by Sir Thomas Malory's *Morte D'Arthur* (and used as late as Tennyson's '*Idylls of the King*') were seen as unhistorical. Historians duly came to take the lead in portraying Arthur as a 'real' person, and he could no longer be shown in mediaeval armour. This was noticeably pioneered by 'Celtic' rather than English historians, the English ones possibly being 'put off' Arthur by the weight of clearly unhistorical literary stories about him from Geoffrey onwards – and not knowing much of the pre-Galfridian Welsh literature. The first major 'Celtic' scholar to consider Arthur as a 'real' person was the Scot W.F .Skene in the 1860s, followed by the Welsh Sir John Rhys in the 1890s, and the first literary studies of the early Welsh references to Arthur seemed to indicate a strong link to the former kingdoms of the North Britons in Rheged (Lancashire/ Cumbria) and Lothian. English historians duly followed this up, but shifted their emphasis towards possible locations in England (particularly for his battles). E. K. Chambers' *Arthur of Britain* (1927) dealt with his possible career and the sources in a sympathetic manner, and sought to evaluate the possible sites for his battles from the ninth-century 'list' in Nennius' *Historia Brittonum*. The 'Dark Ages' sources were now treated as the most likely to be accurate about Arthur rather than the unhistorical, literary concoctions of the post-1066 English and French writers, and the king appeared as a post-Roman warlord shorn of all chivalric paraphernalia.

Robin Collingwood, an archaeologist and brother of the partial inspirations for family friend Arthur Ransome's 'Amazons' Nancy and Peggy Blackett, put forward the theory that Arthur could have held the Late Roman military office of 'Count of Britain' and commanded a cavalry force that routed the invading Saxon infantry (1932).[1] It was developed from an idea of the German O. Zimmer in the 1890s. Alternatively, Sir Edmund Chambers suggested that the mediaeval Welsh literary naming of Arthur as an 'amherawdwyr' ie 'emperor' was an indication that he had held some official 'Roman' office that survived into post-410 Britain, whether this was that of 'Count of Britain' or not. The wide-ranging possibilities of the locations for the famous 'Twelve Battles' of Arthur listed by 'Nennius' c.829 had to be explained logically, and a cavalry-commander using the heirs of a Late Roman cavalry force would be in a good position to use the surviving Roman road-network to move around Britain tackling bands of invaders. As the Angles and the Saxons were well-known to have fought on foot, he would also have a military advantage over them and could achieve crushing victories. The legendary battles' locations were now investigated, most notably by (1868/1896) W. F. Skene, (1928) E. K. Chambers, and (1945) Kenneth Jackson (see Bibliography). Their results differed, with sites ranging from the Scottish Lowlands to the Thames valley. Given the difficult etymology, it was inevitable.

The discovery of an appropriately large 'Arthurian'-era re-fortification of Cadbury Castle in Somerset by Leslie Alcock in the 1960s even seemed to provide a genuine setting for 'Camelot' as a military headquarters within reach of the early Saxon settlements in south-eastern Britain. The project was indeed 'signposted' in its fund-raising as being for that purpose, with a 'Camelot Research Committee' set up to arrange the excavations in 1965 headed by Dr. Ralegh Radford (veteran of earlier Glastonbury 'digs') with the veteran archaeologist Sir Mortimer Wheeler as 'President'. This was presumably necessary to generate publicity, but gave a hostage to fortune –

any post-Roman discoveries were liable to be hailed as 'Camelot' whether or not there was a viable connection to 'Arthur' as opposd to a nameless chieftain. There was no written evidence to connect Arthur to the site pre-Leland. Arthur had been a leading figure of Cornish legend since the first recorded mention of him (as an already famous figure) in the account of the visit of some fund-raising canons of Laon, Artois to Bodmin in 1113. Appropriate sites included the fortified headland at 'Dark Age' port Tintagel (already linked to him by Geoffrey of Monmouth), 'Arthur's Kitchen', and the River Camel that suggested 'Camlann'. The battle at 'Slaughterbridge' on the Camel was linked to Camlann – at least in the minds of the post-Tennyson tourist trade. Logically, therefore, Cornwall – part of the kingdom of Dumnonia – was a probable refuge for Britons who had been driven westwards out of Somerset with tales of the local King resident at Cadbury. Alternatively, Cadbury could have formed part of a Dumnonian king's realm as the pre-Roman tribe of the 'Dobunni' do not seem to have existed as a territorial unit after the Roman 'withdrawal'. At the time there was renewed interest in the Arthurian connection with Glastonbury seen in the eleventh-century hagiography of Gildas, where Arthur had come to the 'island' abbey in pursuit of his abducted Queen and her kidnapper King Melwas and Gildas had mediated between the two rulers. This revival was spearheaded by Geoffrey Ashe, who argued in *King Arthur's Avalon* that the mysterious burial of 'Arthur and Guinevere' found by the abbey's monks in 1190/1 could have been genuine and was in a Dark Ages manner, not an obvious twelfth-century forgery.[2] Even if the accompanying inscribed cross identifying them was too convenient to be genuine and its lettering not in sixth-century style, it did not mean that the burial itself was a fake. The hillfort at Cadbury was local enough to suggest that Arthur could have ruled there and been Glastonbury's overlord. In fact, there is no early literary Welsh identification of the presumed 'original of Avalon/ Glastonbury, the 'Isle of Avallach', with Glastonbury – the enigmatic 'Avallach' himself was apparently father-in-law to Maelgwyn of Gwynedd and so presumably North Welsh. The identification of the original pre-Saxon name for Glastonbury, 'Ynys Witrin' (isle of glass or apples?) with Avalon may be based on an etymological coincidence.

The site at Cadbury Castle had already been cited as linked to Arthur by local tradition by John Leland in the 1530s, and this evidence was accepted uncritically without considering whether the Arthurian attribution was of genuinely ancient provenance. Now there was evidence of military structures – new ramparts and a hall – there and clearly some major warlord had used it as a base. Alcock could write confidently that Arthur was the probable builder of the Cadbury fortifications, though later editions of his book were more cautious. Usefully, Cadbury Castle was close to the major Roman road of the Fosse Way and so had military access to routes across Britain. Leslie Alcock was accordingly 'positive' about linking the post-Roman refortification programme to Arthur in his 1970s books, only to express doubts in a 1982 interview after the literary experts such as David Dumville had undermined his main documentary 'prop', 'Nennius', as not proper history. More excitement was caused by the 1990s discoveries of secular remains at Arthur's supposed birthplace of Tintagel Castle in northern Cornwall, hitherto supposed to be only a monastery in the fifth-century, not a Dark Age stronghold unlike Geoffrey of Monmouth had claimed in the 1130s. The site seemed to have remains of buildings for a sizeable entourage, secular or military, of a ruler. In 1998 a stone was found with a reference to a man called 'Artognu' – though this was probably coincidence as the name was not close to the presumed fifth/sixth-century version of 'Arthur' which would have been more like 'Artwyr' or 'Arthwys'.[3] Further discoveries of a larger than expected Dark Age residential site at Tintagel were made in 2016 with a Light-Detection and Ranging survey of the ground. Linguistically, knowledge of 'Dark Ages' terminology derived from mediaeval Welsh enabled Arthur's name to be connected to that for 'Bear' and it could be assumed that this was some form of nickname. The absence of any Roman family of 'Artorii' who could have been connected to a fifth-century warlord could be explained by the hero's links to the less Romanised kingdoms of northern and western Britain. Was he a warrior or chieftain, a brilliant commander in the service of the post-Roman authorities but not actually a 'Roman' himself? In this sense he could be contrasted to the undoubtably Roman name and lineage of his presumed predecessor as 'national' leader of the Britons, Ambrosius Aurelianus.

Leslie Alcock's *Arthur's Britain* (1971), summing-up the archaeological evidence and centred on the discovery of the fortifications of Cadbury Castle, was the 'high-water mark' of mid-twentieth-century confidence in Arthur's real existence. Using archaeology rather than later Welsh tradition as the basis for his interpretation, he presented Arthur as a cavalry commander in the Late Roman military tradition, basing his mobile 'striking-force' at Cadbury Castle. Arthur was also seen as a real commander in Geoffrey Ashe's *From Caesar to Arthur* (1960) and *King Arthur's Avalon*. In literature, a 'realistic' Dark Ages warrior-king became the subject of children's novels by Rosemary Sutcliffe (*The Lantern Bearers*, 1959; *Sword at Sunset*, 1963) and Henry Treece (*The Great Captains*, 1956). Treece specifically made 'Artos' a rough Celtic warrior in the service of the Romanised Ambrosius, with his later version of the story in *The Eagles Have Flown* having a young Roman noble whose family had been killed by the Saxons joining his army as he is authorised by the ageing Count Ambrosius to attack the Saxon settlements of SE Britain. The campaign then takes place in eastern Sussex (so as to fit in with the *Anglo-Saxon Chronicle* details of the Saxons taking Pevensey in 91)[4], with the battle of 'Glein' at Glynde near Lewes – near authentic Saxon settlements. But our hero becomes tired of the bloodshed, forms a bond with his Saxon hostage slave, and after his mentor Cai (ie 'Sir Kay') is killed deserts to become a merchant in Gaul instead. He and his Saxon friend then return twenty years later to a peaceful Britain ruled by Arthur/Artos to witness the latter being ambushed and killed by his disgruntled subordinate Medraut (ie 'Modred'). Sutcliffe made Artos the illegitimate nephew of 'Count of Britain' Ambrosius, whose cavalry force rallied the rival British kings to victory and led to him being made 'emperor'. A credible series of military campaigns were created to explain the legendary 'Twelve Battles' of Nennius' list in terms of where 'Artos' could have fought both Saxons and Picts, with the uncomfortable fact that native British ponies were too short to carry armed warriors in a charge explained by the import of Roman cavalry mounts from Southern Gaul. Another 'realistic' version of Arthur as a post-Roman Brittonic warlord, in this case as the regent of the kingdom of Dumnonia, was presented by historical military adventure author Bernard Cornwell, creator of the Napoleonic War hero Captain Sharpe, in his own Arthurian trilogy – *The Winter King* (1995), *Enemy of God* (1996), and *Excalibur* (1997). This featured a mixture of mythical figures (based on real origins) such as Merlin, here a Druid 'shaman', and real-life sixth-century British clerics like St Samson with a struggle between Church and paganism for the ideological 'control' of Britain, with a Saxon in British service (Derfel) as narrator. The retreat from a 'real' Arthur: the literary experts move in. The parallel case of the Irish mythical hero Fionn, and the ninth-century 'political' need to promote an anti-Saxon hero.

The king became the central figure in John Morris' seminal work on Dark Age Britain, *The Age of Arthur: a History of the British Isles AD 350 to 650* (1973). He could be seen as a sort of unofficial 'emperor', temporarily uniting the Dark Ages kingdoms and imposing law and order on the Roman model, and became the central figure in the survival of 'Celtic' society after the disasters of the fifth-century invasions. The mediaeval texts were taken largely at face value as conveying fifth/sixth-century details without contemporary distortions or their own political agendas, though even in this confident interpretation Arthur's precise dates and physical location remained inexact. If Morris' Arthur was a sort of 'emperor', where was he based – the Roman Cotswolds, Cadbury Castle, or a Welsh kingdom? Since then a number of scholarly assaults on the reliability of the Dark Ages written evidence have dented this argument, with a comprehensive reinterpretation of the sources' motives and accuracy. In fact, doubts over the reliability of the crucial Welsh evidence (e.g. Gildas) had been expressed by the literary experts Hector and Norah Chadwick as early as 1932 – though they still believed in an 'original'. As the experts on early Welsh literature turned their attention to 'Arthurian' texts in Welsh, the context (and dates) of the latter were examined with unflattering results. In 1966 R.W. Hanning argued that Gildas was writing literary polemic not 'history' and could not be trusted.[5] This 'revisionism' could then go on to attack the very existence of a historical 'Arthur' – at least in the terms suggested by the sources. D. Kirby and J. Williams led the reviewers' assault on Morris' 'Age of Arthur', complaining in their article in the 1975–6 edition of 'Studia Celtica' that it was:

> 'a tissue of fact and fantasy, which is both misleading and misguided'[6]

David Dumville warned in his article on 'Sub-Roman Britain: History and Legend' in *History*, vol. 62 (1977), that Morris had taken no account of the failings and unhistorical rationalisations of myth by the sources, and that no non-expert should tackle Morris' work as they would be seriously confused.[7] Dumville, Philip Rahtz (in his review of C. Thomas' book on Arthurian Tintagel in *Cornish Archaeology* 1993), and Oliver Padel

('The Nature of Arthur' in *Cambrian Mediaeval Celtic Studies*, vol. 27)[8] are particularly sceptical that we can rely on any of the ninth- to twelfth-century Welsh sources. Their arguments sought to present the crucial Welsh 'Dark Ages' documents as written later than was earlier supposed, with contemporary politics or 'nationalist' mythology in mind, and thus not 'historical'. The points at issue often relied on interpretations of the literary language of the sources to decide when they were written via evolution of the words used. But what if a writer had been self-consciously 'antiquarian' in his use of language and used out-of-date not contemporary terminology? The ninth-century authors were seen as being as guilty as Geoffrey of reinterpreting 'Arthur' in terms useful for their own agenda – and it could be argued that they had even 'invented' the Arthurian campaigns to inspire their contemporaries with a narrative of how a British warlord could defeat the Saxon enemy. In this critique, Morris and Alcock had taken the accuracy of the early texts for granted and were unaware of their over-riding literary, not analytical purposes. In this vein, Dumville's ally Charles Thomas argued that serious investigators of the 'real' fifth- and sixth-century should rely on the facts of archaeology and leave the unproveable literary claims about named rulers alone as resting on too shaky foundations.

Mythographers, led by Oliver Padel in his 1994 study, argued that the Welsh mediaeval Arthur's group of 'heroes' was a local version of the definitively legendary Irish national protector Fionn, supposed commander of the 'regiment' of heroic warriors at the court of the third-century Irish 'High Kings'. Arthur and his men acted as the protectors of Britain against supernatural menaces, much as Fionn did in Ireland, and legend concentrated on his adventures against them not on any supposed military campaigns. Indeed, Fionn – like Arthur – was educated by a mysterious wise tutor before coming to court as a 'nobody' to claim his rights, and later faced his brotherhood of warriors breaking up as his lieutenant (Diarmait) had an affair with his wife (Grainne). Fionn unhistorically fought the ninth-century Vikings of Lochlainn (Norway) in literature – so did Arthur fight an unhistorical foe too? Arthur was thus a heroic figure of more than human feats like Fionn, who came to be placed in history as a result of ninth-century literary fabulation rather than actually living in the early sixth-century. Even the very early reference to him as an unsurpassable warrior in the 'Gododdin' could be taken as an indication of his superhuman prowess, not his being a military commander.

The new dynasty of Merfyn 'Frych' ('the Freckled') of Gwynedd in the 820s was as keen as Geoffrey to promote the idea of a heroic warlord uniting the British, and recent Mercian incursions into early ninth-century Gwynedd made it useful to play up Arthur's role as a Celtic leader who had defeated the Saxons. He thus served to show the Welsh what could be done against the national enemy by a general who united their disparate kingdoms into one army, and the more numerous and dramatic his successes the better. It was thus plausible that 'Nennius' collected all the stories of late fifth-century and early sixth-century Welsh victories or indeed others whose date was unknown – and ascribed them to one man. The practice of successive writers shamelessly reassigning battles to different commanders is known from other instances – and indeed seems to have affected the 'battle-list' for Arthur, with at least one battle otherwise assigned to Urien of Rheged c. 580. But did 'Nennius' merely exaggerate Arthur's reputation in useful contemporary terms, or create a whole story like Geoffrey was presumed to have done? The latter is often assumed now and is broadly the conclusion of Nicholas Higham, not least as 'Nennius' was not an objective 'historian' as we would now see the genre (i.e. in the tradition of the secular Roman historians from Tacitus to Ammianus) but had a religious background and purpose. It was possibly rather patronising for modern 'scientific' – and thus objective – historians to assume that because a 'propagandist' like 'Nennius' had a contemporary political motive for creating a successful sixth-century warlord Arthur and lacked reliable sources they indulged in wholesale fraud, unable to comprehend how to write 'proper' history. They may not have been 'objective', but does that rule out accepting any of their details? This is not to deny that 'Nennius', as much as Geoffrey, was indulging in literary creation rather than faithfully transcribing earlier documents – and that his Arthurian campaigns were 'spin' for the court of ninth-century Gwynedd. It also had a religious element, comparing Arthur to Joshua, as proposed by Nicholas Higham. The religious and 'national' elements of the text complemented each other, as in Bede's work and in Paul the Deacon's eighth-century history of the Lombards. (This parallel was pointed out by R. Charles-Edwards, 'The Arthur of History', in Rachel Bromwich, ed. *Studies in Old Welsh Poetry* 1991).[9] But could Nennius' book be taken as being as 'historical' as Bede or Paul are usually assumed to be? It was written in the same manner of a 'national' history, but was much more lacking in specific detail and was as full of the supernatural as Bede (and, unlike Bede, not just miraculous stories concerning saints but secular rulers too). David Dumville denied Nennius' comparibility to Bede in his riposte to Charles-Edwards. Nennius' account of Romano-British history is certainly minimal, and his knowledge of fifth-century events limited and influenced by credulity (as in the story of Merlin and Vortigern). If he had any genuine historical chronicles to call on, these would have been Church not secular ones. But why assume, from a loftily 'objective' late twentieth-century viewpoint, that Nennius was incapable of including any accurate history in his account? Or that his non-analytical purpose condemns all his material? The second piece of 'Nennian' writing on Arthur, the list of 'Mirabilia' ('Wonders'), is indeed a collection of folklore and unlikely legend, but recent analysis of its language means that it is now doubted if it (especially the Irish section) was by the same hand as the Nennian 'history' work.

The number of 'Arthur'-linked place-names in western Britain have been taken by enthusiasts for his reality as proof of his nationwide importance in the non-Saxon areas of post-Roman Britain. They extend across Wales, Cornwall, northern England, and southern Scotland – with plenty of geographical features, e.g. 'Arthur's Oven' on Bodmin Moor, 'Arthur's Stones' (the Gower and Dorstone, Herefordshire), and 'Arthur's Seat' (Edinburgh). The etymology was ancient, as shown by 'Nennius' mention of certain sites in Wales in his 'Mirabilia'. The Welsh sites certainly pre-dated the 'Arthurian revival' set in train by Geoffrey of Monmouth. The only comparable number of sites ascribed to such figures were the Devil and Robin Hood in England. But they could now be explained as having been assigned to a legendary hero rather than a man – and Padel pointed out the number of sites assigned in Ireland and Dalriada to Fionn. They were also in remote locations, suggesting the role of Arthur as a divine figure of the 'margins'. They did not 'prove' anything about the existence of a British warlord, and could have been ascribed to a god who later became mistakenly treated as a genuine historical figure and been spread by wandering Britons over generations from the sixth-century to the tenth-century. The shadowy Welsh god 'Artaius' provided a candidate with the right name; and from Classical myth there was the similarly-sounding 'Arcturus' ('bear-ward'), the brightest star in the constellation of Bootes ('the herdsman') next to the 'Great Bear' in the northern skies. Arcturus was supposed to be a legendary king of Arcadia, 'Arcas' – son of Callisto, who the jealous Hera turned into a bear after Zeus seduced her. (Arthur was legendarily the son of Igraine, seduced by Uther Pendragon.) Was this why the 'Great Bear' came to be known in Wales as 'Arthur's Wain'? Was Arthur originally a 'sky-god' figure, a mixture of Classical and Brittonic figures?

Padel argued that the name was more common in areas settled by the Irish in the fifth-century, and thus could reflect the Irish tradition of turning early gods into secular heroes (e.g.Fionn Mac Cumhaill and Cuchulainn). To him, the precedent of Fionn was particularly important, given that an 'original' third-century AD Irish warrior defending the High King's court at Tara was given Viking opponents who were not active until the late eighth-century and was then transferred to settings in Scotland as Irish settlers emigrated to Argyll. In Welsh myth Arthur fought giants and witches as well as human enemies. Both were involved with legendary boar-hunts; and both had their wives abducted by their followers. If Fionn had been given chronologically impossible battles by Irish writers, why not Arthur too? Indeed, it was argued by modern scholars that the whole edifice of a third-century 'High Kingship' in Ireland was a literary creation of Dark Ages polemicists seeking to create an ideal past, and that the legendary Fionn was at the most an 'ancestor-figure' of a small local tribe in the lands around his 'military base' at the Hill of Allen. Place-names now connected to Fionn, such as Skye and 'Fingal's Cave' on Staffa, have no historical link to a warrior who originally came from central Ireland; the Scottish link was created by Irish emigrants to Argyll from the fifth-century. The main protagonist of this interpretation was D.O' hOgain, in *Fionn Mac Cumhaill: Images of the Gaelic Hero* (Dublin, 1988). So the 'High Kingship' of Arthur and his family could have been invented centuries later too, and place-names given to him outside his original area of 'action'.

On this analogy, could a minor local 'Arthur' have been turned into a national Welsh figure from the ninth-century? Could Arthurian place-names also have been created in areas unconnected to any 'original'? In fact, the basis for this theory is doubtful – the Irish did not settle as far East as Gwent or Herefordshire which have 'Arthurian' sites such as a stone at Dorstone, 'Arthur's Walls' near Newport, and Penarth near Cardiff, or in Powys which has 'Arthur's Chair' near Llangollen. There are 'Arthurian' sites in eastern Gwynedd, e.g. the alleged site of Arthur's execution of the rebel/bandit Huil son of Caw at Ruthin – though this piece of folklore is dubious as Ruthin was only founded in the 1280s and is not an ancient site. The many 'Arthur' names in the Cornish landscape can hardly be attributed to Irish influence given that the latter only settled in parts of western Cornwall. This theory assumes a close influence from Irish literature on ninth-century Wales – more likely for Dyfed in the South-West (which had Irish settlers and dynasts) than for Gwynedd whose Irish settlers in Mon/Anglesey were traditionally expelled by dynastic founder Cunedda in the fifth-century.

And what about the northern sites associated with Arthur, such as 'Arthur's Seat' at Edinburgh, the 'Round Table' at Stirling, the legend of Arthur and Modred at Meigle in Perthshire, and the story of him surviving asleep in a cave near Melrose? These were not areas of Irish settlement; if Arthur was an 'Irish' phenomenon he would have been expected to have place-names created for him in the Irish settlers' territory, Dalriada (Argyll and Lochaber) in Scotland and Dyfed in South-West Wales. Fionn, indeed, was 'Scoticised' as 'Finn Mac Cool'; Arthur however only had connected place-names in the 'Pictish' region of Perthshire and 'English' Lothian South of the Firth of Forth, not in Dalriada.

At best, the multiplicity of 'Arthur' place-names showed that he was seen across Wales, Cornwall, and north Britain as a roving hero with a warband rather than a 'fixed' ruler or general in one area. Nor was 'Arthur' appropriated for a powerful ninth- or tenth-century dynasty of 'High Kings' as was Fionn, their supposed commander-in-chief. Fionn was used then for contemporary political purposes, but neither Merfyn of Gwynedd or Hywel of Dyfed sought to present Arthur as an ancestor or general of their kings in the way that Fionn was made the military commander of the 'High Kings' at Tara. No Irish writers attempted to make 'marginal figure' and 'roving commander' Fionn a king; so why was 'Irish hero' Arthur made one? Was this because Arthur already had a 'fixed' literary setting as a king that they dared not replace? Or was the concept of Arthur as a vaguely 'British' leader – not a leader of specific kingdoms – a reflection of his obscure origins in myth? Arthur did however serve as a useful heroic figure from the misty past to inspire present 'national' feeling from the ninth-century, and Nennius kept his origins obscure and dated him vaguely to some decades after Vortigern.

The argument could be extended into 'deconstruction' of the late twentieth-century enthusiasts' own reasons for wanting to believe in a historical post-Roman 'restoration of order' by a great king. Was their longing for an inspiring 'Arthur' a reaction to the similar chaos and trauma of the Second World War – Arthur as Winston Churchill? The generation of Alcock and Morris had built him up, so the next generation knocked him down as enthusiastically as the tabloids turned on celebrities or biographers to revealed sordid stories about their subjects. There was surely an element of 'nihilism', going beyond scientific investigation, in the way the theorists were unwilling to trust any source and picked away at every piece of evidence. This did valuable work in exposing shaky foundations and revealing early 'historians' ulterior motives in writing, but it went beyond that to leave nothing standing. There must be a 'caveat' about the late twentieth-century demolition of the evidence in literary sources. It is arguable that a historical figure may be built up to answer contemporary needs, but this need not extend to complete fabulation about him. Logically, it could be asked why the 'deconstructionists' were so keen to deny Arthur's reality. Did they have some 'need' to ridicule any concept of a heroic ruler who had united his people as a fitting comment from a cynical age? Were they too keen to throw the baby out with the bathwater? The lack of extant original documents from the early 'Dark Age' period is a problem, and elaborations for contemporary political reasons undoubtably occurred, especially with 'Nennius' who was once seen as a reliable source. But how much lay behind the embellished stories?

'Nennius' can be reassessed, putting him more in the category of Geoffrey of Monmouth, but had he really 'invented' Arthur? He had not invented 'Vortigern', recorded in the fifth-century hagiography of St Germanus, so why should he have invented his other principal subject? Nor could Gildas' silence about Arthur be considered that damning, as Gildas had other concerns than an Arthurian panegyric (see below). Gildas was not writing a historical work, and only used evidence that was part of his argument that the sinful Britons had deserved their misfortunes. Gildas did not state that Ambrosius won the 'Arthurian' battle of Badon, as some sceptics implied – he had merely said that Ambrosius led the British campaign which culminated at Badon. Any realistic explanation of Arthur has to focus on the Welsh material rather than the chivalric king created by mediaeval writers, though in both cases it now seems that a 'need' for a heroic king ruling over a triumphant kingdom caused the story to be promoted in contemporary terminology.

Chapter 5

Arthur and Associated Romances. Totally Myth, or Some Genuine Facts Too?

(1) The Quest for the Holy Grail

Welsh and French origins; how both could have influenced Chretien de Troyes

Though Arthur as a successful battle-leader is of far older provenance, the quest of the 'Holy Grail' to which he and his knights were closely connected by Malory's time does not appear earlier than the later twelfth-century works of Chretien and his main continuator, Robert de Boron (author of *Joseph of Arimathea*, *Merlin*, and *Perceval*). The first story was in Chretien's 'La Conte du Graal', the third of his Arthurian romances, which he left unfinished. It introduced Perceval (as will be seen, a vague figure from sixth-century north British/Welsh history) as an 'innocent' brought up in ignorance of the knightly world or his male relatives by his presumably traumatised widowed mother in a remote forest. He is inspired by meeting some wandering knights to make his way to Arthur's court, where his lack of military and courtly social skills is shown up and he is mocked (especially by Kay, already in his 'bully' role). Despite his lack of military training he is somehow able to kill the insolent visiting 'Red Knight', and after he receives a proper knightly education he commences a series of semi-symbolic adventures. Warned by his tutor not to ask too many questions, he is directed by a mysterious lordly fisherman – the first appearance of the 'Fisher King', who has some sort of injury – to seek shelter at a nearby castle. There he witnesses the unexplained 'Grail procession' of a youth with a bleeding lance and other attendants with gold candelabra and a maiden bearing the Grail (not described but some sort of dish). A banquet follows, but – as we later learn, due to Perceval not asking questions about the procession – all the participants vanish overnight, leaving Perceval to find his way out alone. The event is later explained to him by the 'Loathly Damsel', who calls on Arthur's court for help and says that if Perceval had asked the right questions all would have been revealed and the 'Fisher King' would have been healed.

A quest by various knights to help the maiden follows, but Perceval's story is left unfinished and much of the text deals with Gawain's adventures instead. The story of Perceval and Gawain is continued by the so-called 'Four Continuations' of Chretien's text, written in northern France between c.1190 and 1220 with the second and fourth ascribed to Gautier de Denain. The latter versions had already been overtaken by the work of Robert de Boron, *L'Estoire du Graal*, in the late 1190s – the first to bring in Joseph of Arimathea and the 'pre-history' of the Grail between the Crucifixion and Arthur's reign. Lancelot was added to Gawain as a major protagonist in the Arthurian knights' quests for the Grail in 'Perlesvaus/The High History of the Holy Grail', a Flemish tale of c.1215 which was the next major development of the story after Robert de Boron's. This also had the notion of all the knights being summoned to Camelot to be issued a challenge concerning the Grail (this time by a maiden with a cartload of heads of knights killed due to Perceval's not asking the right questions at his first Grail encounter). The French 'Quest of the Holy Grail', c.1215–20, second book of the so-called '*Vulgate Cycle*', then introduces the Grail's appearance at Camelot at the Pentecost feast, and Lancelot's son Galahad and cousins Bors and Lionel.

Chretien's work had not made it clear that the 'Grail' was connected to the Last Supper or Crucifixion, merely that it had holy powers of feeding its company and that the right questions needed to be asked concerning it by the 'pure in heart and deed'. Perceval's mysterious upbringing and saintly 'simplicity' foreshadowed that of Galahad in later versions; and the idea of Perceval the Grail-achiever as the 'best knight in the world', able to heal the sick, was later to be transferred to Lancelot. The idea of a magic Otherworldly receptacle – initially a cauldron not a dish or cup – that could sustain any number of its devotees was Welsh in origin, not French, and thus may have come to Chretien via Brittany. It was not Christian either – and hence provided evidence for the 'Sir James Frazer'-style school of early-mid twentieth-century mythographers to show that the 'real' Grail story was of 'pagan' spirituality which the Church had sanitised. This added fuel to the arguments of pro-'pagan' enthusiasts to 'revive' the 'real' cult as representative of pre-Christian Britain, and for the centre of 'alternative' spirituality which developed at Glastonbury from the 1920s.

One of the earliest versions of the story is in the tale of 'Bran the Blessed' in the Mabinogi series written up in the twelfth-century, where it brings slain warriors back to life in a battle between Bran and king Matholwch of Ireland. This tale was unconnected to the later Grail story, and centred on the disastrous marriage between the sister of Bran, the giant king of Britain, and the king of Ireland; the cauldron was one of the wedding-gifts and when the two kingdoms went to war it enabled the Irish to revive their slain warriors. (Bran's half-brother, cause of the quarrel, pretended to be an Irish soldier to gain access to the cauldron and destroyed it).[1] The tale was indirectly linked to the Arthurian story, in that Bran's magical severed head – another commonplace of 'Celtic' myth – was said to have been buried on the 'White Mount' at Tower Hill, London for use as a talisman until Arthur – a Christian – dug it up. Another part of the Bran legend probably influenced the Grail story, as the procession of 'cult objects' associated with the Grail in De Boron includes a severed head. After the final battle between British and Irish, a mass-slaughter like Camlann, Bran's magical severed head accompanies the British survivors to an Otherwordly island (traditionally Gwales off Pembroke) where they are sustained by self-renewing meals like the Grail banquets. The fact that the object of nourishment for the heroes was a magical cauldron which served up food of its own volition, not a cup or platter, was shrugged off as a minor detail. Iron Age heroes feasted from cauldrons full of butchered meat in halls like Ulster's Emain Macha; knightly lords in twelfth-century France used sumptuous dishes (as seen in their inventories). The notion of Bran's reign as a golden age ended by a catastrophic battle where the king was mortally wounded presumably fed into the myth of the Arthurian age being ended by military disaster at Camlann – and Branwen was the cause of the final conflict as Guinevere brought about the quarrel of Arthur and Lancelot. The 'Fisher King' (supposedly so-called from supplying the fish for his relative Joseph of Arimathea's community) may be connected to Bran and the latter name has been used for him. A 'Bran' was known in Welsh legend as connected by marriage to the family of the Virgin Mary – hence a suitable companion for Joseph of Arimathea. This man is dated to the early Roman era, and thus is unlikely to be Bran 'the Blessed' who rules in the remote pre-Roman past when the sea between Britain and Ireland is lower.

It is noticeable that the Grail is always associated with female attendants, not clerics as would be appropriate for a dish or cup connected to the orthodox Catholic mass; the 'Celtic' tradition of priestesses was stronger than the church's restrictions. But this is not to say that Chretien using a maiden to carry the Grail indicated his allegiance to anti-Catholic beliefs. The idea may be due to the power of literary tradition about mysterious ladies serving in ancient sanctuaries over the romancers, rather than any conscious desire to be theologically unorthodox and to defy the church. The dish or cup of the 'Last Supper' had no symbolic importance to the early church, though the concept of the mass – as introduced by Christ at that meal – provided a template for the idea that the Grail's worshippers ate a ritual meal using its powers. The 'magical' transformation of the bread and wine in the chalice used at mass to the body and blood of Christ assumed a new spiritual importance in the twelfth-century, at the time of the first Grail romances, and the formerly 'secret' ritual of elevating the Host was now carried out in view of the congregation. The first artistic portrayals of anyone collecting the blood of Christ in a cup at the Crucifixion also appeared c.1100 – though the male recipient holding the cup is not identified and need not have been Joseph of Arimathea. At the same time, the first semi-'lay' Christian warrior brotherhoods emerged in the Orders of the Knights Hospitaller and the Templars, so the idea of a special order of knights devoted to a holy place or objective was fashionable. The Crusades from 1095 saw personal experience of the cultures of the East by many knights, bringing back new ideas to Western Europe, and interest in Islam with which most of the West had formerly had minimal contact. The events of the life of Christ assumed new importance to those who had taken part in liberating or protecting the sites involved.

The devout 'Grail' writers of the twelfth- and thirteenth-century could logically link up the celebratory meal held by the magic cup's devotees (by pagan warriors at a royal court in the original legends) with the Last Supper. Feasting, important to Celtic legends and made a staple part of Arthur's adventures in the 'Mabinogi' series, was now put in a Christian context and given a theological explanation – but the notion of Arthur's banquets at his hall (Gellywig or Caerleon) was taken over by the twelfth- and thirteenth-century writers for the 'set-pieces' of his Pentecost feasts at Camelot. The 'set-piece' feasts and the recurring notion of a visitor arriving and being challenged by the door-warden was also used in Anglo-Saxon myth, namely Beowulf's arrival at the hall of Heorot – and was taken over by J.R.R. Tolkien for the arrival of Aragorn and Gandalf at King Theoden's hall of Meduseld in Rohan. In the early Welsh tales a notable guest such as Culhwch arrives at the royal banquet to precipitate the main action; in the 'Frenchified' Christian version firstly Sir Galahad arrives to claim the 'Siege Perilous' and then the Grail appears to the assembled knights. In the 'preliminaries' of the Quest, the tale was sometimes introduced with a 'set-piece' arrival of assorted knights at a mysterious castle which turned out to be the site of a supernatural feast where the Grail appeared. In the '*Vulgate Cycle*' this device served to introduce the action, with firstly Sir Gawain (already seen as the epitome of wordliness) failing to pray or ask the right question as the Grail appeared and so 'missing out' on its commendation, but the humble and devout Sir Lancelot behaving correctly. In the tale of 'Sir Gawain and the Green Knight', an English Arthurian story of c.1400, the Knight arrives at Arthur's Christmas feast to issue his challenge and in this, less spiritual story Gawain is the hero who takes it up.

When and how did the 'Grail' first appear in literature?

The idea of a 'Grail' (which word meant 'dish', originally 'graal', in eleventh-century Catalan documents), a symbolic receptacle for the transmission of Divine Grace in the form of a vessel, was in vogue in the mid-twelfth-century. So was the Middle Eastern context. The reasons for its relevance have been mentioned above. The important point to remember is that the Christian Grail only appeared then, not in the fifth- or sixth-century – there is no plausible literary link back to 'genuine' Arthurian times. The earliest reference by a historical writer to the Grail is that of the Flemish monk Helinand of Froidment (near Beauvais), in his chronicle written around 1200. He has an entry under the year '718' for a 'vision' by a hermit of the dish used at the Last Supper, which the latter wrote down; but it is uncertain if he was using the said written account or if this was just another untraceable 'ancient book' like that allegedly used by Geoffrey of Monmouth. The area's lords, the Counts of Flanders, were well-known crusaders from 1095 onwards and Count Philip had been the patron of the first writer of a 'Grail romance',

Chretien de Troyes. Importantly, the first holy relic of the alleged blood of Christ collected at the Crucifixion (not necessarily in a chalice or cup) emerged in Flanders, the relic being given by the authorities of Arab-ruled Jerusalem to Mantua in Italy c. 804 and being passed on by Emperor Henry III (r. 1039–56) to the Counts of Flanders. Another such relic was recorded as being at the abbey of Fecamp in nearby Normandy around 1120, and was 'rediscovered' in 1171 (when Chretien's romances made relics of the 'Holy Blood' fashionable). Possibly the enterprising monks of Fecamp, using such relics to attract pilgrims in the 1170s, gave ideas to those at Glastonbury.

Several suitably ancient vessels, claimants to be the dish of the Last Supper, emerged in that relic-collecting age – the first to have easy physical access to Jerusalem since the Arab conquest in 638 – thanks to the storming of the Holy City by the First Crusade in July 1099. The Crusaders also acquired the magical 'Holy Lance' en route to Jerusalem at Antioch in 1098, with its location 'revealed' in a dream to their attendant holy man, Peter 'the Hermit'. Its appearance was denounced by the attendant Papal legate Bishop Adhemar, who represented the 'official' church, but was taken up enthusiastically by the ordinary 'pilgrims'. It was hailed as the 'miracle' which enabled the besieged army to drive off Emir Kerbogha's attackers; this is presumably the spear which appears in the 'Grail procession' in the Arthurian stories. (A separate spear, containing a nail from the Crucifixion in its tip, was already extant in Constantinople by 1098 and Bishop Adhemar, who had seen it, was duly suspicious of the genuineness of Peter's relic.[2] This had probably been brought from Jerusalem at the Arab conquest in 638.) There is no indication that the Crusaders either expected to find or acquired any holy cup in Palestine after 1099. One 'Grail' cup of unknown origin was extant in Germany before the 1090s, was acquired by the Holy Roman Emperors, and later made its way to the Hofburg Palace chapel, in the collection of the Habsburg dynasty as Holy Roman Emperors; it was still there in 1800. Another one was supposed to have been taken to Spain, and a claimant was transported around the royal capitals of Aragon during the twelfth-century and ended up in Valencia.

Quite apart from the notion of the 'Grail' as the vessel of the Last Supper, a connected imagery arose of it as the vessel (a chalice?) which collected Christ's blood at the Crucifixion – and as such the likeliest person to have

Tintagel Castle. Arthur's legendary birthplace – and a genuine post-Roman high-status residence or trading site. (© *Chris Allen/ Creative Commons*)

Pevensey Castle. A Late Roman 'Saxon Shore' fortress stormed by the South Saxons at the time to which Arthur's wars are attributed. (© *Peter Jeffrey/ Creative Commons*)

Caerleon, the Roman legionary fortress. Another major Roman military site, where Arthur was said by twelfth-century writer Geoffrey of Monmouth to have based his court. (© *Robin Drayton/ Creative Commons*)

Llandaff Cathedral. Held by Welsh tradition to have been founded by Bishop Dubricius/Dyfrig, the man who supposedly crowned Arthur; supposedly patronised by the father of the only sixth-century Welsh ruler called 'Arthur'. (© *Tim Venning*)

Arthur's Seat, Edinburgh. Possibly named as the site of the eleventh of Arthur's 'twelve battles', Mount Agned.

Little Solsbury Hill, outside Bath. Possibly 'the fortress of Badon' and so the site of the greatest of Arthur's victories in legend, 'Mount Badon'. (© *Tim Venning*)

Lidington Castle hillfort, near Swindon. Another possible site for the elusive 'Mount Badon'. (© *Edmund Shaw/Creative Commons*)

Badbury Rings, Dorset. Another strategically vital hillfort with a suitable name near a post-Roman Saxon region, suggested as a possible 'Mount Badon'. (© *Philip Halling/Creative Commons*)

Cadbury Castle hillfort, Somerset. Regarded by the sixteenth-century as Arthur's elusive 'Camelot' headquarters, and with major post-Roman building. More likely to be a royal base for Dumnonia. (© *Graham Horn/ Creative Commons*)

Ogmore Castle, Glamorgan. Site of the mysterious 'Ogmore Stone' referencing a post-Roman land-grant by a king with a name like 'Arthur'. (© *Tim Venning*)

Chapel Hill, Merthyr Mawr, Glamorgan. The cave hermitage of Arthur's presumed cousin, St Illtud, near Ogmore. (© *Tim Venning*)

Arthur's Stone, Dorstone, Herefordshire. One of the mythical Arthurian sites in the southern Welsh Marches. (© *Jeremy Bolwell/Creative Commons*)

Cefn Bryn, Gower. Another legendary Welsh 'Arthurian' stone site. (© *Tim Venning*)

Pass of Camlann, near Dolgellau. A possible location for Arthur's last battle against the traitor Medraut. (© *Richard Law/ Creative Commons*)

Birdoswald Roman fortress, Antonine Wall, Scotland . A possible Northern location for the battle of Camlann, as it was known as 'Camboglanna'. (© *David Dixon/Creative Commons*)

Glastonbury Abbey, Somerset. Arthur and Guinevere's tombs were supposedly found here in 1190, but its Arthurian identity as the 'isle of Avallach' or 'Avalon' is not at all clear. (© *Oliver Dixon/Creative Commons*)

done this was the attendant Mary Magdalene. The mysterious principal female companion of Jesus was accordingly known in some esoteric traditions as the 'Grail-bearer' – but for catching the blood of Christ in a cup which she brought to the west, not necessarily as the guardian of the 'magical' cup or dish of the Last Supper. The Grail became linked to her burgeoning cult in twelfth-century France, a development independent of the notion that Joseph of Arimathea – also linked to the Crucifixion in the Gospels – had had the Grail though some writers chose to try to reconcile the two. Indeed, the linguistic term used for the vessel in literature – the 'San Graal' – has been specified as Catalan/Provencal, thus linking its origin to the area where Mary Magdalene was supposed to have arrived in AD 45 and set up a Christian mission. The tradition that she, Mary the sister of Lazarus, and an attendant called Sarah had landed at Saintes-Maries-sur-Mer in a boat that had borne them from Palestine was certainly extant by the twelfth-century, was written down after 1200 in the 'Golden Legend', and is still celebrated. The culture of the Languedoc was seen as more 'feminist' than the orthodox Catholic world of Italy or northern France (the Cathars had female holy women, 'perfecti'), and so receptive to a greater role for the Magdalene. The first artistic depictions of a 'Grail'-like platter are also Catalan, c.1100. The secular references to 'graals', precious dishes, in Languedoc inventories may well tell us where the word came from as it appeared in culture – but an entire edifice of 'conspiracy theory' had been built on this regional connection. One recent researcher has also linked the development of the association of a Languedoc 'graal' to the dish of the Last Supper with enigmatic late eleventh-century paintings of the Virgin Mary holding such as receptacle in churches in Catalonia – did the Virgin's role become usurped by that of the other Mary present at the Crucifixion, Mary Magdalene?

The hills of Languedoc, inland from the region, were where the heretic Cathars had their strongholds in the later twelfth-century, being protected by powerful lords like the Counts of St Gilles and driving the Papacy to launch a systematic campaign of conversion or extermination in the 'Albigensian Crusade' from 1209. The last Cathars then took refuge in the recesses of the Languedoc and were hunted down by the Inquisition. The Cathars denied orthodox Catholic theology, did not restrict theological knowledge to the clergy, and allowed laymen of ascetic and 'holy' lifestyles, the 'perfecti', to celebrate Mass. Thus anti-Catholic admirers of the Cathars from the late nineteenth-century were able to claim that the fact that the rituals of the Grail were not carried out by priests but by 'angels' implied that the 'Grail cult', originating in Languedoc, was symbolically pro-Cathar and was a deliberate challenge to the church. The Grail was also carried in some romances by a woman, anathema to the church. In fact, the idea of angels not men presiding at a 'mass' seems to have come from the Eastern Orthodox Church, to which the western 'Crusaders' had new access after 1095.

In recent years the Magdalene connection has been revived and linked to the 'real' Grail, with the claims by Henry Baigent and Andrew Lincoln in *The Holy Blood and the Holy Grail* (1982) that 'San Graal' should have been 'Sang Real' – 'Royal Blood' – and that the child who legendarily accompanied Mary Magdalene and Mary sister of Lazarus was her offspring by Jesus.[3] This expanded an earlier investigation into the supposed hidden Templar treasure and other 'secrets' located at Rennes-le-Chateau, deriving from a number of programmes presented by Lincoln in the BBC series Chronicle from 1972–9. There is no ancient authority for this, with or without any supposed genealogical descent to the Merovingian dynasty in the fifth-century or the involvement of the highly dubious 'Priory of Sion', alleged long-term guardians of the secrets (which appears as a society only in papers dated to the 1960s although the Crusaders did establish a priory of this name in Jerusalem). Given that there is no ancient provenance for the 'Priory' which at least one of its 'revealers' later claimed to be an elaborate hoax, there is no historical justification for claiming that the organization was a secret 'Grail cult' behind the Templar order and that the Templars were destroyed as a menace for 'knowing the truth' by the Papacy in 1307. The same applies to any theory that the Priory's eleventh/twelfth-century dynastic leadership (allegedly the family of the first Crusader protector/King of Jerusalem, Godfrey of Bouillon), was the real-life 'Grail dynasty' and had ancient Jewish ancestry connected to the line of Jesus. The twelfth- and thirteenth-century writers who referred to a 'Grail dynasty' made no obvious references to either Mary Magdalene or Godfrey's Lorraine dynasty, as might have been expected were they known to be the 'Grail guardians'. Esoteric references are there – but they are clearly to 'Celtic' myth not to a 'Magdalene cult' or to European royal families.

The 'Grail dynasty' that protected the cup/dish in the stories deriving from De Boron was certainly not meant as a hint at a royal Jewish dynasty in southern France founded by Christ and Mary Magdalene. The most that can be said is that there was some sort of a tradition of a dynasty with Jewish royal blood in southern France by mediaeval times, connected or not to the local sect of the Cathars – who derived their origin from the Eastern Roman 'heretic' sect of the Paulicians whose members were active in the eleventh-century Balkans (as 'Bogomils'). Their secretive bodies of initiates may have given Chretien of Troyes or Robert de Boron ideas for the brotherhood of initiates being served by the Grail. This body of Southern French traditions had no connection to Joseph, 'Avalon', or Arthur and his kingdom. It was relevant to the Arthurian myths in the sense that the intense historical Anglo-French rivalry encouraged patriotic fourteenth- and fifteenth-century English writers to firmly draw the 'Grail cult' into an English context, especially during the Hundred Years War. It was only at this time that the linkage of Grail and Glastonbury emerged; notably the Grail had already been popular by the time of the 1184 fire at Glastonbury Abbey but the monks made no effort then to draw in tourists by promoting its local links and claimed to have dug up Arthur instead. The twelfth-century Grail was not linked to Joseph of Arimathea either.

Chretien of Troyes, the Welsh story of Perceval, and their successors

Whatever the contemporary western European enthusiasm for Christian symbolism and secret initiation connected to a 'Grail', the burgeoning of this new literary cult with Arthurian connections was largely due to Chretien of Troyes. At most, it is possible that his work was preceded by a Welsh version of the 'quest' involving its first achiever, Perceval. The date of this initial British work on the quest, *Peredur*[5] (the Welsh 'original' of Perceval, the name meaning 'Hard Spear'), is unclear – and thus so is its influence on Chretien. It may have been composed before, or after, his great work, though the extant manuscripts are probably early fourteenth-century. It was a 'rougher', less chivalric or Christian version of the elegant courtly concoction that Chretien composed, with the hero as a relative of King Arthur engaged in a search for Otherworldly (superficially) Christian objects that will assist the reconquest of Britain from the Saxons, ie. redeem it from its ravaged state as a 'Waste Land'. (There is a military, rather than a symbolically religious, devastation in this version.) Peredur's quest follows the 'magical' appearance of a procession of symbolic objects, as in the later Grail stories, including the Grail itself – here a dish and with no link to a Fisher King's holy dynasty. The other main objects are a blood-dripping lance – probably inspired by the 'Holy Lance' that pierced Christ's side at the Crucifixion – and a severed head – probably inspired partly by the Celtic myth of the head of Bran 'the Blessed'. The Lance notably appears in the *Suite de Merlin* tale of Sir Balin which serves as a prologue to the Arthurian Grail quest, presenting it as part of the holy relics kept at King Pellam' (or Pelles') castle – its magical useage comes ultimately from the Irish legend of the god Lugh. The Templars' connection with the head of John the Baptist – conceivably the relic of a severed head which they were later accused of worshipping – was another possible source of the association of such objects with holy secrets. Unfortunately it is unclear if the *Peredur* was written before, and could have been used by, Chretien or is a simplified Welsh derivation. The debate over the extent to which the Peredur story influenced Chretien continues, and has been explored (1991) by Rachel Bromwich and I. Lovecy.

Chretien introduced the idea of the 'Grail' to a Europe-wide public in *La Conte du Graal*, along with its custodian the 'Fisher King' and its escort of maidens.[6] He also used the concept of the searcher having to ask the right questions in order to proceed further with the Quest, which Perceval fails to do at first. (It is not known where he got the new name for the hero, which means 'Pierced Vale' and as such has symbolic overtones linked to the Holy Lance and to the 'vale' of the 'Waste Land' which he must penetrate to enter the 'Grail Castle'.) His 'grail' was a golden dish not a cup, but also provided miraculous sustenance. He claimed to be relating a story found in a book given to him by his patron Count Philip of Flanders, but this may be a literary device as with Geoffrey of Monmouth's alleged 'source'. The concept of the vessel whose contents can miraculously sustain a multitude comes from three separate sources – the cornucopia, 'horn of plenty', in Greek myth; the feeding of the Five Thousand in the New Testament; and the magic cauldron of the Daghda in Irish myth. The latter was sought by and helpful to heroes by divine permission in Irish stories, and the concept of the 'searcher' having to traverse a symbolic Otherworldly landscape seems to be Irish in origin. The original 'Waste Land' was however the kingdom of Dyfed in the story of 'Manawydan son of Llyr' in the Welsh tales of the Mabinogi,[7] whose date of formulation is unclear but was probably eleventh- to twelfth-century and which also has a hero asking the wrong question and so precipitating disaster.

The 'Grail Castle' first appears as 'Corbenic' in the *Vulgate* version, the *Estoire del Saint Graal*, c.1220;[8] this may derive from the French 'Cor Benit' ('Horn of Plenty'), i.e. a sort of cornucopia which feeds a multitude, or from a Welsh 'Caer Bannog'. Various sites have been suggested for this, in Wales and northern England, but the linguistic similarities with their names may be accidental. The '*Vulgate*' story also introduces 'King Pelles' as the mysterious lord of Corbenic, descendant of the 'Grail dynasty', and has him trick his visitor Sir Lancelot into sleeping with the king's daughter Elaine so he can be father of the Grail-achiever, Sir Galahad. Later versions mix up Pelles and his son Pellam, with Pelles usually as the 'Fisher King' and he or his son as a guardian of the Grail. Apart from the probable pre-Christian connections, there is also the matter of an elusive 'Bledhericus' cited by Giraldus Cambrensis as a source for the contemporary Grail stories, probably the same man as the 'Bleheris' named by the Flemish poet Wauchier. The name seems likely to be the Welsh 'Bledri', and Edward Owen of the Cymmodorion Society is cited by Jessie Weston in *From Ritual to Romance* as identifying him as the early twelfth-century Dyfed translator Bledri ap Cadifor.[9] Bledri travelled to the court of Queen Eleanor's grandfather Duke William IX, patron of troubadours, in Aquitaine and so could have contributed stories of Peredur to the local poets; he might also be the elusive 'Master Blaise' who is linked to Merlin in the *Suite de Merlin* as his mother's priest, elsewhere as his tutor.[10] ('Blaise' as Merlin's tutor was duly taken up as a name by newspaper strip-cartoonist Peter McDonnell for his heroine 'Modesty Blaise' in 1963, the parallel being with a super-powered 'outsider' trained by a mysterious patron.) He could thus be a 'missing link' between the Welsh stories that evolved into 'Perlesvaus' and the upsurge of Continental versions of Perceval's Grail quest in the second half of the twelfth-century by men who had no obvious Welsh links.

'The Spoils of Annfwn' as a Welsh source for the Grail story

The concept of the dish and its properties had an 'Arthurian' connection in Welsh legend the Otherworldly cauldron sought out by Arthur and his men in the *Spoils of Annwfn*. In that story, however, the quest involves a rescue with magic overtones, not a mystic search for a holy relic that will bring Christian fulfilment to the finder. An overseas voyage is involved as in Galahad's journeys, and most of the protagonists are killed.[11] There was obviously a great deal of symbolism in the story of the voyage to Annwfn; what it meant is unclear. It is probably the origin of the concept of the Quest as the crucial spiritual and physical adventure which will decimate the Round Table brotherhood and open the way to the decline of Arthur's kingdom. The story has recently been described by the controversialists Alan Wilson and Baram Blackett as an allegory for a 'real' Atlantic voyage in Arthur's time, which they regard as the correct placing of the enigmatic voyage of 'Prince Madoc' to America.[12] This, needless to say, is denounced by almost all other historians. The voyager 'Madoc' did not appear as an explorer who reached America until the sixteenth-century, when this had a political explanation as a useful 'peg' on which to hang British claims to have discovered the region before Columbus and thus to have legal grounds to rule it. The main enthusiasts for this theory were connected to the Elizabethan Welsh 'magus' Dr. John Dee, 'cheerleader' for Elizabeth's explorers and colonisers. There was a post-Roman 'fad' for tales of imaginary voyages (not only across the Atlantic) by the peripatetic Irish saints of the sixth- and seventh-century, a genre known as the 'Imrams'. Some Irish saints certainly reached the Shetlands and Iceland, as place-names show – how early is open to debate. But the only reasonably accurate account of a sixth-century voyage across the Atlantic is that in the hagiography of the contemporary Irish Saint Brendan of Clonfert, a central Irish monastery, dated at c.550. The account of Brendan's voyage is equally symbolic with miracles and Divine intervention, and sceptics would prefer to dismiss it as entirely imaginary. But it does seem to refer to phenomena such as whales, fogs, and islands at the correct point in such a journey.[13] The 'Brendan Voyage' of Tim Severin's explorers in the 1970s showed that such a voyage by 'ox-hide' boat was perfectly feasible as far as currents are concerned. The only definite Arthurian connection is that St Brendan's hagiographer referred to the Saint's informant about an earlier voyage as

Barinthus, who appears in Geoffrey of Monmouth's story as the pilot on Arthur's last voyage to Avalon.[14] Geoffrey – or his source – at least regarded Barinthus as a suitable character, of the right date, to navigate the ship for a voyage into the West. The voyage in search of the magical cauldron is far more likely to have been a common 'topos' of 'Celtic' myth which was annexed to a suitable British hero after an Irish 'original' than to reflect any real voyage.

Perceval/Peredur's traditional link to the family of the Virgin Mary in Welsh legend. Is this the origin of the 'Grail Dynasty'?

The basket of Gwyddno Garanhir, able to sustain the world with meat, and the horn of Gwlgawd Gododdin which provides endless drink, appear as tasks set for Arthur and his men as they aid Culhwch to carry out the giant Ynysbadden's tasks in *Culhwch and Olwen*.[15] The date of the Welsh tales is unclear and the current surviving version is thirteenth-century, but it is likely to have been developed from an earlier non-extant text. Perceval, the first knightly Grail-quester was possibly the prince Peredur of York, son of Elidyr (the Roman 'Eleutherius') 'of the Great Host', brother of Gwrci, and descendant of Coel 'Hen' the post-Roman ruler of the North of Britain. He can be dated to c. 570–80, given that the 'Dialogue of Myrrdin and Taliesin' and other early Welsh traditions such as the *Triads* refer to him as fighting in the battle of Arderydd which the 'Annales Cambriae' date at 573 and the latter has him and Gwrci being killed by the Angles in 580. Their warriors were one of the 'Three Faithless Warbands of Britain' who deserted their leaders, in battle against 'Eda' (presumably meant as Ida, founder of the Anglian kingdom of Bernicia in Northumberland, but he died c.559 according to Saxon chronicles). Peredur was eventually to be superseded as the 'Grail hero' by Lancelot's son Galahad (not one of the early Arthurian characters) after an interim period when Gawain was made the central character.

Peredur of York was too late in date for a real-life connection to the court of an Arthur who fought at Badon c.516. His father was supposed to have lost his kingdom in Yorkshire to invading Angles, thus making it a 'Waste Land' and Peredur became a homeless adventurer. Possibly the reference in the Myrddin/Taliesin poems to his fighting for his distant cousin Gwendolleu of Carlisle at Arderydd c.573 was the origin of the idea that he went into the service of the region's greatest warlord, later seen as being Arthur; in any case he was a north British military commander. This is far from the late twelfth- and thirteenth-century concept of Perceval/ Parzival as son of a prince of Anjou, and half-brother to a Muslim lord, developed by Wolfram von Eschenbach – who has a sixth-century Angevin prince (Perceval/Parzival's father) serving the Muslim queen of 'Zaramanc', possibly based on Baghdad, before the Prophet founded Islam or Baghdad was built. Wolfram also introduced Perceval's alleged half-Arab, half-Frankish (and piebald) 'multi-racial' half – brother Fierefiz, as a character, and was keen to play up – or to invent – the notion of the basic Perceval story being found in a mysterious Arabic book in Spain by the elusive wandering scholar 'Kyot of Provence'. In this version, Perceval's landless – and thus by contemporary standards 'socially obscure outsider' background – is made more dramatic by his widowed mother having raised him in a remote forest and banned any contact with the knightly class or military matters, not wishing him to get killed like his father. (Derived from the Greek story of Achilles?) He nevertheless encounters some passing Arthurian knights and is inspired to go to Arthur's court and learn military skills, so she dresses him up in 'low-class' civilian clothes looking like a 'fool'/ jester (an occupation which knights looked down on) in the hope of putting his hosts off helping him – to no avail. Wolfram also invented or popularised Lohengrin (originally in his version 'Lohangeran' the 'Swan Knight', a minor character in his version, as Perceval's son who follows in his footsteps as a questing knight while his brother inherits the hero's kingdom. He is the first known writer to identify Perceval's son with the originally anonymous 'Swan Knight' who in contemporary Low Countries myth came to Brabant to act as protector for its embattled Duchess in the tenth-century and duly became her husband and the grandfather of Godfrey of Bouillon, duke of Brabant and co-leader of the First Crusade in 1099 (and first ruler of the new Kingdom of Jerusalem). This seemed to date Perceval and his son as centuries after Arthur's time, but the anomaly was not noticed – even by Richard Wagner who in his operatic version of 'Lohengrin' placed this story in the time of the German king Henry 'the Fowler' (ruled 919–36). The 'book' which Wolfram cited as discovered by 'Kyot' was probably invented. The mysterious 'Kyot' may have been based on the real-life late eleventh-century troubadour Guyot from Provins in Champagne.

There was no Anjou in the sixth-century for any historical 'Perceval' to come from; the real family of Peredur was the dynasty of the 'Men of the North' founded by Coel 'Hen', the '*Gwyr ar Gogledd*'. This was probably a genuine family descended from a major ruler of the North of Britain, between York and Hadrian's Wall – though questions have been raised over later writers' habit of translating a 'political' descent of rulers into a neat, father-son-grandson line of dynasts. Their traditional ancestor, Coel 'Hen', may have been the post-Roman commander of the Hadrian's Wall area who rallied the local military levies to drive back the raiding Picts and subsequently founded a kingdom. The fact that the great later sixth-century warlord Urien of Rheged (Lancashire/ Cumbria?), contemporary of Myrddin and patron of Taliesin and victor at the battle of Arderyyd c.573, was a member of the dynasty would have meant that it was celebrated by the bards at his court. They may have elaborated the family genealogy and pushed it back to Biblical times to emphasize its importance. It was linked in genealogy to the family of Jesus and thus the 'Grail Dynasty', with a supposed cousin of the Virgin Mary marrying into the first-century British family of king Bran 'the Blessed'.[16] From his date, this Bran was not – despite his epithet – the mythical king who invaded Ireland in a story which survives in the Welsh legends of the 'Mabinogi'.

The fall of York to the Angles of the Humber estuary under king Aelle of 'Deira' around 580 could be linked to the Welsh legend that Peredur's ancestral kingdom had been ravaged by invaders and turned into a 'Waste Land'. This date was established in the Irish monastic annals later used by the tenth-century '*Annales Cambriae*'. Thus the twelfth- and thirteenth-century writers could use the traditional dynastic Palestinian links of Peredur to link the 'Grail Dynasty' to the Grail's achiever, his modernised knightly 'alter ego' Perceval. But it is unclear how old is the Welsh story of the link of the 'Grail dynasty', with or without Christ's relatives, to a British royal line – or if the latter was that of Coel's family or the South-Western family of the elusive Arviragus who supposedly gave the Glastonbury site to Joseph of Arimathea in AD 63. Robert de Boron, writing around 1200, was the first to specify a 'Grail dynasty' of twelve keepers of the holy object from Joseph's times until Arthur's;[17] until then the Arthurian quest had not been linked by this family back to the first century.

Robert de Boron and after. The Grail as a holy stone. The Templar link

Robert de Boron, probably writing at Montbeliard in the Jura, was the first to present the Grail as the cup used at the Last Supper and its association with Joseph of Arimathea and an early Christian mission to 'Avalon' (which eventually became linked to Glastonbury). The early date of the mission had been mentioned by Gildas, but not 'Avalon' or the Grail. At first there was confusion over whether the 'Grail' was a cup or a stone, the 'Lapis Exilis', and what its exact provenance and powers were. Wolfram von Eschenbach insisted that the 'Grail' was a stone, in contrast to Chretien. The reference to it being a stone presumably means a linkage with the mythical 'Philosopher's Stone', another presumed source of mystical secret knowledge. It also links this version of the Grail with the pagan veneration of 'holy' stones that had fallen from Heaven, including such cult- objects as the sacred 'sky-stones' of the Middle East including the stone of Baal/Elagabalus at Emesa brought to Rome by the eponymous Emperor in c.220. The Jewish faith had a holy stone at Bethel, allegedly that on which Jacob had rested his head when he had his dream of the angels descending from Heaven – and in Irish legend this was later taken by refugees to Ireland in the time of (?by) Jeremiah to serve as the royal coronation-stone at Tara. In Scottish legend it was then taken on to serve the kings of Dalriada and Scotland, at Dunadd in Argyll and later at Scone. This 'Grail' stone thus did appear in mediaeval myth as coming to Britain. Wolfram also played up the Islamic connections of the 'Grail' by giving his Angevin hero a Muslim half-brother and siting the hero's Middle Eastern adventures in Islamic lands; this 'Grail' and its protectors were deliberately portrayed as 'multi-cultural'.

In contrast to this, Robert de Boron presented an extensive 'back-story' of the Grail to link it to Christ, portraying Joseph as imprisoned for many years after the Crucifixion and then being released by Emperor Vespasian (commander of the Roman expedition to suppress the Jewish revolt in AD 66–9) to lead a mission to the far West. Jesus presented him with the Grail dish in prison to continue to hold meals with it in celebration of the Last Supper, and its magical sustenance kept the prisoners fed. Joseph's brother-in-law Bron became the 'Fisher King' who led the meals after the mission left Judaea, and his descendant would find the Grail again. It has been suggested that Robert mixed up Joseph with the Jewish historian Josephus, who was indeed released from prison by Vespasian during the Jewish Revolt in AD 66/7 but went on to serve this future emperor, not lead any Christian community. In that case Robert was clearly unaware of the contents of Josephus' history, which show that he was a rebel commander and not the man connected to the Crucifixion.[18] The whole story of Joseph being imprisoned for helping Christ and then performing miracles in prison originates from the fourth-century 'Gospel of Nicodemus', a late Roman story of wonder-working supplementary to the 'Acts of the Apostles' which was popular in the twelfth- and thirteenth-century as seen by its appearance in monastic libraries, that had Joseph healing Vespasian's son Titus and being freed by the future Emperor in gratitude. (The idea of miraculous freeing of a senior Christian from prison came from the experiences of Ss Peter and Paul.)

The intense mysticism of the search for the Grail, its body of knightly guardians, and the potential Templar connections of the Grail 'cult' owed most to the development of the story by Wolfram von Eschenbach in *Parzival*.[19] His patrons, the Counts of Thuringia in central Germany, had crusading links like Chretien's patrons, though his exact background is unknown and he may have been Bavarian in origin. In any event, he came from the world of petty princes, dukes, and counts in south-central Germany in the reign of the great Holy Roman Emperor Frederick 'Barbarossa', who was to die on crusade (drowned outside St Paul's home-town of Tarsus) in 1190. He altered the names of the dynasty of Grail guardians and made Parzival a knight from Anjou and son of its ruler, on what literary evidence (if any) is unclear. It may have been a tribute to the crusading links of the Counts of Anjou, who provided the royal dynasty of Jerusalem from Fulk in 1131–44, or been due to the geographical origin of his stories at their descendant Henry II's court. His descriptions of the heraldic surcoats worn by the guardians of the Grail seem to have been deliberately planned at implying a link with the Templars. The black-and-white Muslim half-brother of Perceval, Fierefiz, was also seemingly a reference to the Templars' black-and-white flag and to their special relationship with the Muslims in the Middle East, a rare example of cross-cultural communication which the story also accepted. Possibly the 'cross-cultural' story was designed to promote understanding of Islam and its secret spiritual heritage in the relatively sympathetic ethos of international relations in the twelfth-century, when the Crusader kingdoms usually co-existed with the local Muslim states (and some zealous arriving westerners were appalled at this).

The explicit reference to the Templars commenced the association of the Grail with the Military Orders – which was to lead to modern suggestions that Templars had found it in Palestine and brought it back to be hidden somewhere on their lands in western Europe. The Templars' secret rituals, religious brotherhood of ascetic devotees, and apparently unorthodox religious beliefs could be linked to a 'cult' that had some similarities with the worship of the Grail in the romances – though too much should not be read into the allegations of heresy and cultic worship produced by the Order's enemies at the time of their suppression in 1307. This owed more to the impoverished King Philip IV seeking any powerful charge of blasphemy he could find or invent to justify destroying them to a truthful summation of their rituals. His charge that they worshipped a severed head may be connected to the Templars studying an ancient legend of the magical severed head of Bran 'the Blessed', possessor of a cauldron that had Grail-like powers.A severed head appears in the 'Grail procession' in *Peredur* and in Wolfram's romance.

Alternatively the idea may be linked to the head of John the Baptist. It has been suggested by Ian Currer Wilson that it derived from the Templars obtaining the 'Mandelion', the cloth bearing a miraculous imprint of Christ's features which the Byzantine general George Maniaces acquired from the city of Edessa in 1032 and which was probably looted from Constantinople in 1204.[20] If the cloth was folded up so that only the head was visible it would appear to worshippers to be a severed head, and it would attract legends as an object of supernatural origin.

The Templars and the Grail cups

It is mere speculation by what could be called the 'Dan Brown school' of writers that the Templars had found any significant 'finds' dating from before AD 70 on the Temple Mount in Jerusalem and hidden them in western Europe, or that their discoveries challenged orthodox Catholic Christianity and gave them special insight into 'lost secrets'. This would explain the literary link between the Templars and the 'Grail guardians' as custodians of secret objects connected to Christ, but so would contemporary European rumours (without any reality to them) about this. There is no proof that the Templars had access to special objects found in Jerusalem, or that literary sympathisers carefully hinted at this by a special 'campaign' by chosen authors to create a symbolic myth of the Grail as a source of mystic fulfilment. Chretien de Troyes – claimed by some hopefuls to be a Templar 'agent' – and all the other authors who built up the Grail story over decades were not chosen initiates of 'Templar secrets'. Nor was there an actual Grail cup dating from Christ's time, a relic that could be hidden in a Templar preceptory somewhere in western Europe as an object of worship. If there had been a cup used at the Last Supper, preserved by the Apostles, it would have been an ordinary earthenware vessel (such as the humbly-born disciples could afford) not a priceless artefact unless it was a higher-status dish or cup belonging to some wealthy Christian sympathiser in Jerusalem. (The site of the Last Supper in an 'upper room' in a building on 'Mount Zion', in a wealthy district of Jerusalem, might suggest the latter.) It might have been decorated later by rich Christians, and if it was preserved as an object of honour and later brought out into the open for public display this could be linked to the reign of the first Christian Roman Emperor, Constantine 'the Great' (d. 337). The latter's mother (St) Helena visited Palestine on pilgrimage in 326 to collect holy objects and locate the sites of the Passion – so a 'Grail cup' might have been 'found' then. Richly-decorated cups and dishes seem to have played a venerated part in Christian worship as far back as the fifth-century, as complained about by St Augustine, but had never been declared to be important because of their provenance as Last Supper relics.

There were various 'Grail cups' at large in the chivalric world of twelfth/thirteenth-century Europe which had somehow been found by pilgrims or crusaders in Palestine, none with overwhelming credentials. The most notable cups on public display were at the shrines of Santiago de Compostella in Spain, dedicated to St James, and at Vezelay and Ste. Baume in France, dedicated to Mary Magdalene. The object in Spain, recognised by the Vatican, was associated with the cup said to have been acquired in the third-century by the Roman deacon and martyr, St Lawrence. Those at the two French sites that disputed the relics of the Magdalene were connected to her worship, and to the belief that she had brought relics from Palestine with her on her arrival in Provence at

Ss Maries-sur-Mer.[21] (The main relic was that of the 'Holy Blood', which was depicted with her in her most significant twelfth-century French stained-glass representations.) The connection with the Magdalene cult could also explain the emerging early thirteenth-century Grail story's reference to Joseph of Arimathea also collecting Christ's blood in the Grail, which action was usually associated with Mary. There was a church of Mary Magdalene at Troyes where she was depicted with the cup that had caught Christ's blood, which may be how Chretien picked up the notion of the cup of the Last Supper being brought to western Europe. Alternatively he may have used the fact that the father of his patron Count Philip of Flanders, the relic-collecting Count Theobald, had acquired a cup, reputed to have been used to collect Christ's blood, on Crusade in 1150. Recent research in Britain has unearthed one mediaeval cup apparently hidden in a statue at a Templar preceptory in Shropshire, a place with links to the 'Crusading' family of Fulk Fitzwarin; but there is no mediaeval literary hint of any such object being venerated as a 'Grail'. Fulk (d. 1247), a semi-legendary outlaw of mediaeval romance but based on a real landowner outlawed by King John c. 1200, seems in real life as well as the 'Romance of Fulk Fitz Warine' to have been a wandering hero who not only held out in the Shropshire forests with his band of outlaws after his conviction – and had enough good social connections to be pardoned later – but may have fled abroad at some point in his adventures. His overseas career as a chivalrous 'knight errant' until his pardon is however unproveable, as is any possible acquisition of a 'Grail cup' by him or his family during the late twelfth- or early thirteenth-century.

The same problem of a lack of any mediaeval corroboration affects the claims of Britain's other, more famous 'Grails'. The most famous is the cup now in the possession of the Powell family of Nanteos in mid-Wales, a late mediaeval wooden artefact. It was apparently retrieved from a post-Reformation hiding-place at Strata Florida Abbey, but the story that Glastonbury monks took it to the latter to escape Henry VIII's commissioners only emerged with an article by an American author living in Aberystwyth around 1900. The same lack of early provenance affects the other English 'grail cup' which appeared in the early twentieth-century, an artefact allegedly found and hidden by the father of its 1906 'retriever' Mr. Wellesley Pole. It was duly moved to the 'Chalice Well' in Glastonbury as the focus for its enthusiasts' admiration. Two more cups – late Roman this time – were retrieved in Syria in the 1930s, and one of them was paraded as the 'Grail' at the 1933 Chicago World Fair. They could have been used by early Christians at secret masses before the Roman Empire legalised Christianity in AD 313. But any 'genuine Grail' known to the Glastonbury monks should have been made more of pre-1539 – and the whole point of the Grail romances is that the holy cup was removed from human lands in Arthur's time.

The Grail phenomenon of the later twelfth- and thirteenth-century bore more resemblance to the mediaeval craze for acquiring holy relics than to a serious search for a real cup of proven authenticity. If the Templars had found a genuine cup while digging up the grounds of Soloman's Temple in Jerusalem in the early twelfth-century, why wait until Chretien's literary works in the 1170s to publicise it? The 'Holy Lance' used at the Crucifixion was also 'found' during the First Crusade at Antioch, and is probably the origin of the 'Bleeding Lance' which appears in some of the Grail romances – though there it pierces the 'Fisher King' rather than Christ. (There was however a 'Celtic' origin too, namely the magical spear of the Irish god Lugh.)[22] If the money-making monks of Glastonbury were keen to show off Arthur's tomb and presented his sword 'Excalibur' to Richard I in c. 1190, why not claim a cup brought back from Palestine was the Grail and put it on show for pilgrims?

The mystics of the Cistercian Order seem to have had an 'input' into the early thirteenth-century development of the Grail story, though probably the deluge of Middle Eastern relics imported to the West by Crusaders helped. The trilogy of works in the *Vulgate* cycle – the *Lancelot du Lac*, *Quest du San Graal*, and *Mort Roi Artu* – refer approvingly to the 'White Monks' and have been seen as written or at least commissioned by the Cistercians and designed to link popular Arthurian romance with Church-approved orthodox mysticism. Presumably the Cistercians were aware of the pagan origins of the cult of a 'magic' dish in Irish/Welsh myth and sought to ensure that it was diverted into safely orthodox Christian teaching. (Their principal early organiser and promoter, St Bernard of Clairvaux, had also been heavily involved with the Templars.) The man originally supposed to be the main author of the *Vulgate* trilogy, Walter Map, was in fact antagonistic to the Order and is now accepted as having died by 1209 when the trilogy was being written. The authors were probably anonymous personnel specially commissioned by the Order, though not necessarily monks.

The connection of the Quest to Camelot began with Robert de Boron's lost *Perceval* (1200s?), where the eponymous hero sits in the 'Siege Perilous' at the Round Table and supernatural events follow to start the Quest.[23] (The placing of the hero at this seat was later taken over for Galahad – but hence the latter had to have a 'Grail Dynasty' pedigree too.) In *Perlesvaus/The High History of the Holy Grail* (Flemish, 1200s) the Quest commences with the arrival of three maidens with a cartload of knightly heads at Camelot. In the next French version, *The Quest of the Holy Grail* (c. 1215), the opening action takes place at Pentecost; the basic story used by Malory is now in place as the inscription on the 'Siege Perilous' identifies its rightful owner, the mysterious Galahad arrives to claim it, and the Grail appears to the knights at dinner. The event is dated at 454 years since the Crucifixion, i.e. the early to mid 480s.[24] The basic story was now established, though it was to be elaborated further by Sir Thomas Malory in the 1460s; the later works on the Grail story by post-Reformation poets (e.g. Tennyson and Swinburne) and artists (e.g. William Morris and Sir Edward Burne-Jones) were a matter of changing interpretation rather than detail. The embarrassment of Malory being an ardent orthodox Catholic required the Victorian 'High Anglican' interpreters to reassure their public that they were not 'closet Papists' producing Catholic propaganda, so the spirituality of the Grail became non-denominational. To the 'New Age' enthusiasts – and to Wagner and the Nazis – it reverted to its pagan 'origins'. Its Christian role was however preserved within an esoteric setting by the – unconventional – 1940s Christian poet Charles Williams, who treated it in 'Taliesin Through Logres' as a talisman of the spiritual ideal.

The sixth-century background of the 'Waste Land' – and suggestions about real-life catastrophes to explain it. Other British links – Powys?

That part of the Grail romances that was linked to 'Sir Perceval' had only minimal links with the central Arthurian stories – indeed, the 'original' of that hero was Peredur, the British king of York around 580. The whole mystical concept of a 'Waste Land' somewhere in Britain whose wounded king and afflicted kingdom could only be healed by the perfect knight was linked to the Grail quest, but with only rare connections to Arthur himself (e.g in *Perlesvaus*) and no specific geographic context within the (notoriously vague) Arthurian British geography. It is now claimed that there could have been a real 'Waste Land' in Arthurian Britain after the great plague of c.547 in which King Maelgwyn of Gwynedd died, but this is too late for the reign of a genuine 'Arthur' though the devastation caused by the plague in the mid-sixth-century may have suggested literary possibilities to romancers. Recently it has also been claimed, on climatic evidence deriving from tree-rings, that a 'darkening of the sun' in the mid-530s attested to by Eastern Roman historians could have caused crop-failures and thus a 'Waste Land' at the time in Western Europe, including Britain, before the plague.[25]

This 'Waste Land' dating is within the time-scale of Arthur's 'reign' in the *Annales Cambriae*, ie before Camlann in c.539, but the gap in history from the sixth-century to the emergence of the 'Waste Land' story at the end of the twelfth-century makes it difficult to assert that an accurate memory of a real crisis in Arthur's time suddenly re-emerged after 650 years at the time of the romances. The only Dark Ages story of the 'Waste Land' is that of Pryderi and Manawydan, which is not one of the Arthurian legends in the 'Mabinogi' series. In this version, an enchanter magically empties Dyfed of its people after he has been insulted and Pryderi and his uncle have to travel to London to find employment. The early Welsh version of the 'Grail story', the tale of Peredur, refers to devastation in Britain which can be put right by the hero achieving his quest – which is set during Arthur's reign. But this is a 'Waste Land' caused by Saxon attacks, not any supernatural cause, though it clearly has symbolic overtones. Unfortunately the problems of dating the text means that we cannot state definitively that the tale of Peredur precedes the first Continental literary romance of the Grail, that of Chretien de Troyes, and is the Welsh 'original' which was not influenced by French versions of the story. But in historical terms the kingdom of Peredur's father, the British 'state' of York which had originally been part of the putative realm of Coel 'Hen' in the fifth-century, was overrun by the Angles around 580. The hero's homeland was thus a 'Waste Land' lost to the invaders and he was a stateless exile, as in the twelfth-century 'original' tale of Peredur/Perceval. This event occurred decades after the traditional dating for 'Arthur', that is the 500s to 530s.

A Grail connection to Powys and the Whittington area, where the Fitzwarin family somehow acquired a 'Grail' cup, was to be made by the thirteenth-century but with no clear earlier provenance. The cross-border cultural contacts between Welsh and English lordships in the complex world of twelfth-century Powys means that the Fitzwarins and their poetic protégés may have acquired the idea that the area was connected to Arthur from the current tale of the '*Dream of Rhonabwy*', set in Powys and referring to Arthur as a local ruler,[26] and from that premise gone on to claim that the Grail had been hidden locally. The Welsh linkage of the 'Grail Dynasty' of Joseph of Arimathea was established earlier, at the latest in the tenth-century, and thus independently of the twelfth-century and early thirteenth-century literary embellishments of Chretien's tales. It exists in the pedigrees composed at the court of Hywel 'Dda', first king of united Gwynedd/Powys/Dyfed, c.950 – which brings about the possibility that Hywel's enthusiasm for the early British Christian Church encouraged the promotion of this notion. The Dyfed genealogies now in the Harleian Mss., of similar date, contain references to Emperor Constantine 'the Great' and the 'True Cross', as was currently being promoted in the cult at Nevern – showing that holy relics with a link to the Dyfed dynasty were now made much of.[27]

The line of Coel 'Hen', the early fifth-century ruler of the north of Britain between York and Hadrian's Wall – that is, Peredur's ancestor – was traced by early mediaeval Welsh genealogists back to a king 'Avallach' or 'Aballach' in the first century, who in turn was linked to the family of the Virgin Mary as well as the mythical king Bran 'the Blessed' (the original of 'Bron' the 'Fisher-King'?). This name became turned into 'Evelake', who by the thirteenth-century was regarded as the pagan – Arab? – king of the Middle Eastern city of 'Sarras' to whom Joseph's party had taken their Christian mission en route from Palestine to Britain. 'Sarras' was later connected to Gaza, on what evidence is unclear – one theory has speculated that the title for the local Jewish community leader, the 'Abalach', was the origin of 'Evelake'. But how would a mediaeval Welsh writer know this?

The Arthurian-era king of the 'Grail Kingdom' was eventually identified as Pelles, who tricks Lancelot into sleeping with his daughter

Elaine in order to produce Galahad, and the 'Grail Castle' as 'Corbenic' (possibly the Welsh 'Caer Bannog', but unidentifiable).[28] This story first appears in the French *Prose Lancelot* of c.1215, where the earlier unnamed 'Fisher King' of Arthur's time becomes Pelles – and thus Elaine brings the blood of the 'Grail Dynasty' to the Grail's achiever Galahad. Elaine is already linked to 'Astolat', but without geographical identification; where Alfred Tennyson acquired the Astolat/Guildford link from is unknown and he may have thought it up. Galahad thus usurps the role and lineage of Peredur/Perceval. The *Estoire del Sant Graal* (French, c. 1230), an adaptation of Robert de Boron's work believed to have been written by or for the Cistercians, identified the destination of Joseph's party as North Wales, implying that the Grail questers were probably heading for that region.[29] Incidentally, this is not South-West Wales, as might have been expected (to link up with the Nevern cult) had this story originated in tenth-century Dyfed. If the story had a Welsh base, its 'original' was clearly in North Wales.

The mention of a Welsh destination probably came from the Welsh legends of 'St Ilid' and the dynasty of Gweirydd/Arviragus. The author of *Perlesvaus* identified the main source of his story as a book at the abbey of 'Avalon' – presumably meant to be Glastonbury, given that by this date Giraldus had made the identification public (c.1193). A holy chapel on a ridge above a long valley which Lancelot visits in the story has been suggested by Geoffrey Ashe as a reference to the Chalice Well at Glastonbury.[30] But this 'source', like the untraceable work of 'Gyot de Provence' that Wolfram von Eschenbach claimed to be using, may only be a literary device to make the tale look authentic.

(2) Gawain and Other Connections

Even the Welsh stories before the flowering of 'Arthuriana' in the twelfth-century included a good deal of myth, though they can usefully be mined for evidence that clearly existed before the works of Geoffrey of Monmouth and give us a 'rougher' and more supernatural leader than the latter's courtly king. The *Preidiau Annwfyn (Spoils of Annwn)*, a heroic poem attributed to Taliesin (who served king Urien of Rheged as a bard c. 560–89) about the quest of Arthur and his warriors to rescue a prisoner from a magical fortress and carry off the cauldron of the Lord of the

Otherworld, was composed some time before the twelfth-century. It dates as early as the eighth-century, according to the work of J.T. Koch, and c. 900 according to Sir Ifor Williams.[31] It is now contained in a fourteenth-century collection, the *'Book of Taliesin'*, in the National Library of Wales (Peniarth Mss. 2). It presents Arthur and his men as heroes who are part of a world of gods and legend. It is clearly non-historical, and shows some similarities with the legend of unhistorical 'King' Bran 'the Blessed' and his quest to retrieve his abused sister Branwen from her husband the King of Ireland (who can revive his slain warriors in a similar cauldron). Arthur and his men sail in the ship 'Pridwen' ('White Shape') to seize the cauldron from its owner, the ruler of the 'Otherworld', which was in some legends linked to Bran's destination Ireland; and their target is the 'Fortress of Glass' ('Caer Wydyr'). This seems to have an 'input' on the later story in the 'Life of St Gildas' of Arthur's expedition to retrieve his wife from Glastonbury, which also has a 'glass' connection in that story ('urbs vitrae', 'town of glass') – but is it the main origin for it? Arthur is spoken of in the poem as rescuing a prisoner called Gweir from 'Caer Sidi', the 'fortress of the fairy-people', and as retrieving a 'speckled ox' ('ych brych'), both being referred to in the *Triads* and both also appearing in the early Welsh tale of 'Culhwch and Olwen'. His companions include Gwynn ap Nudd, otherwise known as king of the 'Otherworld' and placed at Glastonbury Tor in the hagiography of St Collen. The ox is retrieved in a battle at 'Caer Vandwy' – 'fort of the divine place' – which is referred to in the *'Black Book of Caermarthen'* in connection to Gwynn, and only seven warriors return from three shiploads who went to Caer Rigor, the 'frozen fort'. (Only seven British warriors survive the battle Bran fights in Ireland.) The story is thus a complex collection of details that relate to current and surface in later 'Arthurian' stories.

Similar Otherworldy elements are introduced to the other early Arthurian poems *Pa Gur* (*Who is the Gatekeeper?*), otherwise known as 'The Dialogue of Arthur and Glewlwyd Great-Grasp' and *Culhwch and Olwen.*[32] The first is preserved in the 'Black Book of Carmarthen', the second in the *'Mabinogi'* collection. Our extant versions of these tales are from Geoffrey of Monmouth's time, but the Welsh courtly milieu that produced them shows little sign of borrowing from Anglo-Norman literature and they are probably based on pre-Norman local poetry. The first has been dated to c.1100 by Patrick Sims-Williams, c.900 by B.F.

Roberts in 1978, and ninth century by J. Koch in 1996. It is usually called this due to its opening – the arrival of Arthur and Cai at a stronghold and their query of the gatekeeper. The protagonist, evidently Arthur, reels of a list of the followers he has with him and their achievements – some possibly based on real heroes, though not necessarily all dateable to the early sixth-century, and others clearly fictional. They include a warrior who has fought at 'the shores of Tryfrwyd', i.e. the battle of 'Tribruit' referred to in the '*Nennius*' list, and on the 'heights of Eidyn'(possibly the battle of Mount Agned which has been located at Edinburgh) with Bedwyr. The reference indicates knowledge of the 'Twelve Battles of Arthur' in Nennius' list of c. 829. Both battles are however in this version against supernatural creatures – sea-monsters and werewolves – not against Saxons; the latter were clearly of less interest to the eleventh- and twelfth-century Welsh audiences.

Cai is a giant who has fought the mythical 'Palug's Cat', a sea-monster, and Arthur himself has fought a witch in the hall of Awarnach and the mysterious 'dogs' heads' (the same as in Greek myth?) on the heights of Eidyn/Edinburgh.[33] His men include Manawydan son of Lir, the Welsh 'alter ego' of the Irish sea-god Mannanan mac Lir, and Lluch 'of the Striking Hand', i.e. the Irish sun-god Lugh. The foe at 'Tryfrwyd' is 'Gwrgi', 'Rough-Grey', otherwise known as some sort of werewolf,[34] rather than any British or Saxon warlord so this is not the same earthly battle as in Nennius; he is slain by Bedwyr. The poem refers to the exploits of Arthur and his men – a band of roving super-heroes rather than a 'normal' human army – in killing assorted witches, an early example of the Otherwordly females, usually hostile to his court, who appear as 'Ladies of the Lake' and sorceresses in the mediaeval English stories.

An unnamed nephew of Arthur's is apparently linked to the loss of 'Celli', which might refer to Medraut and the attack he made on Arthur's court at Gellywig in Welsh tradition. In the *Culhwch* story, Arthur and his men aid the hero to achieve a series of impossible tasks set by a giant as his terms for Culhwch marrying his daughter. In both, Arthur's men include mythical people with supernatural powers – and also some imaginative names that at times suggest a deliberate degree of parody.[35] We are on safer ground only with those companions of Arthur who appear elsewhere, e.g. in local place-names – Cai is supposed to have come from 'Caer Gai' near Lake Bala and Bedwyr to be buried on 'the steep of Tryfan',[36] either Mount Tryfan in Gwynedd or Dunraven in Glamorgan. There is also the enigmatic son of Arthur, Llacheu, who appears in 'Pa Gur' but not 'Culhwch and Olwen' and who was one of the 'Three Well-Endowed Men of the Island of Britain'. His violent death is referred to in 'The Dialogue of Gwyddno Garanhir and Gwyn ap Nudd' in the '*Black Book of Carmarthen*' collection, where Gwyn refers to being at the place where 'the son of Arthur, awesome in songs' was killed.[37] Mabon ap Modron, a pre-Roman British god, appears as a human, the ex-servant of Uther Pendragon. Gwri, apparently the same as 'Gweir' who in 'Preidiau Annwfyn' Arthur has freed from 'Caer Sidi', may be the same as Pryderi, the hero of one of the 'Mabinogi' stories. Carados, who plays a minor role in mediaeval stories, is originally Caradoc 'Vreichvras' who ruled in Gwent, and Owain/Yvain is the late sixth-century ruler of Rheged.Elements of Irish legend are also present at times, most notably in the origin of the 'beheading game' that is central to *Sir Gawain and the Green Knight* in the Heroic Age '*Bricriu's Feast*'. One modern theory has it that this concept of Arthur, the protecting hero with a magically-powered warband who fights supernatural foes, is derived from the Irish legends of Fionn and his 'Fianna'.[38] It is certainly true that Arthur's mythical collection of warriors is as eclectic as Fionn's in gathering figures from different centuries and different stories.

This 'superhero' Arthur even fights a battle with walking trees – the 'Cad Godeu' referred to in the poem 'Golychafi Gulwyd' in the *Book of Taliesin* and in *Triad* no. 84 (as one of the three great 'Futile Battles'). The latter involved the 'branchy trees' of a forest animated by the semi-divine 'Children of Danu' (from Irish myth, again), apparently joined by Arthur, fighting the forces of Annwfyn, the 'Otherworld'.[39] (Is this a possible influence on J.R.R. Tolkien and his 'Ents' who fight against the wizard Saruman and his Orcs at Isengard and Helm's Deep?) This appears to be the battle of 'Caer Achren/Ochren' referred to in 'Preidiau Annwfyn', a conflict fought over a white roebuck (a sacred animal) and a greyhound pup' and possibly occurred in the forest of Celidon. Due to this, it has been suggested recently that this was the origin of the 'battle of the Celidonian wood' in the Nennius' battle-list. Did the Welsh or the Irish stories come first – and does the presence of so many 'humanised' Irish gods in these early Welsh 'Arthurian' poems place him in the same category? The question of gods humanised also appears in the early myth of the hunt for the 'Twrch Tyrwth', the giant Irish boar, across South Wales, where Arthur led a force of heroes to stop its depredations. One version of this story is annexed to the extant manuscript of the 'Gododdin', and there are references to it in 'Culhwch and Olwen' and in Nennius' list of 'Mirabilia'. The latter include a stone bearing the footprint of Arthur's hound Cabal ('Horse' – as it was the size of a pony?) near Rhyader.

3. Gawain or Gwalchmai in myth and history

Arthur and some of his men may be real people who have attracted stories giving them these powers and adventures, but the 'originals' have been distorted and mythical personages introduced even at this early stage. Even Cai has supernatural powers, and in 'Culhwch and Olwen' he can stay underwater for nine days. Similar superhuman powers were given to Gawain, originally 'Gwalchmei son of Gwyar' (not 'son of Llew' or of 'Lot', significantly). In 'Culhwch and Olwen' he is Arthur's sister's son ; he is one of Arthur's 'Six Helpers' who take the lead in fulfilling the tasks. In the *Triads* he is one of the 'Three Well-Endowed Men' of Britain', implying a sizeable landed inheritance. His father is not named; his mother is Gwyar, Arthur's sister. Roger Loomis has traced the use of the personal name 'Walwanus' (from 'Walwen', another alias of Gawain's) to southern Italy and Sicily in the late eleventh-century and early twelfth-century, before Geoffrey of Monmouth's hugely popular book so presumably reflecting local awareness of his legend. Did this come from Breton myth, Bretons being part of the Norman knightly settlement of the area as the Hauteville dynasty took it over post-1050, or from travelling Welshmen? Loomis and others connect Gwalchmai (Gawain)'s legendary powers and adventures with a mythical Irish solar hero called Cu Roi, king of Munster, whose powers waxed and waned with the sun. Cu Roi plays the role in *Bricriu's Feast* that Gawain does in the *Green Knight* poem, accepting the challenge from a threatening visitor to the royal Court, and his name would have translated into Welsh as 'Gwri' – the 'alias' given to Pryderi, mythical prince of Dyfed, who has some of Gwalchmai's superhuman attributes, in the 'Mabinogi' tales.[40]

By the time of William of Malmesbury in the 1120s – again, before Geoffrey of Monmouth – Gawain was believed to have ruled in Galloway, the north-west part of the kingdom of Rheged to which

Gwalchmai's father Llew/Lot and his relative Arawn had been restored by 'Arthur' in Welsh legend.William reported that the burial-site of 'Walwen', Arthur's nephew, had been found in 'Ros' in the time of William II – when Norman lords were overrunning north-east and south-east Wales. This was originally supposed to be 'Rhos' in Clywd, but is now identified by Patrick Sims-Williams ('The Early Welsh Poems' in Rachel Bromwich, A, Jarman, and B.Roberts, *The Arthur of the Welsh*) as in Pembrokeshire. Both areas had a place known as 'Peryddon', where the 'Songs of the Graves ' said Gwalchmai was buried on the seashore. There was a 'Walwain's Castle' near the site in Pembrokeshire. The tomb was supposed by William to have been fourteen feet long, another indication of its occupant's mythical stature.[41] The assumed link of Gawain to Galloway may have arisen from the latter being called 'Walweitha' – to a non-expert, the land of Walwen?

The story of Gawain being killed in battle by Modred as Arthur returns to Britain from his interrupted Gallic war emerges in Geoffrey of Monmouth's version,[42] and was to remain definitive; given the tradition of Gwalchmai's burial in Dyfed or Clywd on the Irish sea coasts, this *could* derive from a genuine memory of the 'original' being killed in a battle as the 'real' Arthur returned to his revolt-hit Welsh kingdom from an Irish war. But the occupation of these areas by French-speakers around 1090–1100, as the Arthurian stories were spreading, would argue that at least some of the new arrivals knew of Gawain as a Welsh hero from romances and were keen to search for evidence of his deeds. Gawain, along with Lancelot and Tristram, was an important enough character to collect his own group of romances in the late twelfth- and thirteenth-century. He initially played a large part in the Grail quest, as befitted the leading knight at Arthur's court, and Chretien portrayed him as a kindly and honourable knight who assists Percival to develop his skills at Arthur's court but is eventually outclassed by him. This version of Gawain involved his falling in love with a mysterious itinerant 'Haughty Lady', later called 'Orgeluse' by Wolfram von Eschenbach from the French term for this quality, who scorns his love and sends him off to tackle a mysterious castle across a dangerous ford. It seems from what a locally expert knight then tells Gawain that she was intending to get him killed, but he presses on regardless, discovers a logical psychological reason for her cold-hearted attitude, and even offers to fight the champion who has killed her previous admirer; she eventually warms to and apologises to him. Later they marry. The extant version of Chretien's story is incomplete and does not contain the 'happy ending'; the extant ending comes from the later development of the story in south-central Germany after 1200 by Wolfram von Eschenbach. The concept of a haughty lady who for unknown reasons scorns and humiliates 'our hero' but who he patiently serves until all is explained was later transferred to the adventures of Sir Gareth, his younger brother.

The idea of a flawed Gawain as being outdone in virtue by the successful 'Grail-seekers', commenced by Chretien, developed much further in later romances, to Gawain's discredit – though it was logical that the 'new' heroes would need a contrasting figure against whom to match themselves and the long-established Gawain fitted the bill. In *The High History of the Holy Grail* (Flemish, c. 1200) he was the knight who played Perlesvaus/Perceval's usual role of being the first to witness a 'Grail procession' at the magical 'Grail castle' but failed to ask the correct question. The first and second continuations of Chretien's unfinished 'Perceval' had Gawain as a contrast to the hero, a flawed character who could not achieve the Grail Quest, but in the third continuation (by Gerbert de Montreuil, c. 1230) he is presented for the first time as a compulsive womaniser whose lechery is a major cause of his failure. A minor French romance, 'La Vengeance Raguidel' c. 1220, also portrays him as an incompetent, as he forgets to take the broken-off spearpoint found in the murdered Raguidel's body with him on his quest to find the killer and has to return to Arthur's court to collect it.[43]

At least Gawain was also the only knight apart from Lancelot to attract a whole series of his own poems – in France as well as Britain – starting with '*La Mule Sans Frein*' ('The Mule Without a Bridle', 1190s?), which introduced his participation in a 'beheading game' and so may be a link between 'Bricriu's Feast' and the 'Green Knight' story. Then came '*La Chevalier a l'Epee*' ('The Knight with a Sword'), c.1215, which introduced the story of Gawain nobly rejecting the temptation to sleep with his host's womenfolk – a daughter, not wife as in the 'Green Knight' version – and '*Les Enfances de Gawain*' ('The Childhood of Gawain'), c. 1225, which followed up Geoffrey's brief reference to Gawain having been educated by the Pope. In the Dutch translation of the *Vulgate* 'Suite de Merlin' by Lodwijk van Velthem (c. 1326) he and his brothers are still the principal knightly supporters of Arthur as a young king, presumably based on Geoffrey of Monmouth. A positive opinion of him as the ultimate chivalrous hero also appears in the works of Wolfram von Eschenbach – and the principal detractors of Gawain's role were mostly French. He was gradually excluded from the role of principal knight at Arthur's court in Lancelot's favour during the thirteenth-century, and even came to be held up as an example of excessive worldliness in contrast to Perceval and Galahad; this first appears as a factor in the '*Vulgate Cycle*' Grail romance, where his misfortunes lead to a holy hermit advising him to go home as he is too worldly to find the Grail. The *Mort le roi Artu* (1215/35) has him as the chief example of reprehensible worldliness at Arthur's court. By Malory's version Gawain was an enigmatic figure, noted for his lechery and jealousy, who was at feud with Lancelot over the latter killing his brother(s) while rescuing Guinevere from the stake after her condemnation (a twist to the story introduced in *Le Mort Roi Artu* c. 1230, so French). This version was used by T.H. White in '*The Once and Future King*', where Gawain is a brusque and somewhat impetuous figure (with a thick Scottish accent as befits a prince of Orkney) who usually does his best to be chivalrous but is hampered by his temper and his honour-linked fondness for feuding. He is not as grudge-driven as his twisted brother Agravaine but does nothing to rein in the latter.

As with the case of Modred as Arthur's jealous illegitimate son, the psychological development of Arthur's nephews into complex, worldly, grudge-bearing figures who will ruin the Round Table was only apparent in the early-mid thirteenth-century French versions. The English stories did not move in this direction until Malory. Gawain's partiality to family feuds in Malory may have been a comment by the author on contemporary feuding nobles at the courts of Henry VI and Edward IV, where a desire for vengeance for past wrongs and 'tit-for-tat' killings undermined attempts to reconcile the great lords in the 1450s and 1460s; Henry VI vainly tried to reconcile his murderous lords from seeking vengeance for past killings with a 'Love-Day' in 1458. In the Malory version, the original accidental killing of King Lot (Gawain's father) in a tournament escalates into a family feud involving the killer, King Pellinore, and his son Sir Lamorak set against Lot's sons – and later Gawain pursuing Sir Lancelot for the accidental killing of his brothers Gareth and Gaheris. The story was updated by T.H. White.

Gawain was also the 'original' of the landless young knight who does not know his parentage and has to prove himself at Arthur's court. This first appears in one version of the 'Bel Inconnu' story, the French *Les Enfances Gavain* (c.1220); an alternative, the first *Le Bel Inconnu* (c. 1180), had the hero as Gawain's son. The character later became Gawain's brother Gareth by Malory's time, with him being bullied as a 'low-born' newcomer to court by Sir Kay. There were also occasional references to Gawain's being brought up at Rome in the Pope's court, which story first appears in Geoffrey of Monmouth and the *Brut Tyssilio*.[44]

4. Other remote antecedents for the stories. The Alans or Sarmatians – and the second-century Roman general Artorius Castus?

Recent research has also shown that even some classical Greek, Lydian, and Sarmatian legends about obscure heroes with names linked to 'Artus' were annexed to Arthur's name and crop up in the most unlikely places in the mediaeval romances.[45] The 'Artus' (or 'Arcas', son of the goddess Callisto) figure in ancient Greece was particularly linked to the isolated Peloponnesian region of Arcadia, regarded as the home of a distinct ethnic population of ancient origin and thus possibly retaining ancient legends that had spread across Europe as far as – or from – Scythia (the steppes North of the Black Sea) in pre-historical times. The connection may also be significant because of the association of Arcadian king 'Arcas' with the star Arcturus and his mother Callisto with the 'Great Bear' constellation, as mentioned earlier. C. Scott Littleton (with Anne Thomas) pointed out the 'Alan' (Ossetian) origins of some Arthurian tales in an article in the *Journal of American Folklore* in 1978, and then explored this further with another scholar who had independently reached similar conclusions, Linda Malcor. In *From Scythia to Camelot* (2000) they have demonstrated that 'Alan' legends lie behind some of the stories of the magic sword Excalibur and the adventures of Lancelot (inspired by the hero Batraz?), together with the concept of the 'Holy Grail'. The 'Lady of the Lake', Lancelot's mysterious 'kidnapper' as an infant and later protectress, may be Alan in origin – or at least come from an ancient legend common to both 'Celts' and Alans. The Alans, one of the elusive wandering nomad peoples of the steppes in Roman times, now survive as the Ossetians in the Caucasus, a distinct ethnic group resisting incorporation into neighbouring Georgia, but under Rome contributed mercenaries to the Imperial army. They suggest that late Roman settlements of Alan mercenaries in northern Gaul enabled these stories to descend to the local contemporaries of the twelfth-century romancers, not least as Celtic Bretons as well as Normans were prominent in the new post-1066 nobility for whom Geoffrey of Monmouth and others were writing. The area was also close to Anjou which Wolfram, on uncertain authority, claimed as Perceval/Parzival's homeland – did Wolfram hear 'Sarmatian'-derived Angevin stories of a hero seeking a magical vessel and link this to the story of the British Peredur?

'Sarmatian' warriors from the lower Danube were part of a Roman force commanded by the general Lucius Artorius Castus in northern Britain in the 170s – from which it has been argued that his victories could have led the soldiers' descendants, settled on Hadrian's Wall, to mix up his campaigns with the myths of their ancestral heroes. The 'Artorius Castus' identification of Arthur was first alleged by Kemp Malone in an article in the *Journal of English and German Philology* back in 1924, but was revived by new work in the 1990s. Artorius Castus himself, commander of the Sixth Legion at York, later took troops to Armorica – where Arthurian myth also sprang up. His use of the 'Sarmatian' tribal mercenaries could have led to their own Danubian myths of semi-divine superheroes being adapted to tales of his feats. As early as the mid-late 1920s Sir Edmund Chambers considered this fact as evidence for Malone's theory and for Artorius Castus being an 'original' for Arthur, but he dismissed it as unlikely given the time-gap from c. 170 to c.500. Linda Malcor has however seen it as significant, though there is no proof of it. In the hunt for any Roman figures with a name that might transmute into 'Arthur' if turned from Latin into a Brittonic language, he is the only 'Artorius' to have been found.

There was probably some annexation of stories concerning the Irish/Welsh sky-god 'Artaus' to the warrior-king who had a similar name,[46] it being more likely that a god would be involved in supernatural quests like that of the 'Cauldron of Annwfyn'. But the attempt to link Arthur personally to Artorius Castus as the only known 'Artorius' commanding troops in Britain is extremely dubious given the time-lapse. This man, the legate of the VI Legion based in York around AD 185,[47] may have had the right name and fought in the right area to contribute to the legends;

he came from Dalmatia, and had served earlier with Sarmatian troops on the Danube so he could have brought a contingent of them to Britain to fight on Hadrian's Wall and their descendants could have adapted tribal legends to fit his achievements. But his date is far too early. This Arthur was never an independent ruler who fought the Saxons, though he presumably fought the 'Picts' (i.e. the northern British tribes living in modern Scotland) and possibly the Irish. He also seemingly led his troops on a Roman expedition in Armorica, though not to fight any of 'Arthur's stated foes (the Empire or the Saxons). Why would this obscure second-century general appeal to the political demand for a 'British' hero to inspire the men of Gwynedd against the Saxons in the 820s, as seen in 'Nennius' myths about him? In looking into etymology as the base for the legends, the argument used for this man – that 'Arthur' was a British linguistic derivation of the Latin 'Artorius' – has however acquired serious backers, including even David Dumville (cautiously).[48] But it is difficult to extend this to claiming that the name was connected to a Romanised British god.

It is more promising to consider the Brittonic/Gallic word for 'bear', derivative from 'arto', 'arth' in Welsh, and to consider the name 'Arthur' as originally a nickname based on the strength and ferocity of the animal – appropriate for a warrior. Indeed, the Early Welsh poem 'The Dialogue of Arthur and the Eagle' refers to him specifically and repeatedly as 'Arth Gwyr', 'Bear of Men'.[49] Whether this was his 'given' name, by which he was known to contemporaries, is another matter. Gildas, our only sixth-century source, continually uses nicknames for rulers like 'Over-King' Vortigern, 'Dragon of the Island' Maelgwyn, and Aurelius Cynan 'the Dog' – not to mention Cynglas from Dinarth, the 'Bear's Fortress'. One mention by him of Cynglas/Cuneglasus, king of north-east Gwynedd and the Vale of Clywd and one of his five 'tyrant kings' targets, as a 'bear' has led to hopeful claims that this meant that Cynglas was Arthur – though in fact this ruler seems to be dated too late as he succeeded his cousin Maelgywn in Gwynedd in the late 540s. The question of nicknames has also led to a modern theory that the name derives from 'ardd', i.e. 'high', and is no more than a personalisation of the rank 'High King' – i.e. Ambrosius as the supreme late fifth-century Romano-British commander? Nicholas Higham has argued that Ambrosius was 'too Roman' a warlord to fulfil the needs of ninth- and tenth-century patriotic

Welsh bards, and so his victories were transferred to a 'British' figure.[50] But the early Welsh 'historicisers' were hardly anti-Roman, or why was Roman Emperor Maximus (Macsen Wledig) so important to them that he even had his own 'Mabinogi' story?

The general question: how 'historical' are the Welsh stories of ancient times?

But that is not to deny a kernel of fact behind it all, or that Welsh bardic tradition could transmit accurate facts through several centuries before the stories were written down. The undoubted embellishment need not mean that there was no 'original' except for some obscure god or invented hero, as some modern sceptics have insisted. All the major heroes of bardic tradition from the post-Roman period, e.g. Urien of Rheged and his son Owain of Rheged and the other great warriors of the north, appear to have been real people and are placed in the royal genealogies. If the propagandists of Welsh claims to Britain in the ninth- to eleventh-century were looking for a hero to be used as a political weapon, why not choose Urien – already a major figure in the *Triads*, the patron of the poet Taliesin, and a leader of a coalition of British kings to defeat the Angles of Bernicia in the 580s – as their exemplar? Or why did 'Nennius', a clerical figure working in Gwynedd and (as per Padel's theory) a 'national revival' propagandist for King Merfyn c. 830, not choose the well-known and successful 'Pendragon', King Maelgwyn of Gwynedd? Because of his ambiguous attitude to the church? The exclusion of Urien from the role of chosen 'national' hero may be due to his Northern British, not Welsh, origins; but in that case why was the 'local' Welsh warrior-king Cyndylan of Powys not chosen?

Fiction seems to have crept in far more for *earlier* figures – it is notable that the garbled legends of the Roman period that survived to mediaeval Welsh literature, e.g. the '*Dream of Macsen Wledig*' about Emperor Magnus Maximus, are at variance with the reliable Latin sources. The stories of Septimius Severus and his fictional 'Wall' and assorted 'independent' British kings during the Roman period that were taken up by Geoffrey of Monmouth are seriously inaccurate. In the lists of Arthur's men, British demi-gods such as Mabon appear and he interacts with the divine Gwyn ap Nudd and the Irish god Manannan/ Manawydan – and possibly with the fictional 'Mabinogi' hero Pryderi.His sphere of action was thus taken as including the figures of post-Roman myth. The early stories of Welsh history in the collection that came to be called the *Mabinogion* due to Lady Charlotte Guest's 1840s translation, those of Bran king of Britain and Pwyll prince of Dyfed (Pryderi's father), are not about historical figures. Patriotism clearly came before a meticulous search for reliable Roman historians, and where written evidence was lacking the gap was filled by guesswork or whatever served the political purposes of the author. But this cannot be used as an argument for all mediaeval Welsh literature concerning 'ancient history' to be entirely or 99 per cent fictional in basis.

If 'gods' like Pwyll and Arthur were exact parallels, why did Arthur alone attract a multitude of place-names? Pwyll was after all placed in a specific kingdom, i.e. Dyfed. Nor did they become accepted by ninth/tenth-century writers as historical figures whose careers could be dated in the *Annales Cambriae*. Why then should Arthur be spuriously placed in a fifth- and sixth-century context, alone among these mythical rulers – unless the writers regarded him as more genuinely historical? And if he was invented as a mythical warrior-hero to fight the Saxons, why do more ninth- and tenth-century stories not refer to his Saxon-slaying exploits? The 'Welsh equivalent of Fionn' argument can be turned on its head, to point out that Arthur's legendary 'pre-Geoffrey' exploits did not centre on slaying the national enemy; Fionn was given unhistorical ninth-century enemies, i.e. the Vikings. If he was created as the Welsh equivalent of Fionn, why not create a coherent account of his battles as the centrepiece of his 'story' rather than only Nennius bothering to refer to them? 'Culhwch and Olwen' and other stories centred on 'domestic' Welsh 'action'. The authors of these stories seem to have regarded the Saxon wars as irrelevant. It is surely too self-assured to insist 1000 years later that Arthur 'must' be as unhistorical as Bran or Pwyll, just because he was placed in a non-historical mileu.

Chapter 6

Arthurian Connections – Persons and Artefacts. Arthur's Queens, Knights, and Swords: Their Development

Guinevere or Gwenhwyfar: the three Queens?

(a) The Welsh original

The likelihood is that there is a kernel of fact behind the Arthurian myth, however much it was embellished between the sixth-century and the twelfth-century. The kernel, however, is much smaller than was suspected during Alcock and Morris' work, and it is less likely that most of the 'peripheral' figures of the myth are based on real people. But conversely, even the archetypes who appear elsewhere may have latched onto genuine people whose story suited (or was changed to suit) the role allotted to them by storytellers. Genuine figures behind the stories may include not only a successful warrior-leader of around AD 500 but other associated figures who are persistent parts of the myth from the earliest Welsh legends. One of the most important of these is Arthur's wife, named Gwenhwyfar ('White Shadow' or 'White Enchantress') in the earliest Welsh stories and in the (tenth-century?) lists in the *Triads*. P. K.Ford, in 'On the Significance of Some Arthurian Names in Welsh' in *Bulletin of the Institute of Celtic Studies* (1983), indeed argues that this name implies an Otherworldly origin.[1] She is placed with Arthur's 'magical' possessions, eg. his ship, spear, and shield, in 'Culhwch and Olwen' as one of the gifts that he cannot give to Culhwch.[2] Her father in the early Welsh myths, 'Ogyrfan', later became 'Leodegrance', and her name was Latinized by Geoffrey of Monmouth around 1135 as 'Guenhumara'. Some later Welsh sources call Ogyrfan a giant. But is the important fact that she was placed with 'magical' possessions, i.e. was 'magical' too, or just that she was treated as another of Arthur's 'trophies'?

The *Triads* (no. 47) gave Arthur three wives all called Gwenhwyfar, the daughters of Cywryd of Gwent, Gwythr son of Greidawl, and Ogrfan the

Giant.[3] This seems unlikely and has been connected to the 'triple' nature of 'Celtic' goddesses – maiden, mature wife and crone. Perhaps several 'Arthurs' and their wives were conflated. The 'three chief mistresses' of Arthur, led by Indeg (still a Welsh name), did not survive into mediaeval legend. Arthur's illegitimate sons did however appear in garbled versions of their original names; 'Amr' and possibly 'Llacheu' were both known to Welsh legends. The violent and tragic death of at least one of them was also a staple of pre-Geoffrey stories; by the early ninth-century 'Nennius' list of 'Marvels' included the burial-site of Amr in Herefordshire and the story that Arthur had killed him.[4] 'Llacheu' is one of the 'Three Well-Endowed Men of the Island of Britain' in the *Triads* (no. 4), and is mentioned in 'Pa Gur' ; 'The Dialogue of Gwyddno Garanhir and Gywn ap Nud' refers to Gwyn, originally a god, being present at his death (probably in battle).[5] The location of Llacheu's death was placed by the twelfth-century at 'Llech Ysgar', possibly near Oswestry. His renown as a paragon of warriorship was also apparent in later poetry, eg by the twelfth-century Powys bard Cynddelw. His name may have been an eponym meaning 'The Glittering One', and as such is linked by one modern theory with the mysterious 'Nowy' or 'Noah' who is also referred to as son of Arthur. Nowy is named in the tenth-century genealogies as a prince of Siluria, son of Arthwys, but another man with this name was a seventh-century ruler of Dyfed. By the mediaeval English romances only 'Loholt' (presumably derived from 'Llacheu') survived as Arthur's son and also had a violent end, being killed by Sir Carados according to the early thirteenth-century '*Vulgate Cycle*' and by Sir Kay according to the 'Perlesvaus'.[6] It is clear throughout that none of these adult young warriors were considered as Arthur's heirs in any 'factual' scenario in sixth-century history which lay behind the stories, although some modern writers (e.g. Baram Blackett and Alan Wilson) have controversially claimed that 'Nowy' or Llacheu – the same person? – was a legitimate son by an early wife, killed in battle during Arthur's reign. The death of this prince cannot be linked to the notable death of a 'very noble young man' at the battle of Llongborth, recorded in Welsh poetry;[7] he is unnamed though some have suggested he could be Gereint of Dumnonia.

The second of the three Gwenhwyfars of Welsh legend in *Triad* no. 47 was the daughter of Count Gwythwr from Leon in Brittany – a name close enough to 'Uthyr' to cause suggestions that it was Arthur's father-in-law, not his father, who was really 'Uther' and an early source muddled them up. Gwythwr may be the 'Vendumaglos' buried at Llanilltern near Cardiff, but this is uncertain. Another – the third Queen – was the daughter of an 'Ogrfan'; her brother was according to the *Triads* killed at Camlann.[8] Ogrfan has been plausibly suggested as the origin of the garbled name 'Leodegrance', Guinevere's father in the thirteenth- and fourteenth-century romances; by mediaeval times he was located at Knucklas in Powys.[9] Another 'Caer Ogrfan' was recorded by Thomas Pennant in 1773 as a name for a fort just south of Oswestry, and Steve Blake and Scott Lloyd in *The Keys to Avalon* controversially interpret the site of Gwenhwyfar's abduction as nearby Valle Crucis rather than Somerset (with 'Dyfnaint' as a part of Powys rather than Devon).[10]

A mediaeval poem in the *Myrvynian Archaeology* of 1870 refers to the abducted Gwenhwyfar as being the second of the three[11] – the one allegedly connected with Meigle, Perthshire (see below) – and her abductor King Melwas as from 'Alban'. The *Triads* have Gwenhwyfar as a worse adulteress than the three most famous 'Unfaithful Wives of the Island of Britain', on account of the political stature of the man she betrayed – showing that a least one story of her willing participation in an abduction or affair was a staple of Welsh literary tradition. She was also involved in one of the 'Three Harmful Blows' (*Triad* 53), namely her being struck by sister, Medraut's wife Gwenhwyfach, and *Triad* 84 had her being responsible for one of the 'Three Futile Battles', Camlann, by quarrelling with her sister. The 'Three Unrestrained Ravagings' included the attack launched on Arthur's court at Kelliwig by Medraut, during the course of which he struck Gwenhwyfar, and the retaliatory ravaging of Medraut's lands by Arthur[12] – suggesting a story of the 'run-up' to Camlann which has not survived. Is this where Geoffrey of Monmouth acquired his story of Modred trying to overthrow the regency in Arthur's absence in Gaul and living in sin with Guinevere?

There is a 'Croes Gwenhwyfar' near Llangollen, though it is uncertain if the holy nature of the area might indicate that she retired to a local nunnery after Arthur's death. By the time of the twelfth-century romances she was said to have embraced the monastic life after Camlann, and a possibly sixth-century poem calling on her to repent for her crimes implies that she was alive for some time after the battle. A local Glamorgan tradition has one of the Gwenhwyfars buried at

Llanilltern – a name derived by Blackett and Wilson from 'the church of the alternative monarch', i.e. Arthur as co-ruler with his aged father Mouric. (A stone reading 'Hic iacet Gwenora' supposedly disappeared in the nineteenth-century.) Another burial-site is St Julian's, Newport, while a rival Scottish tradition has one of the queens running off with the locally-based Medraut and being torn to pieces by Arthur's hunting-dogs at Meigle near Perth.[13] This may be the origin of, or merely a derivation from, the legend of the queen's adultery which was to be so important to mediaeval romancers – the 'Glastonbury' story of the queen being abducted by King Melwas (in the eleventh-century hagiography of Gildas) makes her a passive and innocent victim. In the *Chevalier de la Charette* (Chretien de Troyes, 1170s) the queen is still the victim, of a 'Meleagant' who is clearly derived from Melwas. By the French *Prose Lancelot* of c.1215 Guinevere and her courtly admirer Lancelot are not only 'Lady' and 'Knightly Admirer'/rescuer but lovers.

(b) Later developments – and the role of Eleanor of Aquitaine

As suggested earlier, quite apart from the development of the idea of 'courtly love' by the mid-twelfth-century troubadours of Languedoc the myths may have been boosted by the real-life behaviour of Henry II's Queen Eleanor. As strong-minded and capable of controlling her destiny as Guinevere, she was also a major heiress (Duchess of Aquitaine) sought for political marriage by rival kings. In her case her soured relationship with her husband led to encouraging her sons to revolt against their father rather than adultery, but she was also sought out by kidnappers and protected by knightly devotees (most notably in the 1168 incident by the chivalric paragon William Marshal, subject of a contemporary biography which may have given writers ideas for the career of Lancelot). William's role in saving Eleanor from the would-be kidnapper Guy de Lusignan (later King of Jerusalem by marriage) in 1168 has echoes of the Meleagaunce incident, which in its Chretien version was written up within a decade or two; and like Lancelot William was to be accused of adultery with a 'Queen' (the wife of Henry II's heir, the 'Young King'), in 1181. Chretien's patroness was Eleanor's daughter Marie de Champagne.

Eleanor's memorable career included being separated from and imprisoned by the infuriated Henry in 1173–89, reminiscent of Arthur arresting Guinevere for adultery. She was later chosen as regent of

England (in her son Richard's absence on Crusade, like Arthur's absence in France when Guinevere is his regent) – but by the magnates to replace an unpopular nominee of her son's, not by the King himself. In 1202, aged around eighty, she was being subject to attempted kidnap like Guinevere – by her own grandson, the ironically-named Arthur of Brittany, with her son King John hurrying to her rescue like an unlikely Lancelot.

The story of Guinevere being put on trial for adultery, sentenced to death, and rescued by Lancelot at the cost of several of the knights' deaths in the melee formed the opening of the climax of the 'final version' of Arthur's story. In Malory, it is the disaster that breaks up the Round Table and starts the war between Arthur and Lancelot, giving Modred his chance to stage a revolt.[14] But it is not of early provenance. The episode of the Queen's trial first appears in the French *Prose Lancelot* of c.1215, but features the mysterious 'False Guinevere' not the real Queen (an idea of a 'double' deposited on the unsuspecting King which can be traced to the Classical story of a 'false Helen' being given to Paris in place of the real one after they fled Sparta en route to Troy). The later *Mort Roi Artu* of c.1250 introduces the idea that it was one of Arthur's nephews – Agravaine not Modred – who told the King about his wife's affair in order to ruin her and Lancelot. It also presents the death-sentence and rescue, and the King's siege of the lovers at Lancelot's castle of the 'Joyous Guard' subsequently supposed to be Bamburgh Castle due to its name, 'Din Garde' in '*Nennius*' book).[15] By Malory's version the story had Guinevere being put on trial for adultery twice, the second occasion being connected to Meleaguance finding evidence that seemed to suggest that she had slept with a wounded knight in her entourage while she was at his castle in the 'Chevalier de la Charette' incident; she had also been accused over a knight eating a poisoned apple intended for Gawain.

Guinevere suffered something of a literary eclipse in the nineteenth-century revival of Arthurian works, probably due to discomfort over her well-known association with Sir Lancelot. She was not a suitable heroine for Tennyson, who had an uncomfortable attitude towards assertive women and preferred the chaste 'Maid of Astolat' (who dies for hopeless love of Lancelot) or the nun-like sister of Sir Percival who assisted the Grail-seekers. Nor would Queen Victoria be likely to approve of an adulteress. But the twentieth-century saw Guinevere restored to prominence, though her character and role in the T.H. White tetralogy are somewhat uneasy as if he did not know what to make of her. She was the heroine and principal protagonist of Sharon Newman's '*Guinevere*' (1981), Gillian Bradshaw's '*Winter's Shadow*' (1982), and Persia Woolley's '*Child of the Northern Spring*' and '*Queen of the Summer Stars*' (1987 and 1990).

(c) Cai and Bedwyr (or Kay and Bedivere) and other knights

Early lists of King Arthur's companions including Cai, probably the Roman 'Caius' ('Sir Kay'), and Bedwyr ('Sir Bedivere'), along with others who did not make it to the mediaeval list of 'Knights of the Round Table', appear in the poem '*Pa Gur*' (*Who is the Gatekeeper?*) in the (early thirteenth-century?) manuscript of the *Black Book of Carmarthen* and in the legend of Culhwch and Olwen.[16] The latest dating from the language used puts these earlier stories as being composed in the ninth-century. They would seem to have been a staple of oral Arthurian tradition before that, and to indicate that the mid-twelfth-century claim by Wace that Arthur purposely collected the most notable warriors from across many lands derive from a Welsh tradition. Cai and Bedwyr, indeed, are more prominent in early Welsh stories than in the Anglo-Norman and Malory cycles; Cai is referred to five times in '*Pa Gur*?' and Bedwyr twice, and four and six times respectively in the eleventh/twelfth-century hagiographies (where they are the only companions of Arthur to be mentioned by name). Cai is given superhuman status, particularly in the list of heroes in 'Culhwch and Olwen' where he can breathe underwater and do without sleep for nine days and nights; he could also magnify himself into a giant, in which form he appears in local place-names (e.g. the pass of 'Gwrwyd Cei', 'Cei's Armspan', in Snowdonia) and had a mythical battle with a sea-monster, 'Palug's Cat'. Bedwyr appears in the 'Stanzas of the Graves', along with Gwalchmai, March ap Meirchion, Gwgawn 'Red-Sword', and Gwythyr.[17] By the post-Geoffrey Anglo-French stories the mythical Lancelot has taken over as Arthur's chief knight, Cai is a surly steward who makes life difficult for the would-be knight Gareth, and Bedwyr only appears at Arthur's last battle. The villainification of Cei commences in the works of Chretien de Troyes, who has him as a bad-tempered and spiteful show-off who his hero unhorses at their first encounter in '*Erec et Enide*' (c. 1165). From then on it was downhill all the way, as in Chretien's 'Lancelot' Kay is the incompetent escort whose mistakes enable Sir Meleagant to kidnap Guinevere, the 'Prose Lancelot' has him as a poor warrior who other knights can easily beat in combat, and in '*Perlesvaus*' he is a murderous thug who kills Arthur's son Sir Loholt. Robert de Boron ingeniously blamed his bad behaviour on his mother putting him out to 'wet-nurse' with a peasant while she fed her adopted son Arthur instead. The mediaeval Welsh version of the story of Perceval, '*Peredur son of Effrawc*', has Cei as the scornful court 'insider' who tries to belittle newcomer Peredur as in the mediaeval English story of Sir Gareth he is the surly steward who treats newcomer Gareth like a servant, but it is unclear which influenced the other. Kay had to wait until T.H. White for some better treatment; in *The Sword in the Stone* he is boastful and a little deceitful but basically good-natured and aware of his failings.

The story of Bedwyr/Bedivere throwing Excalibur into the lake – which first appears in the 1230s *Mort le Roi Artu*, from a French source – is connected to ancient Celtic ritual, as the number of swords dredged up from lakes and rivers have made it apparent that they were placed there deliberately as some sort of offering – possibly on the deaths of their owners. Recent research has also established an Alan/Sarmatian equivalent, though this may just derive from a common very ancient origin for the practice. It is unlikely that the tales the Alans told on the steppes in the years when they were recruited for Roman service in Gaul (and Britain) in the second-century could have survived intact in the settlers' new West European territories to re-emerge in the literary culture of the twelfth-century. Some may have become assimilated with Irish myths out of similarity to existing stories; the Irish hero Cu Chulainn, for example, was brought up under an assumed name by a protectress skilled in the martial arts, as Lancelot was by the 'Lady of the Lake'.

Cai and Bedwyr were not the only Arthurian warriors to survive into the mediaeval stories, though the Welsh names of the 'originals' tended to become garbled. Among other early literary Arthurian companions, Caradog Vreichvras becomes the mediaeval 'Sir Carados', and confusingly there are two men of this name (one a murderous villain killed by Lancelot). He is no longer a King, and there is no mediaeval reference to the Gwent dynasty of the 'original'. Cynwyl becomes 'Sir Griflet', and Madoc becomes 'Sir Mador'. Arthur's bishop in *Culhwch and Olwen*, Bedwini (referred to in the place-name of a sandbank in the Severn estuary) becomes 'Sir Baudoin' by the time of Malory. Gereint, son of Erbin, is a king of Dumnonia from around AD 500, from approximately the right date. 'Erec', taken up by Chretien de Troyes c.1170 for his tale of *Erec et Enide*, is however the Breton prince 'Weroch' of the 570s.[18] One warrior who does not appear in the Anglo-French versions is Manawydan, son of Llyr, referred to as a wise counsellor and a veteran of the battle of Tryfrwyd/ Tribuit in '*Pa Gur*'[19] – he is a rare example of a 'crossover' from the main 'Mabinogi' stories, as the brother and adviser of their protagonist Bran. (This would technically make him an Iron Age figure, too early for a genuine Arthurian role.)

(d) The origins and development of Sir Lancelot

Llwch 'Llawwynniog' ('of the striking hand') in the Welsh stories is probably a derivative of the Celtic god Lugh, particularly important in Irish myth but presumably also known in the revived local paganism of fourth-century Britain. (The money and effort spent on the shrine of Nodens, a British version of the Irish 'Nuada of the Silver Hand', in fourth-century Gloucestershire suggests wealthy and noble promoters for British paganism.) Lugh, like Lancelot, comes to the royal court which he is to join (the home of the godly 'Tuatha de Danaan' at Tara, later the High Kings' principal court) as an unknown youth with a mysterious background. Nuada is the current king of these gods – a maimed ruler like the Arthurian 'Fisher King', in this case with a silver artificial arm. Lugh is treated dismissively at first and has to prove his mastery of a variety of skills, and later helps the gods win a vital battle over the malevolent race of 'Fomorians' as Lancelot defeats assorted threats to Camelot. Roger Loomis laid out the evidence for Lugh as Lancelot's 'original' in an article in 1951.[20] The notion of Arthurian stories centring on a visitor – sometimes Arthur, sometimes an 'outsider' to his or another court – arriving at a castle (earlier, a hall) and having to answer questions from a 'gatekeeper' and/or 'prove' himself runs right through 'Arthuriana' from '*Pa Gur*?' to the legends of Lancelot, Sir Galahad, and Sir Gareth, and may originate with the role of Lugh as the 'gatekeeper' of the Irish gods. CuChulainn also fulfils this role, as 'watchdog' at the royal hall of Emain Macha in Ulster.

The semi-divine, mythical 'Mabon son of Modron' also appears in the early Welsh lists of Arthur's men, with a youthly god being turned into a secular hero. *Triad* no. 52 and '*Culhwch and Olwen*' deal with Arthur's warband's quest to rescue him; he is referred to as the 'servant of Uther Pendragon'. His unorthodox background and connection to Otherworldly female patronage resembles Lancelot's. In 1913 Joseph Lot suggested another character in *Culhwch and Olwen*, Llenlleawc, as the original of Lancelot;[21] he was the hero who gained the 'Cauldron of Plenty' in that story so it was a plausible origin for the association of Lancelot with the Grail quest. He is probably the same as Lleminawc in *Preiddieu Annwyn*, and this may be the 'Lleminig' who is one of the 'Three Unrestricted Guests at the Court of King Arthur' in the *Triads*. Lleminawc or Lleminig was known as the 'battle-hound of wrath', suggesting a ferocious warrior, and a member of a junior branch of the dynasty of Powys in the poems commemorating the seventh-century Powys prince Cyndylan.[22] Lancelot was, like Lleminig, a 'guest' at Camelot as a foreigner in the romances, and from the *Prose Lancelot* of c.1215 he is presented as the son of the distinctly unhistorical King Ban of Benoic (probably in France). The French locations suggested for Ban's kingdom, e.g. at Bayonne in Guienne, owe more to post-thirteenth-century linguistic guesswork and association of Arthur's allies with the real-life allies and subjects of the mediaeval English monarchy. At the most, the supposed eviction of Ban from his lands by a king called Claudas *might* be derived from the late fifth-century and early sixth-century conquests of the first great Frankish ruler, Clovis (d. 511), and the 'original' Lancelot might be a local prince whose father had been among Clovis' victims.[23]

Linda Malcor and C. Scott Littleton suggest that the name may derive from an 'Alan' prince, possibly from the Lot region in south-west France which formed part of the Visigothic kingdom overrun by Clovis in 507.[24] An Alan prince from Lot could become 'Lancelot'. This is more reasonable than Laurence Gardner's suggestion in *Bloodline of the Holy Grail* that it was 'del Acqs', 'of the Water', and connected to the supposed 'Grail Dynasty' of Mary Magdalene from Aix-les-Bains in Provence.[25] Any connection of Lancelot with the world of the purported descendants of Jesus, and hence the 1982 book '*The Holy Blood and the Holy Grail*', would need stronger proof than has been found so far; in fact Lancelot's dynastic links to the Grail only emerged as his son Galahad replaced Perceval as the 'Grail-finder' in the early thirteenth-century. More prosaically, in the original French 'let' or 'lot' means 'young' and in

Welsh 'llain' means 'sword'; 'Lancelot' is a vague descriptive appellation, 'Young Lance/Sword', not a personal name found elsewhere in literature or history.

The story of Lancelot being abducted as a baby by an Otherwordly female – later identified as the 'Lady of the Lake' – and kept in ignorance of his real parentage is not in Chretien's original story, '*La Chevalier de la Charette*'. In this version Lancelot is hiding his real name, but with no clue why; he suddenly appears as an anonymous warrior who comes to the aid of Sir Gawain on a quest. The story of his involvement in rescuing Guinevere after her abduction by Meleaguance is as much symbolic as 'action', with him representing the (spiritually) questing knight and the queen the object of his devotion – the Virgin Mary. Lancelot has to overcome his pride, in accepting a 'demeaning' and unknightly form of transport – a cart – to complete his journey after Meleaguance kills his horse. Once he has defeated the abductor he has a night of passion with the queen, but the adultery is incidental to the main thrust of the plot. The story, commissioned from Chretien by Queen Eleanor's daughter Countess Marie of Champagne, was completed by Geoffrey de Laigny so we cannot be certain what Chretien's full intentions were. But it was the Swiss *Lanzelet* (by Ulrich von Zatzikhoven) around 1195 which introduced Lancelot's abduction by an anonymous water-sprite, who brings him up as a knight to take vengeance on her enemies. This story has his fame bringing him an invitation to Camelot, but no adultery with his patroness Guinevere. This version was supposedly based on another of the mysterious Arthurian source-books, given to Ulrich by the Anglo-Norman family of De Morville from the Anglo-Scottish borders. If it ever existed it came from the right area to incorporate surviving legends from the old kingdoms of Rheged, Strathclyde, and Bryniach, the borders also being rich in fairy lore. Abductions by fairies were common in this mythical tradition, as in the Scots borders tale of the knight Tam Lin (kidnapped as a baby by the Queen of Elfland) or in the (allegedly thirteenth-century) disappearance of the poet Thomas 'the Rhymer' from the Eildon Hills in company with the Queen. The fondness of the stories in the former lands of Lothian might just derive from early myths in the sixth-century kingdoms of the 'Gwyr a'r Gogledd' there.

One origin for the abduction may be the Welsh story of the semi-divine hero Mabon son of Modron, rescued by Arthur and his men from Otherworldly captivity in *Culhwch and Olwen*.[26] That story bore some indications that Mabon was originally a god, the 'son of the Earth (Mother)', and the youthfully heroic Lancelot with his mysterious raising by an enchantress could be derived from a mythical origin. The connection with a 'faery' lady in a lake implied a derivation from Celtic myth, given the importance of lake-divinities in those works (possibly Breton given Lancelot's emergence in French not Welsh stories.) The 'Lady of the Lake' was connected with the dynasty of Burgundy according to the *Vulgate* version, on unknown evidence; but her father 'Dyonas' appears to derive from the Welsh sea-god Dylan. She was usually named Nimue and was confused with the similar enchantress Vivian/Viviene, lover and entrapper of Merlin; in the case of Nimue her role became benign rather than sinister. (The 'original' lake-spirit in Ulrich's version is only concerned with her own aims; by the French '*Prose Lancelot*' of c.1215 the Lady comes to the aid of the infant Lancelot and his cousins by rearing them after their fathers die.) Real-life 'Celtic' priestesses associated with water, such as those recorded by Pomponius Mela as living on a Breton island, may have lain behind the legend of the 'Lady of the Lake', and pre-Roman 'pagan' religion in central Gaul was similar to that of Ireland from place-name evidence. Feminist writers have argued that the development of priestesses' role into dark rather than beneficient purposes in mediaeval stories reflected church disapproval of women priestesses. But the malevolence shown towards Lancelot by Arthur's sister Morgan le Fey may derive from Irish myth, where the battle-goddess, the Morrigan, conducts a similar vendetta against Cu Chulainn.

Lancelot's all-white armour might indicate a connection with the similarly-named Lugh, the youthful Irish sun-god and divine warrior. The connection of Lancelot with the magical castle of the 'Dolorous Guard', which he wins in combat with its defenders and renames the 'Joyous Guard', first appears in the *Prose Lancelot*; another French romance, the *Mort Le Roi Artu* of c.1230, introduced the famous episode of Lancelot being nursed by the anonymous 'Maid of Astolat' whose advances he rejects so she dies of grief. The naming of her as Elaine came later; the connection of Astolat with Guildford was an invention of the story's most famous re-teller, Tennyson in '*The Lady of Shalott*'.

(e) King Arthur's swords

Arthur's sword is 'Caledfwlch' in the Culhwch story; this probably means 'hard cutter'.[27] It is probably derived from the 'Caled Bolg' ('hard lightning'), sword of the Irish hero Fergus mac Roich); it becomes 'Caliburn' in Geoffrey of Monmouth's version. The name is presumably connected to 'chalbys', 'steel'. The Culhwch story also gives Arthur a spear, 'Rhongomyant', 'slaying spear'; it becomes the briefer 'Ron' ('slayer') in Geoffrey. Arthur's shield in the Welsh stories, 'Wynebgwrthucher', 'face of evening', becomes 'Pridwen', 'white form' – which in the Culhwch story is Arthur's ship.[28] In neither version is there any indication that Arthur's sword has a supernatural origin or is a sign of his sovereignty; the royal lance is equally important to the Welsh stories and is possibly connected to that associated with the Irish god Lugh.

Arthur assumes the British throne at the age of fifteen, following an interregnum on the death of Uther, in Geoffrey's story. He is brought to the court at the suggestion of the nobles to lead them against the Saxon threat and is crowned by Archbishop Dubricius, interestingly at Silchester which was a genuine Roman town (Calleva Atrebatum) possibly still extant c.500 but was a field by Geoffrey's time.[29] For once, Geoffrey does not place events at a town important in Welsh myth (Caerleon) or still used in the twelfth-century (Winchester/Venta, St Albans/Verulamium, Lincoln/Lindum, and Carlisle/ Luguvallium). Does this indicate that Geoffrey was using a genuine early Welsh source which recorded an event from the time when Silchester was still occupied? But there is no hint of any magical 'test' of Arthur having to pull a sword out of a stone. This, like the Lancelot stories and much of the 'accepted' version of the Merlin story, is French as far as can be traced. Chretien does not deal with the origins of Arthur's kingship, but Robert de Boron refers to Arthur drawing the sword from the stone in his 'Merlin'. From then on this test of kingship becomes central to the story, and as Arthur's foster-brother Kay's character darkens he becomes capable of attempting to pass off Arthur's success in drawing the sword as his own.

'Excalibur', which Merlin locates for Arthur in a lake after he has damaged his original sword, appears in the *Suite de Merlin* in the 1230s, and is thrown back into another lake after his last battle in the contemporary *Mort le Roi Artu* – suggesting that the sword's connection with lakes is French (Breton?) in origin. The recent research into Alan myths has shown that their hero Batraz had a similar sword which had to be thrown back into a lake on his death – with the warrior ordered to do this evading his duty at first as Sir Bedivere does in the Arthurian version.[30]

(f) Medraut or Sir Modred, Arthur's nephew – and his brothers

The traitor called Medraut ('Sir Mordred') who was killed in Arthur's last battle appears as early as the ninth-century in the *Historia Brittonum* attributed to Nennius and is named as the other participant in the battle of Camlann in the early tenth-century *Annales Cambriae*. (It does not say, however, that the two were fighting on opposite sides.) This Medraut is not specifically identified as Arthur's nephew, the son of Gwyar/Anna and King Lot/Llew of Lothian; he could alternatively be the Medraut ap Cawdraf who appears in the genealogies of Gwent and lived at Miskin, North-West of Cardiff.[31] This Medraut was a logical 'original' for a character who is able to launch an attack on the Queen's court – at Caerleon? – in Arthur's absence, particularly if Arthur is seen as a ruler in or near South Wales as in the Welsh myths and hagiographies. But the story in the *Triads* of a quarrel between Guinevere and her sister, Medraut's wife, did not survive into the twelfth-century and thirteenth-century Anglo-French stories. The French writers were probably unaware of it, quite apart from the fact that it was at odds with their creation – if Arthur and Medraut were father and son they were unlikely to have married sisters. In some twelfth-century Welsh references Medraut is treated as a generous and honourable man, not a villain; the first unambiguous Welsh reference to his villainy is in Tudor Aled, post-Malory in date. Thus it has been suggested that Geoffrey invented the idea of him as a traitor (or fused two characters into one?). One possible inspiration was William 'Clito', nephew and would-be challenger of Henry I in the mid-1120s; another were various feuding princes of Powys.

Geoffrey presents Medraut unambiguously as Arthur's nephew, trusted with the regency during his uncle's Gallic campaign and treacherously revolting and trying to seduce Guinevere, and from then on his role in the finale of the saga is fixed. As of the French '*Estoire de Merlin*' of the 1230s, Modred is conceived by the lustful Arthur deceiving his half-sister Anna (later Morgause) into thinking that he is her husband King Lot.[32] This was a re-telling of how Uther seduced Arthur's mother Ygerna/

Ygraine, the wife of Duke Gorlois of Cornwall, in Geoffrey's story – and may have been intended to show how one generation's sins were repeated by its successor.

Arthur's other 'original' nephew Gawain, in his earlier incarnation as 'Gwalchmai' ('Hawk of May'?), has a contrasting brother called Galchavad – possibly an early equivalent of the mediaeval feuding brothers Balin and Balan. The brothers of Gawain and Mordred – Agravaine, Gaheris, and Gareth by Malory's version of the tales – appear only in the thirteenth-century, starting with Agravaine's role in exposing Guinevere's adultery to Arthur in the *Mort Artu* in the *Vulgate* version c.1215. Originally, in the *Mort le Roi Artu* c.1230, it is Gawain's brother 'Gaheriet' who is accidentally killed by Lancelot as he rescues Guinevere from the stake, thus sparking off his blood-feud with Gawain. In this version Gaheris is the brother of Sir Mador, and accidental victim of a poisoned apple intended for Gawain which is blamed on Guinevere; Gaheris and Gareth become Lancelot's victims in the melee around the stake later. The 'Orkney brothers' indirect responsibility for the fall of the Round Table by exposing Lancelot and Guinevere now became a 'staple' of the literary developments of the stories, with Medraut/Modred as the ultimate 'baddie'. Any psychological investigation of Modred's motives had to wait until the twentieth-century, when T.H. White presented him as a physically and mentally twisted character, possibly influenced by the Shakespeare version of Richard III. His Modred was jealous of the successful and accomplished Lancelot, but also psychologically scarred by his monstrous mother Queen Morgause; and the concept of Modred's mother as the principal cause of his problems was taken up by Rosemary Sutcliff in '*Sword at Sunset*'.

(g) The Triads *as a source of the legends*

The *Triads* and the 'Celtic' hagiographies also provide the initial kernel of the story of Guinevere's adultery (though not with Lancelot) and/or abductions, notably in the *Life of Gildas* where the saint mediates after King Melwas carries her off to Glastonbury Tor.[33] In this version it is Arthur who turns up with his army to blockade the abductor's headquarters, rather than Lancelot on a lone rescue-mission. They also include some stories that did not survive into the English version such as her rivalry with her sister, Medraut's wife, and the part that quarrel played in the final conflict between Arthur and Medraut. A poem attributed to 'Myrddin' calls on Gwenhwyfar to repent her crimes and links this to Camlann, indicating the queen's role in causing the final battle – which by the late Mediaeval version had developed into the notion of her adultery with Lancelot leading to a blood-feud between him and Modred's family.[34] The *Triads* hint at other vanished stories of an Arthurian 'cycle' in their identification of certain heroes' exploits.

There were two stages in the development of the extant *Triads*, as analysed by Rachel Bromwich (1978, see Bibliography), and a development of Arthur between the two has been detected. Around twenty-six of the ninety-six mention Arthur, with the 'caveats' that in some cases he is 'added on' to a list of the three people in question as outranking any of them (suggesting a later interpolation?) and in other cases the nature of the subject (eg the Grail) suggests a post-twelfth-century not sixth- to tenth-century creation. The 'ranking' of Arthur's Court is extended, now turning it into the pre-eminent centre of power in Britain, and new members are added to it who are definitively post-550 – including Owain ap Urien of Rheged and the poet Llywarch 'Hen'. There are also problematic and hard-to-place names, such as Arthur's 'chief elder' at his Northern Wales court, 'Garthmwyl Wledig', who may be the eponymous resident chief of the extant fortress of The Gaer near Garthmyl in Powys – whence Arthur marches to the battle of Badon in the twelfth-century 'Dream of Rhonabwy' – but who is not named in any other Welsh traditions as a holder of the rank of 'Wledig' (ie a regional overlord). The 'chief elder' at Arthur's West Wales court at 'Mynyw', ie St David's, is Maelgwyn, best known as king of Gwynedd in the north – does this mean that he was really Arthur's adviser at this court before he became king (c. 520)? The 'chief elder' at Arthur's court in 'Cerniw' (Cornwall or S.E. Wales?) is 'Caradawg Vreichvras', ie a shadowy prince linked to the royal dynasty of Gwent in the early-mid sixth-century. Two of the bishops at the court are real figures of the early-mid sixth-century – 'Dewi Sant' in the west and Bedwini in Cerniw.

In general, the collection seems to be aware of Arthur as a great warrior and 'protector', but there are no references to the battles in Nennius' list – but several to Camlann. One group of warriors in the *Triads* is the troop of 'incontinent' soldiers led by the Breton prince Alan Fyrgan, cowards who ran away from their post before Camlann. One hero, Iddawc, is a legendary 'embroiler' who distorted Arthur and Medraut's messages to each other to drive them to war, and others are survivors of Camlann.[35] The mass-slaughter at Camlann has an ancient Welsh origin, though the precise number of seven survivors suggests poetic licence due to the magical number concerned. Seven men returned from Bran's legendary battle in Ireland, and seven from Arthur's expedition to Annwfyn. The 'final' version of the battle established by Malory, with only three Arthurian knights surviving a day's fighting, has been suggested as being influenced by the bloodbath at Towton Moor in the 'final' battle between York and Lancaster for the English throne in spring 1461 which Malory may have witnessed. Significantly, there is a strong link to Brittany in the Welsh Arthurian legends, with a number of Arthur's knights (e.g. Riwal) and relatives (Amlawdd) coming from there. This suggests that versions of these legends survived in Brittany to be brought to England after 1066, and could be used by Geoffrey of Monmouth whose story has a strong Breton presence. The name 'Arthur' re-surfaces as a personal name in Brittany in the later ninth-century. There was also the enigmatic 'Artuir ap Bicor' the 'Briton' of unknown origins, who the Irish '*Annals of Clonmamacnoise*' say in the entry for 624 killed Irish king Mongan mac Fiachna – but a 'lament for Mongan' attributed to an Ulster king says that Mongan was killed by the men of Kintyre, ie part of Dalriada in south-west Scotland.

Assorted Arthurian knights – including obscure ones – appear in the *Triads* under earlier versions of their later names, eg Llemenig and Drystan. Welsh Arthurian tradition is also the origin of the mediaeval stories that have the King acting as a knight on his own adventures rather than sitting in state in his castles, as the *Triads* have him as a more famous prisoner than the 'Three Illustrious Prisoners of the Isle of Britain'. He was held captive in the 'prison of Caer Oeth and Anoeth' until rescued, presumably a memory of some poem about his adventures. His captor, the 'Wen Pendragon', has been suggested by Baram Blackett and Alan Wilson as a Saxon warlord (the 'White Dragon' being the Saxon symbol in the legend of Merlin at Dinas Emrys), and the name of the prison meaning the place which is 'concealed and revealed' rather than the more mystic 'past and future'. They believe that Arthur was not actually imprisoned but 'shut up', i.e. besieged in a fortress by the Saxon commander, until rescued by his cousin Goreu ap Custennin. (Genealogically, Custennin is presumably the Constantine who ruled Dumnonia in the fifth-century and/or Ambrosius' father.) The fortress is supposed to be one close to the coast to enable a surprise Saxon attack, with an adjacent cave which a river entered and then left again so it was 'concealed and revealed' – in their view, the coastal fort and cave at Merthyr Mawr, Glamorgan.[36] This seems a little tortuous for a logical military explanation of what may be a reference to a legendary story with Otherworldly overtones that had accrued by the ninth- or tenth-century. Anyway, according to the hagiography of Illtud the Saint was occupying the cave in Merthyr Mawr hill around 500 – which means that there was unlikely to be a contemporary fortress at the same location.[37]

Chapter 7

Interpreting the Early Written Evidence. 'Legend' and Propaganda Not History?

The first written evidence – Gildas and Aneirin

It is unfortunate that the only contemporary writer, Gildas, does not mention Arthur – or give a nickname or pseudonym that can be identified as referring to him. In his '*De Excidio Britanniae*', 'On the Ruin of Britain', his account of fifth-century history proceeds from the 'proud tyrant', i.e. Vortigern, to Ambrosius Aurelianus and so to the battle of Badon, and then to the situation when he wrote (usually assessed as c. 545). There is no reference to any 'national' ruler of the Britons after Ambrosius. At most there is an oblique reference to one of the five kings he condemns, Cynglas the 'tawny butcher' of north-east Wales, as 'charioteer of the Bear's stronghold'[1] (Dinarth in Gwynedd?), a fort presumably occupied at one point by a man called 'the Bear'. This has been latched upon by 'Arthurians' as possible evidence for the 'Bear', ie 'Arthur', as being king Cynglas, son of Owain 'Dantgwyn' ('White-Tooth') of Clywd from the royal house of Gwynedd and cousin of King Maelgwyn who ruled from c. 520 to 547/9. In reply Kenneth Jackson, in 'Gildas and the Names of the British Princes' (*Cambridge Mediaeval Celtic Studies* vol. 3) and Nicholas Higham regard it as a coincidence[2] – and the 'Bear' of Dinarth need not be a man or, if indeed he was a warlord, a recent one for the fifth-century. But did Gildas 'have' to mention Arthur at all in his book? He was writing polemic about current bad rulers not a panegyric for a good one, and his approval for past rulers was clearly centred on Ambrosius (as a symbol of Roman civilization and order?). Some warlords were evidently responsible for the peace and strong government after the Saxon revolt, which had degenerated into misrule by the time that Gildas wrote – though it could have been Ambrosius alone. He complains that contemporary British kings pretend to do justice but harbour thieves at their courts, and that queens are whores and magistrates are corrupt.[3] But by definition there was thus a stable if exploited politico-legal framework for these people to misuse, and the chaos of the mid-fifth-century Saxon revolt indicates that some authority had restored order since then. Ambrosius the 'Roman' could have done it all, and it is more likely that one leader would have had the 'vision' of an ordered society – and the military ability to enforce it – than a nebulous coalition of rulers doing so. Gildas' complaint that the current generation of rulers has not lived through the 'storm' of the Saxon attacks implies that the restoration of a stable administrative system took place under the previous generation, i.e. around 500–20 at the latest.

But such an administrative system does not necessarily mean that the 'creator' (or restorer) of it ruled as a sort of 'Emperor' as John Morris has suggested in his *The Age of Arthur*. The title of 'emperor' is used of Arthur in the probably ninth-century 'Gereint fil(ius) Erbin', where his men are referred to as fighting at the battle of Llongborth under the command of the 'emperor (ameraudur), the ruler of battle', and later in the twelfth-century '*Dream of Rhonabwy*'.[4] But this could easily be meant in its original Latin sense of 'supreme military commander', an appropriate and unusual epithet to use for someone known to later centuries as a military overlord. It need not have political connotations. There had been a stable administrative system of civil and military leadership, and town councils in the 'civitates', in existence when the Roman Imperial authority had lapsed in 410. The rural aristocracy could have maintained leadership in southern Britain at least until the devastating Saxon attacks testified to by the Gallic Chronicle around 442. In the less 'Romanised' areas of north and west Britain, the tribal units and kingship of pre-Roman Britain would seem to have been revived. But the lapse of time since the end of the post-Roman world in the 440s would make it unlikely that the British authorities could reconstitute the administrative order of c.410–440 in the later fifth-century, though a 'national' leader brought up in the Roman tradition – Ambrosius, from Gildas' account – may well have attempted it. Logically, any era of peaceful governance in Britain c.500–40 was likely to have been achieved as a result of military success co-ordinated by one warlord (or by two warlords in succession as believed by 'Nennius').

Gildas' dating

The traditional picture of a strong and vigilant 'emperor' Arthur controlling his subordinates across Britain that we should expect from John Morris' optimistic picture of his power is not that of misrule and injustice in Gildas' book. However, the statement in Gildas (chapter 25) that the kings and churchmen who had witnessed the 'storm' of the great Saxon attack and its miraculous defeat, men who had 'kept to their proper stations', had died and been succeeded by inferior figures[5] would seem to indicate that some decades had passed since the victory at Badon. By this definition, Ambrosius the heroic war-leader has been dead for some time when Gildas writes. There had also been some sort of 'partition' of the island with the Saxons, under which the British could not visit some Christian shrines in the east of Britain[6] – indicating a successful British leader or leaders who could conclude a treaty from a position of strength. The only known Roman Christian shrine in the east of the island was at St Albans, where (coincidentally or not) Geoffrey of Monmouth places a major battle between British and Saxons in Arthur's youth. Gildas' targets, the current wrongdoers in office, had only lived through 'calm' not the previous 'storm' and accordingly relaxed their morals – which argues that he was more likely to be writing in the late 530s or 540s than earlier.

Gildas is not renowned for his accuracy about fifth-century history, on which he is confused regarding the nature of Roman rule and their leaving Britain. He has little idea about the true course of events during the Roman occupation, ascribing the building of Hadrian's Wall to Magnus Maximus in the fourth-century, and none regarding the supposed 'Wall of Septimius Severus', from which it is evident that he did not use a currently extant written source for events before his own lifetime. He would have been able to speak about events of his own lifetime more accurately, but has a habit of substituting generalisation for facts or names – indeed the polemical nature of his work would make this logical. Apart from Ambrosius, he rarely calls people by their real names but by puns – e.g. 'superbus tyrannus' for Vortigern, the 'over-king' of the mid-fifth-century, or 'Caninus' ('the dog') for Aurelius Cynan/Conan, one of his foes who probably ruled in the 540s. On this basis, it is not at all damning that he does not refer to Arthur who was not relevant to his argument – unless the 'Bear' who Cynglas *may* have served as a charioteer was meant to be him. Recent archaeological 'fieldwork' in British agriculture of the fifth-century and sixth-century also suggests damningly that Gildas' picture of chaos, devastation, and the abandonment of homes and land by Britons fleeing hordes of ravaging Saxons in the mid-fifth-century is seriously exaggerated. The work of Petra Dark should be mentioned here,[7] plus the current argument that a change of the nature of 'valued objects' buried with the dead in fifth-century graves in lowland Britain may reflect a change of trade or fashion not of the ethnic origin of the people using them. There is simply no evidence that farms were abandoned across the country after invasion and returned to scrub and forest until the Saxons cleared them again, as a reading of Gildas would suggest. Indeed in some areas the occupation of 'Romano-British' farmsteads merges seamlessly into 'Anglo-Saxon' habitation on the same sites with no new buildings either, as at Mucking in Essex – and the wooden buildings put up post-400 could be either 'British' or 'Saxon', with modern writers such as Francis Pryor doubting if there was any cultural let alone ethnic 'break'. So where does that leave myths of Arthurian-era warfare? Or was 'Germanic settlement' (or a change in culture brought by a smaller number of incomers) in East Anglia unusually stable compared to wherever 'Arthur' fought and Gildas wrote? The basic facts of Gildas' portrayal of two waves of Saxon attack – one immediately after the end of Roman authority in 410, one a generation later – are independently verified by the contemporary *Gallic Chronicle*, which dates them to 410/11 and 441/2.[8] The latter source however is unreliable for precise dates by the 440s, and we can only say that the writer linked the Saxon attack to the Vandal conquest of Carthage in 439 as it appears in the same paragraph and so was presumably within a few years of that event.

Gildas' obscure prose also makes it difficult to place his dating of the 'Arthurian' campaigns with certainty. He states that the battle of Badon, their finale, occurred forty-four years after an event he has mentioned. But the poor Latin makes it unclear what he means when he says that 'this begins the forty-fourth year' and then refers to him knowing it as it is the date of his birth.[9] Bede took it as meaning that Badon was forty-four years after the Saxon landing, i.e. 44 years from Hengest's arrival in 449[10] (which makes Badon occur in 493, far earlier than in the *Annales*

Cambriae). Alternatively Gildas means 44 years after the commencement of Ambrosius' campaigns against the Saxons. This would have occurred some time after Ambrosius had deposed Vortigern, which is usually placed in the 450s. If he means that he was born in the year of Badon 493 would make more sense than 516/18 as a birthdate for a man who was at St Illtud's school with Maelgwyn, an adult ruler in the 520s, around 500 (according to whatever evidence lay behind the 'Life' of Illtud, c. 1120). The critics of the historicity of Gildas' hagiography prefer to believe that Gildas' presence at lltud's school was invented in order to annex it for his prestige as a famous scholar, or vice versa.

Rodney Castleden has argued that the battle might be forty-four years from the landing of Aelle, the first 'Bretwalda' (ie Anglo-Saxon regional warlord), at Selsey in Sussex in 477 – i.e. 520/1, closer to the Welsh annalistic date for Badon.[11] In that case again, Gildas would have been the right age to be a contemporary of Maelgwyn as a pupil at Illtud's school and was more likely to be born in the year of the start of the war than the year of Badon. But need the (later ninth-century dating) of the landing of Aelle in southern Britain to set up the kingdom of Sussex mean the opening of the 'British vs Saxons' war that led to Badon, or was this event really only an obscure and insignificant local one?

Gildas is traditionally supposed to have been active enough to travel to Ireland in c. 565, having been summoned there to deal with church indiscipline by 'High King' Ainmere, and to have died around 570 (572 according to the *Annales Cambriae*).[12] This might argue against the alternative explanation of the '44 years' reference – that Badon occurred when he was aged forty-four and that the famous year of his birth was not Badon but that of the start of Ambrosius' campaign. If he was alive to 571/2 it is unlikely that he was born 44 years before a battle dated around 516, i.e around 472. But the *Annales* seem to be fairly accurate about other dates in their sparse records for the fifth- and sixth-century, although our extant version of them is tenth-century, and their compilers at the court of Dyfed presumably used what local written records were available (?at the monastery of St Davids?). Their Badon date of 516/18 would seem to be probably accurate within a few years – remembering that it may only be a date within an 'Easter cycle' that commenced in 516/18 not that actual year. It is now argued that the way in which the Welsh – and early Saxon – chronicles were written was based on dividing time by a period of years, a new 'Easter cycle' commencing when the festival occurred on a certain date. Thus the events of each 'cycle' were noted down under the date on which the period commenced; Badon may just have been in the 'cycle' commencing in 516/18.

Gildas does *not* say that Ambrosius was the commander at Badon, though this has been inferred by modern writers such as Oliver Padel; he only states that Ambrosius started the British campaign which ended at Badon.[13] It is always possible that the problem of the dating may have been exacerbated by inaccurate copying of the original text by a Dark Ages writer, probably a monk at a monastery such as his own probable foundation at Rhuys in Brittany. The existing text preserved in the British Library is dated from c.1100, and even so has suffered damage from the fire at its earlier home at Sir Robert Cotton's library in Westminster in 1731.

Gildas' location: close enough to the events he describes to have accurate information?

Gildas' 1120s(?) hagiographer Caradoc of Llancarfan (Glamorgan) presents him as the brother of the disruptive northern warlord Huil, son of Caw, who Arthur executed at Ruthin after he raided North Wales. The stone marking the alleged site of execution still exists, but unfortunately Ruthin was only founded in the 1280s though the stone could have been brought there from elsewhere as a treasured local relic. Nor does the story linking the episode to Ruthin appear in Welsh literature until the works of Ellis Gruffydd in the 1510s (i.e. post-Malory), so its origin is shaky. Caw was said in Gildas' eleventh-century Breton *Life* to be a ruler around Are Cluta (Dumbarton), the father of a family of saints, and was called 'Caw of the Wall' in the Welsh elegy *Mawrnad Uthyr Pendragon.* Presumably Hadrian's Wall is meant. According to the hagiography of St Cadoc the latter was returning to South Wales from founding a monastery in Scotland when he was visited by Caw's ghost on the hills of 'Bannauc' and asked to give him a Christian burial to save him from returning to Hell, where he had been sent for his piracy. This 'Caw of Prydain' had been located in the 'Clywd' valley – but name-specialists Steve Blake and Scott Lloyd suggest that this was the river Clywd, in eastern Gwynedd, not the Scottish Clyde. This Caw may or may not be the 'Lord of Cwm Cowlwyd' ruling in Edeirnion (Northern Powys) in the *Llanstephan Manuscripts* and similarly in the 1530s *Chronicle* of Ellis Gruffydd – presumably the Caw recorded in local tradition by William Camden in the sixteenth-century as building Caer Gai near Lake Bala.[14] Perhaps this Caw was not the father of Huil, who is shown in legend as a raider attacking Wales' coasts from overseas – and on geographical grounds the Caw from Powys is a more likely father for a Saint active in southern Britain and Brittany than one from remote Galloway (though the latter area did have a notable monastery, at Whithorn, to educate a future saint). In '*Culhwch and Olwen*' both Caw and (temporarily) Huil have served in Arthur's warband. A stone found at Llanfor near Caer Gai refers to 'Cavo' (Caw) son of Seniargius.[15]

Assuming that one of these attributions was not a case of mistaken identity by later writers, a 'Caw' may have ruled in North-Central Wales and Huil could have been son of someone with a similar name, later mistakenly identified as the same man. But identifying him with Gildas' father is relying on what may be just coincidence. The sceptics would prefer to argue that the attribution of Gildas the author to Gildas the son of any 'Caw' is guesswork by later writers, confusing two men with the same name, or even outright mythology. The differences between the two 'Lives' of Gildas, one Welsh and one Breton, have been such as to imply that they were dealing with two different men. The Breton one had him founding a monastery and dying at Ruys in Brittany; the Welsh one had him as abbot of and dying at Glastonbury. There was also a difference of opinion over whether he was educated in Gaul or Ireland.[16]

There is however also evidence of Gildas' family in a Glamorgan inscription. Gildas was the grandfather of a contemporary of St Cadoc (St Fili, founder of 'Caerphilly') who was granted land at Ogmore by a South Wales king called 'Arthmail', possibly 'Arthur' himself. (Cadoc, as will be seen, was regarded by his eleventh-century biographer as the son of a man helped by Arthur, a local ruler of unspecified territory in South Wales.) 'Arthmail' is not 'Arthur' – but is the latter a 'bear' nickname for a man with a similar 'given' name? Cadoc's dates are fixed by his biographies at c.500–70, so the date of this grant is definitively early-mid sixth-century. Thus the 'Ogmore Stone' (see below) would suggest strongly that Gildas was a contemporary of or older than Arthur. Gildas' hagiography makes him a pupil of St Illtud at Llanilltud Fawr (Llantwit) around 500 as a contemporary of Maelgwyn of Gwynedd, making it likely that he was born before 485/90. (Some writers believe the Ogmore Stone's script is later – but this does not invalidate it from being an accurate copy of an earlier inscription.) There has been speculation that it was Arthur's execution of Gildas' brother Huil (the two are at feud in '*Culhwch and Olwen*') that caused Gildas to seek to avoid having to praise him in the account of Badon and its results of peace and prosperity, though this explanation only appears in late mediaeval writings and the omission may have been simply due to the fact that Arthur was not the subject of Gildas' attack on bad rulers so he had no reason to refer to him. And if Huil was not Gildas' brother after all, this theory is invalid. (A mediaeval Welsh story that survived into the Brut traditions has Gildas destroying all his favourable works about Arthur in revenge for Arthur killing his brother Huil, but it is uncertain how reliable this story is. Caradoc's '*Life*' assures the readers that Gildas forgave Arthur for killing Huil.)[17] The fact that Gildas' extant hagiographies are eleventh/twelfth-century has led some commentators to question their reliability, but there is no reason why accurate facts about his parentage and education could not have been remembered in local monastic records and used by his biographers, Caradoc of Llancarfan and a Breton monk – though two 'Caws' could have been mixed up. Given their locations, Caradoc would logically have used records at Gildas' contemporary Cadoc's nearby monastery or at St Dyfrig's see of Llandaff and the Breton author used extant records at Rhuys where Gildas died.

Gildas' purpose in writing his polemic was clear – to denounce the 'degeneracy' of contemporary Britain c.540 and blame the Anglo-Saxon conquest on its moral failures. His tone has usually led to him being portrayed as a monk, though this may be a later assumption. He was very sparing with his praise, usually reserving it for 'Romans' like Ambrosius (who represented the traditional order of the departed Christian Empire) not 'illegitimate' modern rulers. His model would appear to have been the attacks on equally 'degenerate' Judah c.600 BC, ahead of its conquest by the Babylonians, by Jeremiah in the Old Testament – a literary model which he would have known intimately as a monk. According to his interpretation the British deserved the same sort of 'Babylonian Captivity' which befell the kingdom of Judah in 586 BC, as Divine vengeance for their wickedness, and it has been argued that his polemic was regarded as valuable learned justification for the Anglo-Saxon conquests by the latter's historian Bede. When British military fortunes revived in early ninth-century Gwynedd, the patriotic writer 'Nennius' had to concoct a suitable riposte to embolden his countrymen and show that, contrary to what Gildas said, God was on their side – and he duly chose Arthur as his subject.

The 'Gododdin' evidence: a question of dating?

The paucity of written evidence is a problem, but it is evident that Arthur was a name to be conjured with as a great warrior by the time that the *Gododdin* was composed. In this 'Trojan War'-style epic of heroic failure by a British attack from the kingdom of the Votadini (ie Lothian) on the Anglian kingdom of Bernicia c.600, the catalogue of its heroes referred to a warrior who 'glutted the black ravens but was not Arthur'.[18] As this is the first dateable reference close to Arthur's time and a North British one at that, it has been played up as evidence that the 'original' was a major figure in the region's 'folk-memory' by c. 600 – and therefore presumably local. The poem survived in two different versions in the *Llyfr Aneirin*, dated around 1250, now in Cardiff Public Library. It was composed to commemorate the failed campaign of a force of British heroes (traditionally 300 of them) from disparate kingdoms who were recruited by Mynyddog 'the Golden', lord of Din Eidyn, to attack Bernicia. The warriors fought an unsuccessful action at 'Catraeth', where all but a few (supposedly one or three) were killed. Most scholars would accept Ifor Williams' identification of the site in 1938 as Catterick in north Yorkshire, the Roman fort of 'Cataractonium',[19] where a cavalry force of Britons moving south on Roman roads would have been able to strike at an important strategic junction protecting the trans-Pennine route into Rheged. (John Gwenogfyn Evans in the 1900s suggested Anglesey as an alternative venue, but this seems too far west for a battle with Bernicia c.600. In 1869 John Stuart Glennie suggested 'Calathros'/'Galtraeth' near Linlithgow, far closer to Din Eidyn i.e. Edinburgh.)[20]

The problem lies with the dating of the two different texts, of which version 'B' contains the reference to Arthur (verse 38). Analysis of the text containing this reference on linguistic grounds indicates that it is probably from c.600 rather than being that part of the epic which was composed in its extant form in the eighth- or ninth-century, and thus is not an interpolation. (See the edition edited by Ifor Williams, published in Cardiff in 1938, and Kenneth Jackson's article in *Antiquity*, March 1939.)[21] This has been backed up recently in C. Cessford's analysis in 'Northern History' in 1997, and J.T. Koch has argued persuasively that an 'original' and parts of the extant text can be dated to the seventh-century.[22] Unfortunately none of the stanzas whose language Koch identified as definitely seventh-century include the one where Arthur appears – though this is not to say that the extant version of the latter was not 'modernised' later from a seventh-century original. Oliver Padel argues that the context of the reference – Arthur as a mass-killer appropriate to a warrior who glutted the ravens with his victims – suggests that the poet had read the 'Historia Brittonum' reference to Mount Badon so must be post-829. Thomas Green argues that the notion of Arthur as an unsurpassable warrior in this stanza implies that the poet knew he could not be outmatched because he was superhuman, not a genuine commander.[23] This first reference to a renowned warrior 'Arthur' is not proof that he was an earlier warlord of the Northern kingdom of the Votadini/Gododdin, as some interpreters have claimed including Alistair Moffat in *Arthur and the Lost Kingdoms* (1999).[24] More certainly, Arthur was clearly celebrated by them and their bards as a standard for heroism – meaning that if he was not a leader of the Votadini his exploits were great enough to be commemorated across several kingdoms. This argues against him being some sort of obscure minor Welsh or Cornish chieftain who only fought small local battles – such a man would hardly have achieved the 'reclame' over centuries that Arthur did. If he was a Dumnonian warlord from Tintagel who fought in southern Britain, why did his reputation matter to the warriors of the Gododdin in Lothian? But if he had mainly fought the Picts and Irish in the Firth of Forth area and the Borders, where there was no Saxon settlement in the fifth-century, why did his name become attached to Saxon wars?

Whoever Arthur was, he was notable enough for his name to attract stories in a way that men as great in power as Maelgwyn or Urien did not. These great rulers of major kingdoms have definite links to long-lasting dynasties, unlike Arthur, and both led coalitions of kings. Maelgwyn's kingdom, Gwynedd, was the leader of the Welsh principalities in the twelfth- and thirteenth-century when the majority of Arthurian stories were being written; he was remembered as 'Pendragon' and thus a forerunner of current Gwynedd rulers like Owain Gwynedd and Llywelyn 'Fawr'. So why did the Welsh legends centre on a dynastically obscure war-leader instead? It is certainly arguable that 'Arthur' was chosen precisely because he had a better reputation than Maelgwyn, who was one of Gildas' villainous kings and was cast in an equally bad light in the legend of Taliesin. A patron of pagan bards and Druids, he was not even a suitable Christian hero – though Urien of Rheged was and he was eclipsed in later memory by Arthur. Arthur's god-like name may have helped to attract stories originally belonging to mythical figures. But the adherants of the theory that he was an entirely mythical figure like 'Fionn mac Cumhail', alleged commander of the third-century Irish 'High Kings' warband the 'Fianna', argue that he attracted such stories because he was already known as a mythical figure who had Otherworldly adventures and could not be 'tied down' to one Welsh kingdom. Alternative explanation for why he was an 'outsider' to Welsh dynastic politics are that he was an illegitimate son of a king, son of a minor noble (Uthyr?), and/or from one of the kingdoms obliterated in central England or Cornwall by the Anglo-Saxons in the later sixth-century.

Arthur as a god of early Welsh legend?

The similarity of his name to that of the sky-god Artaius (originally from Gaul) has enabled sceptics such as Oliver Padel to argue that the latter provided much of the attributions and the place-names that became attached to 'Arthur'. It is not clear how important Artaius was to the Welsh between the sixth-century and the ninth-century when the legends were presumably forming, ahead of the 'Nennius' collection written around 829. Why should one minor god – not even the principal god of the pre-Christian pantheon – become so popular among the ordinary populace that so many place-names linked to him survived and he was written into Dark Ages literature? Those other gods who did become part of literature – Bran, made a pre-Roman king of Britain, and the elusive Pwyll of Dyfed – did not have this impact. Nor did they become connected to a mass of place-names and put into the historical record of post-Roman Britain; Arthur alone appears in place-names from Cornwall to Scotland. Bran was a prototype 'King of Britain' who fought the national enemies – in his case, the Irish – and became involved with Otherworldly treasures (a cauldron), but he was carefully kept in the pre-Roman era. One clue may lie in the early Welsh 'Englynion y Beddau', the 'Stanzas of the Graves', apparently composed around the seventh-century and listing unusual geographical features across Wales that were identified as the burial-sites of – usually mythical – heroes. Sites were identified for Arthur's warriors, such as Bedwyr, but: 'Anoeth bit bed y Arthur' – 'the world's wonder, a grave for Arthur'.[25] So even at this early date Arthur's place of burial was unknown, with the implication that he was immortal. Was it this which set him apart and led to him being taken up as an immortal hero? But the lack of a known burial-site need not imply that he had never been a historical figure, as the fact could be due to the unusual circumstances of his departure from military events. It could have been due to a deliberate act by his supporters, to cause hope of his return once he had recovered from his wounds at 'Camlann'.

Arthur with a ninth-century – tenth-century Welsh political purpose

It has been suggested by later twentieth-century Welsh literary scholars that the growth of 'Arthuriana' from the ninth-century reflects more on the contemporary situation in Britain than on the real sixth-century, and that the idea of a powerful 'over-king' was attractive to storytellers at the time of the real-life 'super-national' Saxon rulers Athelstan and Edgar or the reviving Welsh kingship of Hywel 'Dda'. Athelstan, king of England in 924/5–39 and the first ruler to claim overlordship of both Wales and Scotland, required his junior colleagues to come to his court in England and witness charters as his vassals – was this the inspiration for the collection of vassals around 'Arthur' seen later in Geoffrey of Monmouth's work? A Breton connection from Athelstan's time for the lost 'original' of Geoffrey's source has been suggested in a 2016 article for 'Arthuriana' by the American scholar Edwin Pace, the then count Alan of Brittany having been brought up in exile at Athelstan's court. Athelstan's wars against the Viking kingdom of York in Northumbria could have inspired tenth-century tales of Arthur fighting in the area on behalf of a south-based kingdom which anticipated Athelstan's kingdom of Wessex – and Athelstan laid claim to be a ruler of all Britain like Arthur. The Norse were Athelstan's foes and he conquered their Northumbrian realm (927), then making the Scots his vassals (934); hence the story of Geoffrey of Monmouth of Arthur conquering Scotland and Norway? Edgar had a special coronation in Bath – the possible site of the battle of 'Mount Badon' – as king of all Britain in 973, with his Welsh and Scots fellow-rulers as his vassals; hence Geoffrey's account of Arthur's coronation as king of all Britain? Possibly the 'anti-English' coalitions of Welsh, Scots, and Vikings created to combat the new Kingdom of England created by Edward 'the Elder' and Athelstan in 911–27 used Arthur as a literary inspiration, although the main Welsh 'unifier' of the era, king Hywll 'the Good' (of Dyfed 904–50 and Gwynedd/Powys 942–50) stayed out of this attempt to revive 'Celtic' power. Arthur could thus be used to encourage the mixed army of anti-English warriors who fought Athelstan unsuccessfully at Brunanburh in 937 and then backed Olaf Guthfrithson's attack on 'England' after Athelstan died in 939. This is certainly the context for the militantly anti-Saxon prophecies of the 'Armes Prydein' around 930–40, which look back to when the Welsh ruled all England and hope for their restoration to power – but Arthur does not appear in this collection, whose hero is the seventh-century ruler Cadwaladr. Arthur was thus not the automatic inspiration for every work of anti-Saxon polemic of the early-mid tenth-century.

Supposedly the Welsh writers of the tenth-century could have responded to their Saxon foes' new 'imperial' realm across Britain by constructing an imaginary 'empire' for Arthur in the sixth-century, to console themselves that they had priority in the claim to have founded a kingdom of all Britain. The court of the reviving kingdom of Gwynedd in the 820s had reason to promote a successful pan-British warlord who had united the land and defeated the Saxons, as had the court of Hywel 'Dda' in the mid-tenth-century (though in the latter's case without military aggression). Gwynedd/Powys and Deheubarth had one sovereign in 942–50, 986–99, 1018–23, and 1055–63, making a leader of their British ancestors in the sixth-century seem a relevant figure. This was especially so with king Gruffydd ap Llewelyn ap Seissyll, who united Gwynedd/Powys and Dyfed in 1055 and then attacked the Anglo-Saxons successfully in Herefordshire, regaining control of the lands west of the Wye. But why in this case did the legends crystallize around Arthur rather than Urien or Maelgwyn – or the heroic Cadwallon, crusher of Northumbrian power in 633? Urien and Cadwallon, unlike Maelgwyn, were both known for their battles against the Saxons and were thus suitable heroes for the men of Gwynedd in the 820s and for Hywel's Dyfed.

When did the name 'Arthur' come into fashion?

In the early to mid-sixth-century (if the genealogies of the 'Men of the North' descendants of Coel 'Hen' are accurate) there was an Arthwyr who ruled in the Pennines, probably father of Pabo 'Pillar of Britain', and another Arthwys ap Mar. Both were placed in the extant tenth-century genealogies as several generations after their dynastic progenitor Coel 'Hen'. In the late sixth century a number of rulers with this name appeared, e.g. Arthwys ap Pedr of Dyfed (great-grandson of Gildas' contemporary Vortipor) and prince Artuir of Dal Riada in Argyll, son of the great 560s-80s warlord Aedan mac Gabhran.[26] The latter was not even a Briton but from a Gaelic dynasty of Ulster origin, suggesting that Arthur's fame had spread far and that his was an aspirational name for a great king to give his son. Presumably warriors had been telling tales of Arthur's wars round their campfires or bards had sung of him at the king's court, and the name was thus taken up although this ethnically and politically Irish dynasty did not use any other mainland British warrior-names. Then use of the name in princely dynasties dies out, except for an obscure nobleman, Arthur son of the presumed expatriate Briton Bicor, who was in trouble for murdering king Mongan in 624 (though as mentioned an Ulster story makes the killers Scots from Kintyre), and late seventh-century or early eighth-century kings 'Arthfael' in Morgannwg and Arthoddfw in Ceredigion – suggesting that Arthur's immediate fame had faded. So it would be logical to assume that any 'original' who inspired widely-separated rulers across Britain to name their sons after him lived before c. 550 – ruling out the theory that the 'original' was one of the minor princes of the later sixth-century, either the Dyfed ruler or the prince of Dal Riada.

The princes of the Pennines remain candidates, especially Arthwys son of Mar, but in that case it would need to be explained how by the eleventh- or twelfth-century this 'King Arthur' was relocated into Wales by bards. It is not sufficient to argue that the collapse of the British kingdoms of the Pennines caused the extinction of local Celtic tradition and the escapees to Wales to take their stories of Arthur with them.

Rheged collapsed and became part of Northumbria by the 640s, but no bards relocated the battles of Urien or his son Owain to Wales.

The Cambrian Annals, poetry, and hagiography

The problem of the 'Cambrian Annals'

The *Cambrian Annals* were compiled in their extant form in the reign of Hywel 'the Good' ('Dda') in the early tenth century. That king was the first to unite the combined realms of Gwynedd/Powys (in a dynastic union since the 850s) in north/central Wales and Dyfed/Seissylwg in the south-west, being the son of a cadet of the line of Gwynedd who had acquired the latter which he duly inherited in 905. He took over the North too after his cousin's death in battle against the English in 942, and proved a master of the art of 'spin', having a series of genealogies complied to show his rights to inherit each of his realms by descent. The *Annals* may also have been part of a 'nation-building' exercise, rallying the kingdoms' elites around his dynasty; if he did not commission them (he died in 950) his son and successor Owain did. The controversy over their precise date still rages, with current thinking centred on around 954 or 977 as the date of the finalised entries. They were compiled at the monastery of St David's, the bishopric of Dyfed – a site presumably established by 'Dewi Sant' himself in the mid-late sixth-century. But it should not be thought that the annals had been carefully compiled there ever since; analysis has shown that the continuous 'St David's' section of coverage only commenced in 798. Another crucial question is – how much of the detail is a mid-tenth-century scholarly copying of 'original' material from previous centuries, including the sixth- and seventh-century? According to the most exhaustive modern analysis, by Kathleen Hughes, they consist of material from three basic sources – an early Irish religious source, covering the period to 612 and based on the Spanish annals of Isidore of Seville; a northern British source, explaining the large amount of material on local events for the period c.600–750; and a set of local Dyfed annals for the period after c.750, presumably written at St David's in Pembrokeshire where the *Annales* were composed.[27] In that case, the sixth-century material is only a record of what the eighth-century Irish believed had occurred in that era, unless the latter used authentic records written at Irish monasteries pre-600. It is noticeable that these 'Welsh' annals only have seven British entries for the period to 600, and only twenty-three entries for the period 444 – 600; the dating of St Patrick's death (457) clearly comes from one particular Irish source. Most of the entries are of religious obits, not secular ones, showing that they were composed by churchmen, and the term used for the deaths of secular and religious personnel is different; the only two Welsh rulers noted for the early-mid sixth-century are Arthur and Maelgwyn. The use of exactly the same Latin words to describe Arthur's success at Mount Badon as in the '*Historia Brittonum*' of Nennius, c.829, has been suggested by J.T. Koch (1996) as evidence that the annalist copied this reference out from 'Nennius' and was not using an independent source.[28] Granted that Nennius was writing 'propaganda' with a political purpose for ninth-century Gwynedd not scholarly history as we would understand the term (see below), that poses problems for any '*Annales*' material deriving from his work. Nor is there any reference to the campaigns of Ambrosius, despite their crucial value to British survival in the mid-fifth-century – either the annalist had no fifth-century British source or he was not interested in them.Thus, we are not dealing with a reliable, 'undiluted' list of early events in Welsh history.

Given these problems, we still have to make what we can of the '*Annales*'. They refer to Arthur winning his greatest victory at Mount Badon in 'year 72', 516 or 518: 'bellum badonis in quo arthur portavit crucem domini nostri Jesu Christi tribus diebus et tribus noctibus in humeros suos et brittones victores fuerunt'.[29] Twenty-one years later he was killed at the 'strife of Camlann' with Medraut in 537/9: 'gueith camlann in qua Arthur et medraut corruerunt'.[30]

However, the dates cannot be taken as exact as they were compiled in a 'cycle' based on religious tables of Easter dates, each set a specified number of years after its predecessor. Therefore Badon or Camlann could more accurately be said to have occurred in the 'cycle' of years that ended in 518 and 539 rather than definitively in those actual years. Accordingly, it is not even certain that there were exactly 21 years between Badon and Camlann. Sceptics argue that the fact that these two battles were the only military records in the early/mid-sixth-century section of the *Annales* indicate that they were added at a subsequent date to the text by 'Arthurian' promoters, but this is unproven. Analysis of the wording of the entries gives no indication that they differed from, i.e. were added later than, the rest of the text. But much has been made recently of the reference in the Camlann entry to plague following the battle in Britain and Ireland; it has been explained as a monastic annalist seeking to show that the plague was Divine punishment for the sin of civil war. Or did the dating of Camlann arise from the annalist locating the 539 plague in an Irish 'annal' and guessing that this must have been the plague which followed Camlann?

The reference to the Cross presumably originates from some poetic saga of the battle – it is significant that the Cross was an object of religious devotion at the court of Hywel Dda, patron of the *Annales*, as seen from the Cross-linked nomenclature given to places around the pilgrimage-site at Nevern in Hywel's Dyfed. This may have been invented by the tenth-century rather than remembering a genuine event, but does not mean that its implausibility for a sixth-century warrior-king's priorities means that the battle did not take place and was invented too. In fact, there was a notable rise in devotion to holy cults – e.g of the Virgin Mary – in the fifth-century Roman world, as seen by the controversy at the Council of Ephesus in 431 over the 'insult' to the Virgin as 'Theotokos', 'Mother of God' posed by the theology of Nestorius. (Geoffrey has Arthur putting an image of the Virgin on his shield.)[31] The extension of this devotion to the far west of the former Roman lands by the time of 'Arthur', and thus his participation in acts of devotion before battle, are quite plausible.

Ninth-century to twelfth-century Welsh poetry: how early, how reliable, and with a contemporary political undertone?

The early Welsh poems compiled a few centuries after Arthur – the Welsh *Triads*, the *Song of the Graves* (the origin of the claim that his grave was unknown or at any rate 'the world's wonder'), and the legends preserved in the *Red Book of Hergest* and *White Book of Rhydderch*, together with the eleventh-century Lives of sixth-century Saints – depict him as ruling in Wales in the earlier sixth century, but do not specify his dynasty with reference to contemporary rulers. The earliest extant copies of the Welsh manuscripts are thirteenth-century and the Hergest collection is early fourteenth-century, i.e. after the literary inventions of Geoffrey of Monmouth. But this is not 'proof' that the Welsh took up Geoffrey's stories after c.1135 and had no earlier local versions; the extant texts of the Welsh legends are probably accurate (or slightly embellished?) copies of earlier texts, as they show little sign of incorporating mediaeval elements. There is a 'kingdom of England' with its capital in London in the 'Mabinogi' tale of Manawydan son of Llyr so that must have been 'finalised' after London took over as capital from Winchester under the Normans, but there is more significantly little sign of Christianity. The kingly courts, e.g. in *Culhwch and Olwen*, show more similarity to the brutal, boastful, and pagan world of Iron Age Irish myths than to mediaeval courts.There is no evidence of cross-cultural fertilization in the Arthurian 'Mabinogi' stories from the post-1066 Anglo-Norman culture, including that of Breton immigrants; the most comprehensive assessment of its dating from its wording, by Thomas Charles-Edwards in 1970, is some time in the eleventh-century (i.e. pre-Geoffrey of Monmouth).[32] The importance of roving heroes with extravagant claims to super-human powers is reminiscent of the sagas of Fionn and Cu Chulainn in Irish mythology – and, as we have seen, some of the Irish semi-divine figures reappeared in the stories of Arthur. It has been suggested in Rachel Bromwich and D.S. Evans' 1992 edition of '*Culhwch and Olwen*' that Gwyn ap Nudd, the mysterious 'lord of Annwfyn' (the Otherworld) who is treated as one of Arthur's leading followers in the poem, is another 'alias' of Fionn mac Cumhaill himself, the supposed 'humanised god/hero' Irish equivalent of Arthur, both names meaning 'Sacred' or 'Otherworldly' as well as 'White'.[33] Certainly, conflict with giants and witches and superhuman feats are the 'norm', not tales of fighting Saxons (though this may reflect the fact that by the ninth- and tenth-century the Welsh poets and their audience did little of the latter so were usually not interested in it). Arthur's court, the chief court of Britain, is not located in one recognisable Welsh kingdom, but seems to 'hover above' the action with its heroes moving around Wales as and where they are needed. The dates of the extant stories are unclear, but modern research would put some in the ninth-century and there are hints of these sagas in the earlier 'Gododdin'. Even if some details may have been 'modernised' in the last decades before the form of the evidence was 'frozen' by its extant written copies, the alterations were probably minor – so we are looking at stories probably constructed in the seventh- and eighth-century.

The Welsh literary sources that we possess can thus be taken as reflecting the contemporary beliefs of the ninth-century to the twelfth-century, with every likelihood that the courtly bards that had earlier told the tales could transmit genealogical and political facts accurately by oral means for several centuries. To take two examples from Irish oral legend, the legendary histories put the chief fortress of Ulster at Navan/ Emain Macha (confirmed by archaeology) and the racial origins of the last wave of Irish invaders as from Spain (confirmed recently by DNA comparison). Modern writers should not be too dismissive of the accuracy of later written sources which have used earlier oral memories. Nor can the 'reinterpretation' and reimagining of a 'heroic' past in contemporary terminology automatically be regarded as discounting a core of fact. The Greek heroic epics of the Trojan War by 'Homer' (whoever he was, and whatever his date) were long held to have no factual basis. They were composed around 800/750 BC at the earliest, and possibly as late as the seventh-century, and used post-Mycenaean terminology – yet Troy was discovered and names of rulers like the legendary commanders' were found in Hittite records. As far as Britain goes, there is now a similar scholarly scepticism about the alleged details of the campaigns of Urien of Rheged (fl. 560–89) presented in the poems of 'Taliesin' and the campaigns of Cyndylan of Powys (fl. 650s) presented in the poems attributed to Llywarch 'Hen'. Their linguistic terminology may indeed be ninth- or tenth-century, not contemporary – yet this does not mean that the later writers invented all their details. It is more usual for heroic poetry to use genuine names and dates, however distorted by contemporary needs – as do modern 'historical' films. The same can apply to Arthur.

According to the *Triads*, Arthur had 'three tribal thrones' across the lands of the Britons (*Triad* no.1, in Peniarth Mss. 16). These were Mynyw (Menevia, St David's), Celliwig (or Gellywig) in 'Cerniw', and Penryn Rhionydd in the North. There is no indication of how his overlordship related to the kingdoms in question or their kings – Maelgwyn of Gwynedd and Vortipor of Dyfed. Maelgwyn is made a 'chief elder' of Arthur's court, but of the one in St David's not in his own kingdom. The *Triads* are of uncertain date, and so might reflect the political situation of the twelfth- or thirteenth-century when a 'united' Wales was seen as a desirable option (then being led by Gwynedd under Llywelyn 'Fawr' and his grandson Llywelyn 'the Last') and so could be 'projected' back in time to give it a respectable antiquity. The originals of the *Triads* were probably lists memorised by bards to make remembering details easier, and were earlier in origin than the longer Welsh tales in the 'Mabinogi' collection. They refer to Arthur's generosity, with him being more generous than any of the three leading exponents of the virtue, and to his courtiers: the 'Three Peers of Arthur's Court' are Rhahawd, Dalldaf, and Drystan (i.e. the original of 'Tristan', whose name here sounds more like the 'Drustanus' of the memorial-stone at Castle Dore in Cornwall). They make reference to his conflict with Medraut (without saying if this is Medraut ap Llew, his nephew, or Medraut ap Cawdraf) – the 'Three Unrestrained Ravagings of Britain' include that of Medraut attacking Arthur's court at Gellywig and Arthur attacking Medraut in reply. The 'Three Harmful Blows of Britain' include Medraut's wife Gwenhwyfach striking her sister Gwenhwyfar, the cause of the battle of Camlann; this is presumably a reference to the original Welsh poetic saga of the causes of the war between Arthur and Medraut and the battle of Camlann. In the original Welsh version, it appears that the quarrel between the sisters commenced with them squabbling while collecting nuts, a prosaic origin for what by the twelfth-century was seen as the great disaster for British unity – and no reference to Gwenhwyar's sister survived into Geoffrey of Monmouth's version.

The 'Three Unfortunate Counsels of Britain' include Arthur dividing his host into three at Camlann (presumably a flawed tactic that aided the disastrous outcome, as remembered in some now lost poem). The amount of detail on Camlann suggests that by the tenth-century or eleventh-century it was a well-known subject of bardic tales. The 'Three Knights of Battle' at Arthur's court are Cador, Earl of Cornwall, 'Lanclod' (i.e. Lancelot, which suggests that this particular *Triad* post-dates Chretien de Troyes), and Yvain/Owain son of Urien, in reality a figure of the 580s; the 'Three Golden-Tongued Knights' include Gwalchmai son of Llew and Elinwlod son of Madog son of Uther. The 'Three Royal Knights' include Medraut son of Llew and Hywel son of Emyr Llydaw. The 'Three Unrestricted Guests of Arthur's Court' are Llywarch 'Hen' the poet, the warrior Llemenig (one of the 'originals' of Lancelot), and princess Heledd of Powys – which suggests a link with Powys, where the first and third lived in the early-mid seventh-century, but confusion about dates.[34] In the *Yr Afallenau Myrddin* of uncertain date, attributed to the poet-prophet Myrddin who lived in the 570s, there is a mention of Arthur fighting Medraut at Camlann and only seven survivors – and a reference to the 'crimes' of Arthur's wife Gwenhwyfar, presumably connected to responsibility for the battle.

It is notable that Arthur does not appear in some *Triads* where he might be expected to feature, though he is referred to in around 26 of the 96 in the edition by Rachel Bromwich.[35] He is not among the 'Three Battle Leaders', where Urien of Rheged is joined by Selyf ap Cynan (king of Powys and commander at the battle of Chester against Northumbria, 616/17) and the obscure Addeon, son of Taliesin. (But the great commanders Vortimer and Ambrosius are not in the list either.) Urien and Selyf were historical figures recorded in many early sources – Arthur was not. Nor is he among the 'Three Battle Horsemen' despite all the theories that he was a cavalry-commander. The 'Three Bull Protectors of Britain' – a term probably referring to some sort of term of leadership in defending his subjects' wealth, given the Dark Ages warlords' fondness for cattle-rustling as seen in Irish legend are all Northern rulers, namely Urien, his cousin Gwendolleu of Caerluel/Carlisle, and the obscure Cynfawr. This shows that Arthur was not remembered by the tenth- or eleventh-century as a great leader of the Northern kingdoms, which argues against Alistair Moffat's theory that he ruled the Votadini and against the chances of Arthwys ap Mar or Arthwys ap Pabo as the 'original'. Arthur is however a 'ravager' greater than any of the 'Three Red Ravagers' of Britain, albeit also one of the 'Three Stout Swineherds' – the latter possibly deriving from bardic poems about his exploits as a young warrior while protecting his father's estates and livestock from brigands. The original version of the story of Tristram apparently referred to Arthur and his men trying to steal Tristram's lord's pigs – normal practice for restless bands of warriors in search of fresh meat and glory. Some scholars believe that all the references to Arthur being greater in accomplishments than all of the three in certain *Triads* were added to the 'original' at a later date, as a result of people questioning why Arthur was not in the list – and that he had not been in the original list because his fame had grown (or been invented?) since they were compiled.

Nowy, one of the 'Three Learned Men', is Arthur's son – suggesting that the 'original' Arthur has been confused with Arthwys of Dyfed, great-grandson of Gildas' contemporary Vortipor, who had a son and successor of that name. (It is however possible that 'the' Arthur had a son called Nowy and the later prince of Dyfed around 600/620 was called after him.) Arthur's son is also referred to in the Welsh poetry as 'Llacheu', though this has been explained as a sobriquet – 'The Glittering One'? The identity of this man may be distinct from the other son of Arthur known to early Welsh myth, the 'Amhar'/'Amr' supposedly killed by Arthur and buried at a place named after him near Wormelow in Herefordshire according to 'Nennius' early ninth-century list of 'marvels'. All that can be deduced from this mass of conflicting detail is that the Welsh traditions extant when the *Triads* were composed jumbled up people from the fifth-century to the seventh-century without recognising that certain links they made were historically inaccurate. But it is not an argument that Arthur was an invention from legend, even if the exploits of several men were confused.

Arthur and the hagiographers.

In a – 1070s? – hagiography by Lifris of Llancarfan Arthur is a contemporary of St Cadoc (c.500–570), first bishop of the sub-kingdom of Gwynllw (East of Cardiff) and rules a realm that includes the River Usk, i.e. the Silurian lands. There the Saint turns the cattle that Arthur has demanded as compensation for pardoning a fugitive in Cadoc's care into bundles of ferns. However, he comes *to* the river in pursuit of the fugitive from somewhere else, indicating that in this story he is not ruling at nearby Caerleon. Cadoc's story would have been preserved at his own foundation, the early sixth-century monastery of Llancarfan (Nantcarfan) near Cowbridge, so the monks are more likely to be accurate about Arthur's location than the (geographically unknown) composer of the tale of *Culhwch and Olwen* which puts Arthur as ruling at Caerleon. Arthur is supposed in this hagiography to have intervened to help Cadoc's father Gwynllw, prince of Glevisseg, and his bride-to-be Princess Gwladys of Breichiniog escape from her father (Arthur's cousin) so he is presented as being a generation older than Cadoc. Interestingly, when he and his chief followers Cai and Bedwyr are interrupted in a game of dice by the fleeing lovers his instinct is to take the princess for himself and he has to be reminded that he is supposed to succour those in distress[36] – suggesting that the role of the 'knights' as protectors of the weak was well-known by the early twelfth-century but Cadoc's biographer had to reconcile it with an alternative (monastic?) tradition of Arthur as more selfish and worldly.

The story has Arthur and his companions seeing the flight of Gwynllw and his bride from her father from a hilltop, a common opening to Irish legends of Fionn – but that is not 'proof' that the tale is totally fabricated. Arthur's dating is similar in the *Life* of St Illtud, founder of the monastery and school of Llanilltud Fawr (Llantwit), where he is an adult ruler and the saint's cousin when the latter, son of Bicanys, first comes to Britain from Armorica some time around AD 500.[37]

Arthur rules at 'Dindraithov'(Dunster?) in north Devon with Cador, father of Gildas' opponent Constantine of Dumnonia, in the life of St Carantog, and tries to use the Saint's floating altar as a table until it throws the contents off.[38] He is also acquisitive and occasionally hostile in his attitude towards the church, which could be a memory of the 'real' Arthur seeking to exact supplies or land for his men. The incident in the *Life of St Padarn*, where Arthur comes to the saint's cell coveting his tunic and the latter makes the earth swallow him up until he apologises,[39] may refer to the late sixth-century King Arthwyr of Dyfed, where the saint lived at Llanbadarn. This king was the son of Pedr ap Cyngar and great-grandson of Gildas' comtemporary and literary 'target', king Vortipor of Dyfed. In the *Life of St Illtud* the saint, another of his cousins, is critical of his and his men's boastfulness at their ungodly court.[40] In terms of the recognised saintly and royal genealogies recorded around 1100, Illtud was the cousin of the kings of Morgannwg – a clue to Arthur's believed family origins? The dates of Cadoc and Illtud are reasonably precise, with the former dying aged over seventy in c.577 and the latter as King Maelgwyn's teacher around 500–510, so their hagiographers knew when Arthur was supposed to have ruled. The Welsh genealogies made Brychan of Breichiniog, father of Gwladys and grandfather of Cadoc, the son of a princess of Siluria so by this reckoning Arthur – Brychan's cousin – was also linked to that dynasty. This Arthur is not the Arthur listed in the early tenth-century genealogy of Dyfed, although the geographical location of the latter in south-west Wales means that he ruled in the right area. Arthur also appears in an early Breton hagiography, that of St Eufflam (the current written text is twelfth-century), as fighting a dragon on the Saint's behalf – and Thomas Green has pointed out that Arthur wears a lion-skin and uses a club to do so, like Heracles in Classical myth.[41] Could this 'Breton Arthur' have annexed some of the heroic qualities of Heracles, seen as a 'protector god' by the Romans and utilised for propaganda as a template for the Emperors by Diocletian in the 280s? Could the club-brandishing 'Cerne Abbas Giant' in Dorset be a pre-Saxon reflection of the cult of Arthur as well as of Heracles?

In secular Welsh literature, the legend of Culhwch and Olwen places Arthur's court at Caerleon. He similarly presides over a magnificent court with a multitude of vassals and a collection of famous warriors in the tales of Yvain, Peredur, and Erec. The earliest existing manuscripts of these tales, in the '*Black Book of Carmarthen*', is probably early thirteenth-century – but the origin of the stories is no doubt rather earlier. Lugh, Gweir or Pryderi, Manawydan son of Llyr, Mabon son of Modron, Gwyn ap Nudd,Caw, the Saxon(?) Osla 'Big-Knife', and many others appear in a long list of Arthur's men. But despite his increased entourage the story still centres on him as an active warrior, assisting Culhwch to complete his – clearly legendary – tasks for a giant and hunting the legendary boar Twrch Troit. Culhwch's challenger is indeed the 'Chief Giant' so he is an appropriate foe for the chief ruler of Britain. The argument that as 'super-hero' Arthur fights other mythological figures, not Saxons, he was not considered historically as a warlord but as a 'roving righter of wrongs', may be too simplistic, as the tales were arranged to suit their audience – who did not want to hear about battles with Saxons but about 'escapist' fantasy? In *The Dream of Rhonabwy* the poet seems to present Arthur as ruling in Powys, as his realm is looked back on as a 'golden age' in the time of king Madoc ap Mareddud in the mid-twelfth-century. His army is found preparing for the battle of 'Caer Faddon' – presumably Badon – near the River Severn, possibly at the ford of 'Rhyd-ar-Groes' near Welshpool though Blackett and Wilson prefer a site near Ogmore Castle in Glamorgan.[42] This may indicate that the author's patron king Madoc looked back on Arthur as his forebear – but Arthur did not appear in the royal genealogy of Powys, which suggests that contrary to sceptics' imaginings the latter could not be 'forged' to suit political needs as required.

These two tales are later than the early *Triads*, with the *Dream* being composed in the reign of Madoc ap Maredudd of Powys (r. 1132–60). The long list of Arthur's companions in *Culhwch* suggests that his legendary court was collecting a mixture of real and fictional heroes before the time of Geoffrey of Monmouth and Wace – the 'Round Table' knights were a translation of this into a contemporary twelfth-century Norman idiom.

The notion of Arthur as a 'knight-errant' also developed from his heroics in Welsh legends. Giants were also a staple part of the Arthurian 'canon' in Wales, long before Geoffrey's (Breton?) story of the giant of Mont St Michel and the fourteenth-century tale of Sir Gwain and the 'Green Knight'. Apart from the central part of the giant Ynysbaddaden 'Chief Giant' in '*Culhwch and Olwen*', that story refers to Arthur's band killing the giant Diwrnach for his magical cauldron (an adaptation of the story in 'Prediau Annwfyn'?) and killing Dillus for his beard to use it for a leash for hunting-dogs in the great boar-hunt.

The battle-list of Nennius

The details of Arthur's campaigns are recounted in the 'recension' or preface added to the ninth-century Welsh history attributed to Nennius. This was probably done in the ninth century though the first copy of the *Historia Brittonum* which we possess that includes it (at Corpus Christi College Cambridge) dates to 1164/6. (It is not in the earliest version of the text, British Library Harleian Mss. 3589.) David Dumville dates the 'recension' later in his article in *Studia Celtica* (1975/6); more recently Peter Field (in *Studia Celtica* in 1996) believes that it is ninth-century but was left out of the text by early editors for reasons of literary merit.[43] Despite its impressive list of details it is of uncertain reliability given that 'Nennius' is a problematic source. How reliable is a text of the early ninth-century – or later – for events of the sixth-century? Is it meant to be 'historical', or is it a part of a lost literary/oral work of bardic poetry? And what were his motives in writing it?

The author, presumably the Gwynedd cleric of the 820s of that name, admitted that he had composed his work by 'making a heap of' extant material, though this would seem to indicate that – if he was being honest – he transcribed rather than embellished it. Modern critics are more sceptical about his interpretation of the text, and about his political motives. For that matter, can he be trusted to have really acquired his material from other books? (Geoffrey of Monmouth was to make the same claim.) Or if he did use books, and just distort the material, how accurate were they? We cannot assume that a monastic library in 820s Gwynedd would have copies of accurate historical chronicles; the main interest of ecclesiastics was Biblical commentary.

For that matter, 'Nennius' shows more interest in supernatural stories (e.g. his list of 'Mirabilia') than in military history, and clearly connects Arthur with divine backing. The main recent sceptical interpretation is by Oliver Padel in his article in *Cambridge Mediaeval Celtic Studies*, vol. 24 (1994); he thinks that 'Nennius' was writing a patriotic riposte to the attack on British worthiness of Divine backing in Gildas, and doing so for the needs of the aggressive new king of Gwynedd, Merfyn 'Frych'. The founder of a new dynasty in 825, replacing the line of Maelgwyn, Merfyn was seeking to rebuild a kingdom devastated by recent invasion by Mercia and to rally the Welsh behind the leadership of Gwynedd for a counter-offensive; the heroic Arthur was thus a suitable inspiration. Moreover, according to traditional genealogies Merfyn was a prince of the Isle of Man dynasty and so descended from the great poet-prince Llywarch 'Hen' of the later sixth-century, eulogist of Urien and Owain of Rheged – so was Merfyn brought up in a tradition of remembering the heroic struggles of the sixth-century?

'Nennius' used Biblical inspiration as had Gildas. Gildas had modelled himself on Jeremiah, castigating British sins; 'Nennius' used Joshua, the heroic conqueror of the Promised Land and favoured warrior of the Lord, as his model for the Divinely-backed Arthur. In this interpretation, Arthur was called '*dux bellorum*' – 'leader in battle' because that had been Joshua's title in the Old Testament, not because this was some ancient British military office; and it was no coincidence that Arthur fought twelve battles as Joshua had done. This Arthur was a British Joshua, invented by a patriotic churchman steeped in Old Testament material, and not a historical figure whose deeds were being scrupulously collected from existing literary material or annals.[44] It is noticeable that 'Nennius' patriotically included details of the pre-Roman British kings' alleged ancestors, the legendary 'Trojan' kings of Alba Longa (the line of Aeneas and ancestors of Romulus and Remus), presumably to link his story to the '*Aeneid*', and also made reference to the Irish legends of ancestral migrations from Spain. His narrative was thus designed to fit in with both the Bible and with Roman and Irish narrative 'histories'.

A reference in the extant preface indicates that it included material by one 'Rhun', probably the prince and bishop of that name of Rheged in the early seventh-century – and the military successes of the Rheged warlords Urien and Owain against the Angles in the 560s to 590s make them probable enthusiasts for collecting inspiring Arthurian stories at their court. (The reference to Arthur in the *Gododdin* shows that he was regarded as an inspiration for warriors in this time and region.) One modern theory has it that Rhun, or a contemporary at the court of Rheged, was one of the historical writers who Nennius used. Some battles by a second man (called 'Arthur'?) could have been added to the list of the victories against the Saxons in the intervening centuries, though this remains disputed. The contemporary revival in the fortunes of Gwynedd under the new dynasty of Merfyn 'Frych' (ruled 825–844) saw a reassertion of the notion of a heroic single leader unifying the Welsh to fight the Saxons, at a time when the Mercians were raiding across Offa's Dyke to reach Degannwy under king Beornwulf in the mid-820s. The concept of Arthur as a successful battle-leader was thus welcome to the royal court. Arthur could be talked up as a progenitor for Merfyn, and later his son Rhodri 'Mawr' who unified Gwynedd and Powys, and presented as the forerunner of their aggressive kingdom. Accordingly, there was at least a temptation to cast Arthur in terms of the Welsh situation of the 820s rather than to faithfully recount what was relevant to the 520s (if that was even known). The question of Nennius' interpretation of Arthur in ninth-century terminology has been examined in detail recently by Nicholas Higham in *King Arthur: Myth-Making and History* (Routledge, 2002). He follows up Padel's argument that Nennius was creating an inspiring myth of British success on an Old Testament model, not writing 'history' as we would understand it.[45] But even if a misty figure from the heroic past known for defeating Saxons could be used as a model for Merfyn and Rhodri, this is not to say that he was invented. If the new rulers of Gwynedd wanted a template for success, why not choose their own ancestors Maelgwyn – 'Pendragon' and national over-king – or Cadwallon the defeater of Edwin? These men had definitely fought the invading 'Germans', and so were suitable for 820s Gwynedd propagandist works. So why choose Arthur instead? No attempt was made to annex Arthur for the royal genealogy of Gwynedd, which would have been such a propaganda coup that it is likely to have been attempted if at all feasible. Thus we can take it that the Arthurian enthusiasts at Merfyn's court had no conception that Arthur could be Owain 'Dantgwyn' of Gwynedd, uncle of Maelgwyn and father of Cynglas.

A note of caution should be sounded about 'Nennius' chronological accuracy. Quite apart from ignoring Ambrosius, the mainstay of Gildas' account of the mid-late fifth-century, his chronology is suspect. He gives the date of Patrick's mission to Ireland as 438, whereas the contemporary Gallic chronicler Prosper put it at 431. He claims (chapter 28) that the Romans ruled in Britain for 409 years, whereas they landed in AD 43 and 'left' in or around 410 (407 if Constantine III's transportation of troops to the Continent is meant) – 377 years. He may have carelessly muddled the date of Honorius' letter with the number of years between 43 and 409/10. He dates the landing of the Saxons to 429 years before the date when he is writing, the fourth year of King Merfyn (i.e. 828/9), which makes it AD 400. This is clearly not the date either of the first post-Roman attack recounted in Bede (411?) or the admission of the first 'federates' by Vortigern who took the throne in 425. At best it could be the date of the Germanic raids on Britain which the Rome poet Claudian claims his patron, Stilicho the regent of the Western Empire, repulsed as consul in 399 (*On Stilicho's Consulship*). He also refers to the date of the Saxons' arrival as 400 years after the 'Incarnation', which is usually taken as the birth of Christ, and so to AD 400 again – but his earlier reference ('Miscellany', chapter 66) to the consulship of Felix and Taurus as being in this year is wrong as this consulship was in 428/9.

Nennius also appears to be the origin of some of the unhistorical stories in Geoffrey of Monmouth's book – including the landing of the early British ruler Brutus (here a Roman consul, not a Trojan prince) and the claim that the warlike Britons drove the Romans to withdraw by constantly killing their generals. His fondness for unlikely and supernatural events is shown by his credulous collection of 'mirabilia' connected to Arthur – which it has been suggested show that he was seeking to show that his hero could 'work wonders' as Christ and Moses had done.[46] The story of Emrys (Ambrosius or Merlin?) evading sacrifice by 'Vortigern' by showing him the red and white dragons fighting in the pool under the tyrant's castle was duly taken up by Geoffrey of Monmouth. The fact that his 'Mirabilia' include a reference to Arthur's dog Cabal's participation in the hunt for the 'Twrch Tyrwth' across South Wales shows that this story was in existence by the 820s.

'Nennius' also states that Arthur was the leader of the kings of Britain though there were others of nobler blood than he.[47] That hints that he was not of 'regular' royal blood, at least as remembered by the early ninth-century. It is not to say that Arthur was non-royal, as real or suspected bastardy would also have been looked down on by kings of undisputed lineage. But it may well imply that the uncertainty over his birth was already part of legend, with the question centring on his mother – Ygyr/Igraine as recorded by the Welsh stories of the eleventh- or twelfth-century. Igraine was regarded by the Welsh mythographers as the daughter of Amlawdd 'Wledig' and granddaughter of Cunedda, placing her in the later fifth-century.

The crucial part of the 'Nennius' text dates the Arthurian campaign as being in 'those days' when Hengest had died and his son Octha had come from northern Britain to succeed him in Kent. Hengest's death is given as 488 by the *Anglo-Saxon Chronicle*, which is late ninth-century but incorporates details of Hengest's wars which show a familiarity with the 'saga' also recounted by Nennius. The 'battle'list' follows on from Nennius' account of Vortigern's troubles, with notably no reference to the intervening campaigns of Ambrosius. This suggests no close knowledge of Gildas' version in which Ambrosius is pre-eminent as the British leader after Vortigern. It is a summary of Arthurian tradition extant in the ninth-century or even the eleventh-century according to David Dumville's dating of the extant version of the text – rather than an original documentary source dating from Arthur's time, and the author admits that he collected and is transcribing a mass of materials.

The battle-list: a poetic origin? Or a historicization of fiction?

Whether he invented (or just embellished) many details in the process due to his politico-religious agenda depends on how the approach of a 'historian' of the ninth-century (or eleventh-century) can be interpreted. He cannot be conclusively written off as a literary fiction-writer despite his inaccuracies, though some modern writers have done their best. The nature of the list of battles suggests that it may be a transcription of an oral bardic poem, as suggested by H.M. and N.K. Chadwick in *The Growth of Literature* in 1932.[48] This is certainly suggested by the way that the list is laid out – it does not deal with all the battles at the same length, but has a rather odd account of four days' fighting at 'Dubglass' (as counting as four battles) and extra details for the battles of 'Castell

Guinnion' and Mount Badon alone. Why were these two singled out – because they had separate bardic poems dealing wth them in detail? It has been suggested that counting 'Dubglass' as four battles, not one, was a literary device to bring the total up to the required twelve. (Similarly, the '960' men killed by Arthur at Badon could be a literary device, as the number is four times that of the word-length of the poem, 240.) Also, the way the list is laid out in several sections may suggest transcription of a poem written in strict metre where the words were chosen to fit the required structure of the poem, not transcribing accurate data. The list may be an authentic – or embellished – memory of a traditional list of campaigns, or a mixture of campaigns by several men of a similar name mistakenly ascribed later to one man. The custom of bards compiling this sort of list of their patrons' victories is certainly sixth-century, as 'Taliesin' provided similar lists of the victories of Urien of Rheged and Gwallauc of Elmet. A similar list is still extant for the victories of the seventh-century Gwynedd ruler Cadwallon.[49] To Nicholas Higham, the very fact that there are twelve battles suggests strongly that the number was artificially inflated to match Joshua's battles. This is the obvious explanation why the obscure 'battle of Dubglass' is extended to cover four days. But there is little point in analysing the extant text of the 'battle-list' sentences to see if this can be identified as originating in the metre used for heroic poetry, not annalistic prose – as some recent writers have done. Even if the list as it stands came from poetry, this poem could be based on fact – albeit nine not twelve battles, and not all against 'invading' Saxons.

The precise sites are much argued-over, with some historians trying to fix all of them in one particular area; but this reliance on place-names ignores the fact that original sixth-century names may have changed in the intervening centuries. Kenneth Jackson made the first systematic investigation in 1945, and believed that two ('Urbs Legionis' and the 'Caledonian Wood') could be positively identified; later he suggested probable locations for another two. He also suggested that the battle of 'Urbs Legionis' was based, unhistorically, on the later battle of Chester between the armies of Powys and Northumbria in 616.[50] W.F. Skene in the mid-nineteenth century founded one rival school of thought that argued for an exclusively Scottish setting, mostly around the Antonine Wall and the Forth,[51] which would imply battles against the Picts as much as against the Saxons. This is where the historical prince 'Arthur' of Dalriada, son of king Aedan, fought in the 580s – but that could just be coincidence. The Lothian and/or Forth/Clyde region settings seem plausible mostly for the 'Caledonian Forest/Wood' and 'Mount Agned', but proponents of that theory were divided over whether Arthur was a British or Gaelic Dalriadan prince. One claim by Ronald Millar in 1978 even refers to sites in Brittany, which is unlikely given the strong Welsh and north British flavour of the sources – why would the North British creator of the 'Gododdin' poem c. 600 be interested in a Breton warlord as an exemplar for his listeners? Recently Steve Blake and Scott Lloyd have argued for sites solely within Wales, which would argue for battles mostly against fellow-Britons.[52] Mid-twentieth-century historians favoured a range of sites for battles over a wide area across Britain, which 'Nennius' claim of a 'multi-national' force drawn from many kingdoms for a long campaign might indicate. The later sceptics argued that the wide geographical locations merely testify to post-sixth-century bards 'collecting' stories of any notable early battles and awarding them to Arthur. Patrick Sims-Williams (in Rachel Bromwich, A. Jarman, and B. Roberts, *The Arthur of the Welsh: The Arthurian Legend in Mediaeval Welsh Literature*, 1991) argued that many of the battles were from early poetry.[53] But a wide-ranging campaign across several areas of Britain was not beyond a post-Roman warlord on logistic grounds – in the early Anglo-Saxon kingdoms of the seventh-century king Edwin of Northumbria could march south into Wessex in 626 and King Penda of Mercia could cross Northumbria to Bamburgh in c. 644.

There have been various interpretations of 'Nennius' statement that Arthur was 'leader in battles' ('*Dux Bellorum*') of the kings of the Britons, with some scholars claiming this as a formal title in the Roman tradition of the 'Count of Britain' and others that Arthur was not a king as he is not stated here to have been the 'king' but the 'leader' of the Britons. Nicholas Higham believes that it is derived from Old Testament references to Joshua. The use of Biblical language and parallels in 'Nennius', as in other early Welsh clerical writers, which linguists have detected may indeed indicate that any 'real' Arthurian campaigns were reworked in a suitable Biblical manner in the ninth century and so be more literary than historical in their 'Nennina' form. But the mention of '*dux bellorum*' may reflect no more than that Arthur, whether or not holding the rank of a king, led a coalition against the Saxons through force of personality and military skills. If he was the son of the long-lived Mouric of Siluria, who apparently ruled long after his son was adult, he would have been heir to the throne or co-ruler at the time but not yet king as the *Llandaff Charters* have the two of them reigning together for decades. Alternatively, one theory has linked this name to the persona of an obscure late fifth-century king in part of Powys, Riocatus the son of Pascent and grandson of Vortigern (who is called 'Briacat' in the genealogy of Vortigern's family in 'Nennius'). His name actually means 'King of Battles', but there is no tradition of Arthur as having been linked to Vortigern's family. Arthur may alternatively have come from any one of a number of noble or 'royal' dynasties in parts of southern Britain soon to be conquered by the incoming Germanic settlers, and their existence has been lost to history as subsequent generations forgot their submerged 'British'heritage.

The list of the twelve battles, whether or not transcribed from an oral bardic tradition, is:

1. '*The mouth of the river that is called Glein*'. The name is derived from the 'Old Welsh' for 'pure'. The River Glen in Lincolnshire is the most likely, in a campaign against the settlers in Lindsey. The River Glen in Northumbria (near the fortress of Yeavering Bell, later capital of the Anglian kingdom), the Lune (formerly called the Glen) or Leven in Cumbria, the '*Nant y Gleiniant*' river near Llanidloes in Wales, and even Glynde in Sussex have been suggested. Glynde might make sense from the archaeological evidence, given the local Saxon settlements around the River Ouse by the people of the warlord Aelle and the literary evidence of a major massacre of the British at nearby Anderida (Pevensey) dated to 491 by the *Anglo-Saxon Chronicle*. The similarity of names could suggest the River Glyme in Oxfordshire, near another major area of Saxon settlement.[54]

2–5. 'The river Dubglass in the region of Linnuis'. Linnuis is most often translated as Lindsey, as suggested by Kenneth Jackson in 1945, though Leslie Alcock has suggested 'Lininius' (around Ilchester) in Somerset, on a major Roman road (the Fosse Way). Some Scots writers prefer Lennox. Geoffrey of Monmouth places the battle during an early Arthurian campaign against the Saxons around York, which would make Lindsey a likely site if he had access to Welsh material on the campaign which has not survived.[55] The town of Lincoln, a major Roman 'colonia', was still in use through the fifth-century and the Anglian settlements around it clearly did not cause its abandonment. It was thus a logical site for a battle to repel an Anglian or Saxon incursion – from their settlements on the lower Humber?

Dubglass is the Celtic for 'Dark Water', as in the Scottish family name 'Douglas'. Steve Blake and Scott Lloyd suggest the Welsh derivation '*Dulas*'; their favourite is Llandulas near Colwyn Bay but there is another Dulas in Ergyng (near 'Arthur's Stone' at Dorstone) and *Pontarddulais*. There is another 'Dark Water' near the possible landing-site of Cerdic on the Western shore of Southampton Water in Hampshire, and a River Blackwater running into the Water not far from the probable site of Cerdic's battle against the British king 'Natanleod' at Netley Marsh.[56] Any one of a number of sites could have held this name and been renamed by the Saxons – the likeliest candidates must be reckoned by the 'Linnius' connection, not by the etymology of 'Dubglass' alone.

6. *'Above the river which is called Bassas'*. May contain the Celtic word for 'shallows'. Baschurch in Shropshire is proposed by Graham Phillips and Martin Keatman in *King Arthur: the True Story* (which places Arthur's headquarters at the post-Roman town at Viroconium/Wroxeter).[57] Any one of a number of sites could have been called that and renamed by the Saxons. Basingwerk (Shropshire), i.e. 'Bassa's stronghold'; suggested by Blake and Lloyd in *The Keys to Avalon*.[58]
7. '*The wood of Celidon, that is Cat Coit Celidon*'. The forest of Celidon, that is the ancient 'Caledonia', was the name given to the forests of south-east Galloway in Scotland. The name would seem to be easy to interpret. But some scholars prefer to argue that the name derives from a man or another place called 'Celidon', possibly the 'Celyddon' in South Wales referred to in the Culhwch story, the Clywd area (Steve Blake and Scott Lloyd), or the forest of Clun in Shropshire (Frank Reno). Thomas Green argues that it is derived from the mythical 'Cad

Goleu', the 'battle of the branchy trees' where Arthur assisted the Irish demi-gods, the 'Sons of Danu', against the forces of Annwfyn.[59] But there is no need to suggest that an Arthurian battle in a forest need be a battle 'with' the forest.

8. '*Castellum Guinnion*'. Unknown. Arthur is said to have carried an image of the Virgin Mary on his shoulders, but this is probably a mistranslation of 'ysgwydd', 'shoulder', for 'ysgwyd', 'shield'. Notably this feat of Arthur's also appears in accounts of the battle of Badon, so it was presumably duplicated or muddled up by later bardic accounts of one or other battle. The site is likely to be some then-British hillfort that later lost its old name. Using possible linguistic derivations, arguments have been made for:

   a fort in Wedale on the Borders (Alistair Moffat), the 'gwyn' in Guinnion perhaps being translateable as 'pure' i.e. 'holy'. The Saxon name could mean 'dale of woe' from a military defeat. Wanborough in north Wiltshire, the Saxon 'wen' perhaps being derived from 'gwyn'. There is a nearby Roman fort, Durocornovium, which the Saxons could have referred to as the 'white fort' from the nearby 'White (chalk) Hill'. Winchester: 'Caer Guinn'? It is more likely that the post-fifth-century British knew Winchester as a derivative of 'Venta', hence the confusion in Geoffrey of Monmouth's story over which 'Venta' was Arthur's capital. The Wrekin in Shropshire, 'Caer Guricon'. Binchester in Durham (Vinovium, which could translate into Welsh as 'Gwinnouion').[60]

9. The '*City of the Legion*'. Presumably a former Roman legionary fortress, that is Chester or Caerleon (Kenneth Jackson suggests Chester). Chris Barber has suggested that if it was Caerleon, the name 'Cat's Ash' given to a pass overlooking the Caerleon valley may derive from 'Cad Oesc', that is, the battle with the Saxon leader Oesc of Kent.[61]

Another city that had had a legionary base, and which had Anglian settlements nearby by c.500 unlike Chester and Caerleon, was York. Skene's suggestion of Dumbarton in Strathclyde is the least likely, though conceivably the later sixth-century prince Arthur of Dal Riada could have fought there.

10. '*The shore of the river that is called Tribuit*'. An estuary where three rivers meet – it could be anywhere, though the latest researchers have suggested Cardigan Bay or Gwent in Wales. The earliest etymological investigators, Skene and Glennie, suggested a link with the ancient name for the Firth of Forth, and suggested a site near Bannockburn. Chris Barber in *Journey to Avalon* (1993) suggests the mouth of the River Twrc (Troggy) near Caerleon. The River Ribble in Lancashire has been suggested, on the tenuous grounds that its original British name may have been 'Breffrwd'. Kenneth Jackson suggested that the name could be translated as 'broken strand', implying a ford. There is a linguistic similarity to the name of Trebarwith Sands in northern Cornwall – a beach 'broken' by a ford.[62] The battle of '*Tryfrwyd*' is also referred to in another early Arthurian source, a poem in the *Black Book of Carmarthen*. Under the name 'Trywruid' it appears in the poem *Pa Gur* – but as a mythical battle with sea-monsters.[63]
11. '*The mountain which is called Agned*'. Edinburgh has been suggested, following Geoffrey of Monmouth's use of the name 'Mount Agned' for a town which the Scots chronicler John of Fordun identified as that place. Geoffrey refers to Agned as the 'Castle of Maidens', which has been claimed as a reference to the Pictish tradition of matrilinear succession. He also used the name of the 'Dolorous Mountains', derived from the Welsh 'ochenaid' ('sigh'), from which a link has been claimed to the Eildon Hills which are so called in the Scots Arthurian romance *Fergus of Galloway*. The Edinburgh campaign may also have been mythologised in the story referred to in '*Pa Gur*', on the 'mountain of Eidyn'.[64]

    An alternative name for the battle has been given as '*Cad Bregion*', from the name 'Breguoin' in one manuscript of Nennius. Chris Barber suggests 'Cat's Brain Hill' in Gloucestershire, a site identified as 'Cathbregyon' in a marginal note to a copy of Nennius acquired in 1825 by the antiquary Joseph Ritson.

A site near Leintwardine in Herefordshire, the Roman fort of 'Bravonium', is also possible from the place--name, as suggested by Alfred Anscombe. Urien of Rheged also fought a battle at Breguoin, but this is not proof that this battle was annexed for Arthur in later centuries.

12. '*The battle on Mount Badon, in which there fell together in one day nine hundred and sixty men in one onslaught of Arthur, and no one laid them low save himself alone*'.[65] The legendary feat of killing 960 men single-handed is clearly an invention of some poet, but may derive from Arthur's personal warband doing the killing rather than the more usual combined army of the British kings. The story of Arthur carrying the Cross for three days beforehand is presumably a garbled survival from some heroic poem, a mistranslation, or a duplication in slightly different form of the Castell Guinnion battle's account. The cult of the Cross was not present in ninth-century Gwynedd, so Nennius is unlikely to have invented the reference; but its originator clearly saw Arthur as a Christ-like figure. The sceptics prefer to allege that the mythical elements of the numbers killed and the detail about carrying the Cross are 'proof' of its unhistoricity.

Gildas refers to it as 'the siege of Badon Hill, which was pretty well the last defeat of the villains, and certainly not the least'.[66]

Logically, it would seem likely that the crushing victory which the British achieved was due to some major advantage of tactics such as the use of cavalry – and if the battle was on a hill the British would have been better-placed to win by a charge downhill. Gildas, the nearest source in time, refers to it as a siege so it is more likely that the Saxons were besieging the British than the other way round. The site has been linked to any number of places containing the element 'bad-', of which a number survive in England. Following Kenneth Jackson's conclusion that the name would have translated into Anglo-Saxon as something like '*Baddanbyrig*', hence modern Badbury, suitably-named hillforts have been suggested – e.g. Badbury with its hillfort Liddington Castle in Northern Wiltshire (near the crucial 'Ridgeway' track) or Badbury Rings in Dorset. The former, chosen by Rosemary Sutcliff for the battle-site in *Sword at Sunset*, is the more strategically logical.

Blackett and Wilson prefer either Mount Baedan near Tondu in Glamorgan, which has local nomenclature suggestive of a battle (e.g. 'Maes Cadlawr', the 'Field of Slaughter'), or Bouden Hill in southern Scotland. Neither seem logical for a campaign against Saxons. Frank Reno has suggested the Wrekin, and the nearby Breidden Hills could have provided a suitable 'Bad-' name for a local hillfort.[67] There is a strong argument for an early favourite accepted by Geoffrey of Monmouth, Bath, on account of the early Welsh description of the town as 'the springs of Badon' in one of 'Nennius' references in the 820s.[68] The foundation-charter of Bath Abbey in 676 referred to the town as 'aet Badum'. Conceivably one of the hillforts overlooking Bath, such as Little Solsbury Hill, could have been the post-Roman defensive stronghold protecting Bath, the 'fortress of Badon'.

The Welsh–Powys tradition used in the '*Dream of Rhonabwy*' in the twelfth-century regarded the battle-site of '*Caer Faddon*' – presumably Badon – as close to the Severn, a few hours' march from the riverbank; the poem is admittedly late but there is no reason why its author could not use an accurate tradition of where the battle took place. Blackett and Wilson have used this siting of the events surrounding the battle as an argument for Badon being Mount/Mynydd Baedan and site the 'pre-battle' events at a Severn-side ford in the poem at the ford at Ogmore Castle on the North side of the Bristol Channel, around six miles from the ridge.[69] But technically the ford in question is in the Ogwr/Ogmore river, not the Severn, and a long way down the Bristol Channel coast from the mouth of the Severn at that. Nor it is clear what a Saxon army would be doing up the remote ridge of Mynydd Baedan, east of Port Talbot and north-west of Bridgend.

The more accepted interpretation of the poem's geography places the ford, named as 'Rhyd-y-Groes', at a farm of that name near Welshpool on the upper Severn and the battle within a few miles of Caer Digoll or Middletown. But it is not clear why Arthur would have been fighting the Saxons in the heartland of Powys, and it is more likely that the twelfth-century author only guessed at the battle-site. He was clearly placing Arthur in a Powys context as the presiding hero of a past 'Golden Age', so had no reason to bother with any traditions that placed Badon outside the kingdom.

Bath makes more strategic sense for Arthur dealing with a Saxon attack across the Cotswolds or up the Severn estuary, in which case either Bannerdown – the choice of John Aubrey in the seventeenth-century as Badon – or Little Solsbury Hill would be the probable site of the hillfort that was besieged. The Roman road from the South-East passes close to both hills, making it easy for the British and Saxons to use it for quick access to them. The actual town of Bath, 'Aquae Sulis', was probably still functioning to some extent into the fifth- and sixth-century according to Barry Cunliffe's archaeological survey, and was recorded in the *Anglo-Saxon Chronicle* as one of the three fortified towns overrun by Caewlin of the West Saxons in 577.[70] A large Saxon army could have marched across the South of England from the Thames to attack the Cotswolds and aimed for Bath, or a force landed from the sea. There is a reference in the *Annales Cambriae* to a 'second battle of Badon' in 664/5, so if this took place at the same site as the first some scholars have argued that it must be within Wales. No Welsh king was likely to have fought Saxons at Bath, well within Mercia, in 664/5. But the reference does not say that the battle was between Welsh and Saxons.

The 'hunt of the Irish boar': a vague memory of a real campaign?

A further Arthurian campaign has been speculated about, according to the interpretations of the story of Culhwch and Olwen, first referred to by 'Nennius' in the ninth-century and preserved in the (twelfth-century?) collection of tales of the 'Mabinogi'. This refers to the hunt of Arthur, his cousin Culhwch, and other warriors after the '*Twrch Twryth*', the 'Irish Boar', across South Wales from Menevia (St David's) via Presceli and the vicinity of Rhyader to the Severn. It is also in a poem annexed to the 'Gododdin' text. The notion of a hunt against a 'magical' boar, sometimes a transformed human, is (originally?) Irish, where Fionn hunts a ferocious boar in the legend of Diarmait and Grainne – and lets the boar kill Diarmait, who he has the power to heal but does not, in retaliation for Diarmait running off earlier with his wife Grainne. (The Irish legends' boar's name is 'Traith Troit'.) The 'boar' in '*Culhwch and*

Olwen' significantly comes from Ireland, and is chased across South Wales into the Severn estuary. It has been suggested that this refers to a campaign to expel a force of Irish invaders who fought under the banner of a boar rather than a 'pig' as such, the 'boar' being the leading invading chieftain and the nine 'piglets' his sons or lieutenants. The references in tradition to a war with the 'King of Africa' have been used by Blackett and Wilson to suggest that the invaders may have been a force of Germanic Vandals expelled from North Africa by the Eastern Roman Empire in the 530s or 540s.[71] This is very unlikely. Chris Barber has suggested that the conclusion of the 'Irish boar' campaign, involving the expulsion of the enemy into the Severn near Chepstow (the 'Severn Bore' is referred to), could also remember the eviction of hostile elements in the local kingdom of Ergyng – possibly the enigmatic 'Gewissae' (Gwentissae?) linked to later West Saxon founder 'Cerdic'. The whole 'campaign' may be symbolic and/or mythical, and Arthur significantly ended up in mediaeval folklore as the leader of the supernatural 'Wild Hunt' (in France as well as Britain). But a real war against an invader is possible though none of its battles came to feature in the 'battle-list' by 'Nennius'.

It should, however, be pointed out that there is no early origin for the major battle of 'Bedegraine' in which the mediaeval romancers had Arthur defeating his British kingly rivals. This first occurs in the French 'Prose Merlin' of the thirteenth-century, and is an established part of the story by Malory's version, though he places it north of the River Trent in Sherwood Forest.[72] In this version, the battle is the climax of a campaign by Arthur against a coalition of eleven kings, who challenge his right to succeed Uther Pendragon. Their legendary locations imply a group of Northern and Welsh rulers, aided by the Irish, attacking Arthur who is by now in possession of southern Britain (i.e. 'Logres', the later England) – possibly influenced by the real-life Welsh/Scots/Irish attack on national unifier King Athelstan of England at 'Brunanburh' in 937? The origin of this tradition about a battle is unknown, though the Roman fort at Leintwardine in Herefordshire – 'Branogenium', 'born of the raven' (or a King Bran, as at Cwmbran?) – has been suggested by Mike Ashley.[73] It could conceivably be a version of 'Cad Bregion', i.e the eleventh battle in the 'Nennius list', but the names are not that similar.

Camlann – and the location of Medraut's usurpation

The other battle linked to Arthur,' the strife of Camlann where Arthur and Medraut fell' twenty-one years after Badon according to the *Annales Cambriae*, is equally uncertain. It has been linked to any number of places containing similar place-name elements. The name may be 'Camboglanna', that is 'Crooked Bank' in Middle Welsh. It has been placed as far north as Camelon in the Forth valley in Scotland by Stuart Glennie, citing an ancient tradition of Arthur fighting there with the Pictish ruler Modred, and at the Roman fort at Cambolanda (Birdoswald) on the Antonine Wall by O.G.S. Crawford (1931).[74] It was placed as far south as the River Camel in northern Cornwall (where however the hopefully-named 'Slaughterbridge' nearby seems to refer to a battle in the 820s) by modern Cornish enthusiasts, assisted by an enigmatic inscribed stone which when fully investigated turned out not to refer to Arthur at all. Queen's Camel near Cadbury Castle hillfort in Somerset is Geoffrey Ashe's favourite.

Geoffrey of Monmouth placed the battle on Salisbury Plain, a version continued in the late mediaeval retelling by Sir Thomas Malory, but with no clear historical tradition behind it except a probable mistranslation of Arthur's landing-site at 'Porth Hamo' as Southampton. If the traditional story – extant by the *Triads* – that Medraut attacked Arthur's court while he was away fighting is correct and refers to a foreign expedition, it should be somewhere near a coast. As Welsh tradition says that Arthur was campaigning in Ireland rather than in Gaul (Geoffrey's version) the coast would be the west coast of Wales – or just possibly the Bristol Channel, also within reach of Queen's Camel. Similarly, Arthur's loyal nephew Gwalchmai/Gawain is supposed to have been killed in battle as Arthur landed on his return. (Geoffrey and his successors placed this at Dover.) His traditional burial-site is either in Pembrokeshire or near Rhos by the lower Dee; the *Stanzas of the Graves* locates it at 'Peryddon' (which Steve Blake and Scott Lloyd claim to be Rhos).[75] He is unlikely to have been buried far from where he was killed, which would rule out the south coast.

Medraut himself may have been either Arthur's nephew, the son of Llew/Lot of Lothian and brother of Gwalchmai (as continued into English mediaeval stories), or Medraut ap Cawdraf of Gwent. The latter, living at Miskin near Llantrisant according to Glamorgan tradition, is more likely than Arthur's nephew to have married the sister of Arthur's wife or to have been local enough to make 'Caer Wynt' (Caerwent?) his headquarters during his usurpation, as cited by the twelfth-century *Brut*. If this tradition is accurate, Medraut would have centred his usurpation in South-East Wales and Arthur could be expected to have marched on his headquarters from the coast opposite Ireland, being intercepted somewhere en route. Medraut is given by mediaeval Welsh genealogies as marrying (St.) Cwyllog, the daughter of Gildas – the sister of St Cennydd (of Llangennith in Gower). But it is not clear that this can be used as evidence for the dating of Gildas as a generation older than the Medraut who died at Camlann c. 539; either Medraut ap Llew or Medraut ap Cawdraf – one of whom was the rebel – could be meant.

An alternative, rather surprising East Anglian connection for Medraut was suggested by John Morris in *The Age of Arthur* (p. 140) and taken up by Philip Holmes in *King Arthur: the Military History* (Cassell, 1996).[76] It centres on the only record of the name 'Medraut' outside the Arthurian stories being as the father of St Dyfnauc/Domnoc in that figure's hagiography, and links the latter with the British 'Domnoc' who Bede says founded Dunwich in Suffolk. The latter was close to the vanished Late Roman 'Saxon Shore' fortress of Walton Castle, whose English name could mean 'Welsh town' – so Holmes suggests that a body of British troops were placed there under Medraut and/or his son to watch the local Anglian settlers. This is ingenious, but depends on too many improbabilities or coincidences. The only sons of Medraut named in early tradition were the boys murdered by Constantine of Dumnonia in a church, which would suggest that they had some claim on the latter's throne and were unlikely to be the sons of a man ruling in Suffolk. The name of Domnoc's father is probably coincidental.

The current favourite site for Camlann among 'Celtic' scholars is the Pass of Camlann 6 km. East of Dolgellau in mid-Wales, favoured by Graham Phillips and Martin Keatman (in *King Arthur: the True Story*, 1992). Chris Barber prefers Cadgamlan on the south coast of the Lleyn peninsula.[77] Both would make sense if there is any factual basis for the Welsh tradition that Medraut usurped the throne while Arthur was fighting Llwch 'of the Lakes' (a possible 'original' for Lancelot) in Ireland. Arthur would have landed either in Lleyn or around Aberystwyth on his return, and been confronted en route to South Wales. Another North

Wales site identified as 'Camlann' by the mediaeval period was Cwm Lan, on a mountain-pass in Arfon – close to the hillfort at Dinas Emrys and the legendary cave where the King and his knights were supposedly asleep until they were needed again. (The legend may owe something to the myth of the 'Seven Sleepers of Ephesus', known in England by the time of Edward 'the Confessor's hagiography in the mid-twelfth-century.) Peter Bartrum has written about this site for the battle.

The traditions cited in the *Triads* make it apparent that casualties at the battle were regarded as being every bit as severe as in the mediaeval version, even if it was poetic licence that only seven men survived. (By the Malory version there are only around three survivors among the knights, led by Bedivere and his brother Lucan.) Rodney Castleden (*King Arthur: The Truth behind the Legend*, 2000) has identified another site with a suitable etymology near Dolgellau, the 'Pont ar Gamlan' at the confluence of the rivers Eden and Mawddach 6 km. north of Dolgellau.[78] This was a site on the crucial 'Sarn Helen' military road suitable for an ambush, perhaps by Medraut in alliance with Maelgwyn of Gwynedd. It is unclear if the reference to Maelgwyn's treachery to Arthur's family in a poem attributed to Taliesin is contemporary, or if it implies that the king of Gwynedd allied himself to Medraut.

Chapter 8

Camelot and The Round Table

Camelot – the potential sites

(i) 'Caer Melyn'? Blackett and Wilson on Camelot and the Table

The myth of Arthur's 'Camelot' owes more to Chretien of Troyes and his peers than fifth- or sixth-century fact, and the only large Roman town with a similar name – Camulodunum (Colchester) was either in ruins or under East Saxon control by the early sixth-century. The name of 'Camelot' itself first appears in Chretien's 'Lancelot' then in the early thirteenth-century French '*Quest of the Holy Grail*' and the '*Prose Lancelot*'; it is not in Wace. They may just have adapted the name of Camulodunum as the 'capital' of Roman Britain in Tacitus' '*Annals*' and a useful south-eastern fortified town to site an Arthur ruling on both sides of the Channel. But it has been asserted by modern Welsh linguistic scholars (professional and amateur) that the 'real Arthur' could have lived at a much more modest hillfort known as 'Caer Melyn' i.e. 'the 'Yellow Fort'. Much has been made of this in trying to find a site with an appropriate name – though there is no mention of 'Caer Melyn' in the *Triads* so it was clearly thought unimportant in the ninth- and tenth-century. Blackett and Wilson have linked this name (1985, see Bibliography) to an obscure site on the southern slopes of Cefn Onn ridge overlooking Cardiff, a nameless fort at what was originally called 'Yellow Wells Farm' near Lisvane, which was in a good strategic position above the main route from south-west Wales to the Severn crossing. It was in the centre of an area protected from raiders by a network of forts and signal-stations, not far from Machen (associated with Arthur in mediaeval Welsh legend) and the hillfort of 'Arthur's Buttresses'. They claim that the privileges granted to the local 'commote' derive from it being the principal residential centre for the Silurian monarchs including Arthur. They also claim that the name of the 'commote', 'Cibbwr' or 'Cybor', derives from the words for 'mutual action' ('cy') at the 'table' ('bwrdd') – suggesting that the area was a meeting-place for important people at a royal table.[1] This could be the origin of the legend of Arthur's 'Round Table', at which the shape of the table meant that there could be no disputes over precedence or more 'senior' seats. But even if the name of Cybor does imply that the cantref contained a senior royal site, there is no clue as to how far back this status existed or if 'Arthur' initiated it. It could have originated at any time in the history of independent Morgannwg from the fifth-century to the eleventh-century, and the hillfort in question is too small to have been more than a minor estate of the local kings.

Unfortunately for their argument, there is no record of Arthur being linked to a 'Round Table' before the mid-twelfth-century, when it first appears in the work of Wace. Robert de Boron says it was designed to prevent quarrels over precedence. There is no trace of it in the Welsh legends extant in the twelfth-century which were written up in the 'Mabinogi' collection, where Arthur and his men feast in an ordinary manner. 'Celtic' mythological scholar Roger Loomis thought that there was an ancient tradition of kings and their great lords feasting at a round table, to prevent disputes over precedence. Layamon, c. 1190, refers to the Table as the work of a Cornish artificer after a fight over precedence among the knights; Robert de Boron in *Perceval* presents Merlin as its inventor, in honour of the table used at the Last Supper. The story that it was presented to Arthur at his marriage to Guinevere by her father Leodegrance is a later development. Robert de Boron has Merlin create 52 places – those for Arthur and 50 knights plus a vacant seat, which probably echoes the place left vacant at the table used at Christ's 'Last Supper' after one apostle (Judas) had been expelled from it. Later in the book Robert has Merlin create new knights after Arthur has lost 100 in battle, and refer to the reasoning behind the vacant seat, namely that it is to be left vacant for the 'most excellent' of the knights who is still to join the King's knightly fellowship – and Sir Galahad duly fulfils this criteria. Robert also has the knights' names appear miraculously at their places, which was used by later writers.[2]

The original number of knights was 12, in Robert de Boron's works, i.e. the same number as the Apostles. This was raised to 50 later – 48 plus Arthur plus the vacancy (for Galahad). Layamon claimed there were 700 and the Vulgate *Lancelot* that there were 150. Chretien lists 50 and states that he has only named a fifteenth of the total, i.e. c.750 in all; Malory lists 127 by name. In the Welsh versions, *Culhwch and Olwen* refers to 220 names (some duplicates) but the fifteenth-century *Pedwar Marchog ar Hugain Llys Arthur* names 24 including Bors, Galahad, Gwalchmai, Gawain, Lancelot, Owain (i.e. 'Yvain', the one connected to Gower), Tristan, Llywarch 'Hen' (a late sixth-century poet-prince of Rheged), Modred, Perceval, and Sanddef.[3] Only Kay/Cei, Bedivere/Bedwyr, Gawain/Gwalchmai, and Urgan/Urien are surviving figures in the original 12 from Welsh legends. 25 names appear on the fake 'Round Table' made in the thirteenth-century for Winchester Castle, whose commission and placing (by Henry III?) suggests that he regarded Winchester as 'Camelot'. They bring in Galahalt (Galahaut), Lamorak, Lionel, Palamedes, Ector Demaris, and Dagonet among other names well-known by or as a result of Malory's version. The table was only decorated after 1509 for the young Henry VIII, so the choice of names presumably come from Malory. The concept of a chivalric 'Round Table' had entered current culture across the knightly world by 1223, when the name is first used for a tournament in Cyprus staged by the powerful Ibelin family – linked to the Angevin dynasty's cousins the kings of Jerusalem. In 1252 there is the first reference to a knight being killed at a 'round table' event, evidently a potentially dangerous knightly joust or melee, and in 1281 the chronicler Walter of Guisborough has the first record of a 'round table' event held for knights at Warwick Castle. Edward III incorporated the 'Round Table' concept into his development of Windsor Castle and the Order of the Garter based there.

The Glamorgan hillfort-system – protecting the King's headquarters?

The same argument against a definitively Arthurian origin applies to the system of inter-linked hillforts that were allegedly erected in the area to defend the heartland of Arthurian Siluria. This is a pet theory of local authors Baram Blackett and Alan Wilson, who have ingeniously traced a layout of forts (and smaller signal-stations) across Glamorgan and Gwent, all within signalling-distance of each other and seemingly surrounding 'central' locations such as Pentre Meurig in the west and the area of Caerleon in the east. They maintain that this was a system of lookouts for foreign invaders across Silurian territory, and note that one near Caerleon is known as 'Arthur's Walls'.[4] (Given the story of Arthur as the ruler at Caerleon in '*Culhwch and Olwen*', the name probably arose from that story's local link.) Evidently an able and powerful king must have had the ingenuity and resources to carry out this sort of planning. But even if a complex system of hillforts was established at some date centred on the area around Caerleon (with another system centred on Pentre Meurig?), it cannot be proved that this was post-Roman from the 'Arthurian' era or that it centred around the 'original' of Camelot. Again, it could have been set up at any date in the history of the kingdom of Morgannwg and been aimed at keeping watch against the Vikings instead of seaborne Saxon or Irish raiders.

Other possible sites – and Cadbury Castle. Camulodunum?

Chris Barber prefers the hillfort at Llanmelin near Caerwent, which unfortunately has not yet been excavated.[5] This is at least nearer to the Severn and two major Roman towns, Caerwent and Caerleon, and easier of access for a ruler campaigning across Britain along Roman roads. A Welsh site for 'Camelot' would make more logic than the English candidate of Cadbury Castle, a hillfort massively reconstructed some time after the Roman withdrawal by some powerful ruler which was cited by John Leland in 1540 as being known as Camelot by locals and has had renewed support since Leslie Alcock's archaeological discoveries there in the 1960s.[6] There was great excitement at the time about it being 'Arthurian', and certainly its size and impressive defences and hall suggests a royal residence. But Cadbury's name derives from 'the burgh of Cador', the ruler of Dumnonia around 500, and he is the likeliest candidate for restoring the fortress. The tradition noted by Leland could have arisen at any time over the previous centuries of Arthurian literary works and legends in England, connecting him personally to a place vaguely remembered as the seat of a 'Dark Age' British ruler. Nor is the local village-name of 'Queen's Camel', not recorded until the sixteenth-century, 'proof' that it was associated to Camelot or to Guinevere. Some writers prefer to think that Leland created the identity of Cadbury as Camelot, as a guess aimed at bolstering Arthur's historicity for political purposes. His employer Henry VIII, self-proclaimed 'emperor' within the British Isles and defier of Rome, had every reason to play up Arthur as his illustrious predecessor and exemplar – though he allowed Arthur's shrine at Glastonbury Abbey to be vandalised.

It is very unlikely that 'Camelot' was the major Roman town with the nearest name, 'Camulodunum' i.e. Colchester in Essex. The name is exactly correct – but it is probably coincidence, possibly due to thirteenth-century French poets knowing this to be a major Roman town suitable for a great ruler (from Tacitus?). This site is favoured by John Morris as close to the areas of campaigning against the Saxons in East Anglia and Kent/Sussex,[7] but even if the fifth-century Saxon artefacts found in the area do not mean a Saxon 'conquest' this early the town – if still inhabited – was surely too exposed to enemy attack to be a viable base. There is no indication of post-Roman building on the site. Steve Blake and Scott Lloyd go back to the second French Arthurian romance to mention 'Camelot', the *Perlesvaus* of c.1210–15, and argue that it could have used a genuine early Welsh tradition as the original manuscript was owned by the Fitzalans of Oswestry and the text may thus have been composed for them. The text sites Camelot at the entrance to the kingdom of 'Logres', which according to the twelfth-century *Brut Tyssilio* (or *Y Brenhinedd*) was bordered by the Severn.

From the time of Geoffrey of Monmouth – who may have used Welsh texts – 'Logres' was taken to be the original name of England before the Saxon arrival, with Geoffrey dividing up the island of Britain into the three ancient realms of 'Locrinus', Camber (of Wales) and Alban (of Scotland). In the Welsh text *Enwau Ynys Prydein* ('The names of the Island of Britain') Lloegyr, i.e. Logres, is clearly meant to be England with 'Llundain' as its principal episcopal see and the Hafren (Severn), Thames, and Humber as its main rivers but it is not clear if this text pre-dates Geoffrey's work. Accordingly Blake and Lloyd agree with the editor of the 1937 edition of *Perlesvaus* that Camelot has to be in the Severn valley. They then point to the existence of a River Camlad flowing into the Severn near Montgomery to indicate that Camelot was the post-Roman hillfort which the Normans later took over to build the castle and town of Montgomery.[8] Again, like Llanmelin this site had reasonable access to the Roman road-system across Britain – with the first major town being Viroconium/Wroxeter which was occupied and saw building-work around 500. Viroconium is more logical a site for Arthur's headquarters than Montgomery, given its easier access to the road-system across south-central Britain. If the traditional link of Arthur and 'Logres' derives from pre-twelfth-century Welsh tradition rather than Geoffrey's imagination, it might explain why Arthur is not unequivocally placed in a Welsh dynasty that still ruled in the twelfth-century. This territory around the upper Severn valley had been lost to the Anglian kingdom of Mercia in the mid-seventh-century, so no local tradition had survived to be recorded as Arthur became fashionable in the twelfth-century.

Gellywig – in Cornwall or 'Cerniw'?

The *Triads* place Arthur at three main residences – *Caerleon* in Gwent, *Kellywig* in 'Cerniw', and '*Penryn Rhianedd* in the North'. All are Welsh, at least in most modern scholarly interpretations though the Cornish have long held claim to Gellywig – whose name means 'grove in the wood' so it could be anywhere. (Just because there are 'Kellywigs' in Cornwall does not mean that one of them is 'the' Gelliwig, as similar place-names undoubtedly existed in lands ruled by the British in the sixth-century but then lost to the Saxons and re-named.) But this does not mean that Arthur was remembered accurately by mediaeval (c. 1100–1200) Welsh writers as the early sixth-century overlord of the region, merely that by the time this 'tradition' was written down he was being used as a symbol of their ancient unity – for contemporary political purposes. If the great hero Arthur had unified and ruled all Wales and had been superior to the local princelings, this justified the attempt to unify the region by the rulers of Gwynedd, especially Llywelyn ap Iorweth (reigned 1194 – 1240) in the early thirteenth century, as his 'heirs'.

The three names of his courts certainly seem to refer to distinct regions. If Penryn is specifically named as being the Northern royal residence, the others are presumably the 'central' and the 'southern' ones. Caerleon is in South-East Wales, but is it the central or the southern residence? Penryn may be Dinarth near Penryn Bay in Gwynedd, assuming that the 'North' means the North of Wales not of Britain. The chief elder in the North is given as 'Gyrthmwl Wledig' – an odd title as the epithet of 'Wledig' is usually restricted to major commanders known to history, such as Macsen/Maximus, Emrys/Ambrosius, and Cunedda. *The Songs of the Graves* give this Northern chieftain's burial-site as Celli Frifael in Gower, but the name is similar to that of Garthmyl (the Gaer fort, near Welshpool) so he has been suggested by Mike Ashley as its commander.[9]

Gellywig – or Kellywig – in 'Cerniw' is more contentious. There is still a Gelliwig Farm in Lleyn, though this seems too near the Northern site 'Penryn' for a court that is presumably Arthur's residence in South or West Wales. Some Welsh scholars would argue that Cerniw is a region of Wales – possibly the area around Cardiff or in eastern Powys – rather than the long-favoured Cornwall. The latter identification was first made by translator Lady Charlotte Guest in the 1840s, but 'Cerniw' or 'Kerniw' is an authentic mediaeval name for Cornwall that has survived into modern Cornish. Baram Blackett and Alan Wilson (in *Artorius Rex Discovered*) cite assorted documents that refer to princes of a 'Cerniw' that seems to be South-East Welsh rather than Cornish – it is connected to Arthur's court bishop Bedwin, King Brychan of Brycheiniog, St Cynfarwy (of Llechgynvarwy, Gwent), and Glywys 'Cerniw' the grandfather of St Cadoc (who reigned in Gwent). Culhwch encounters the men of 'Cerniw' in his adventures in the area of Ystrad Yw (near Brecon) with no indication that they are Cornishmen far from home rather than locals. Cunedda's father Einion/Eternus – of the royal line of the Votadini in Lothian, not connected with Cornwall – is named as prince of 'Cerniw' in the early fifth-century, and Bledric 'tywyssog Cerniw' of around 600 is an ally of King Morgan of Glamorgan and Brochwael of Powys against Aethelfrith of Northumbria (victor of the battle of 'Catreath'), at a time when no Cornish prince is likely to have been able to campaign that far north.[10]

Geoffrey of Monmouth's linkage of Arthur to Winchester as 'Kaerguentid' probably originated in Welsh tradition concerning a 'Caer Wynt', which it has been argued that he mistranslated. It may have originally referred to a place in Wales such as Caerwent or Viroconium/Wroxeter. Steve Blake and Scott Lloyd suggest Corwen in Gwynedd,[11] but this is too isolated a site, the name is not derived from the ending 'Wynt', and it was not even a town in the post-Roman era. It is possible that the Roman town of Venta Belgarum, i.e. Winchester, was still held by a British prince around 500 but it is likely to have been far too near the lands of Saxon settlement to have been a secure residence for a British warlord. There was an early Saxon village settlement nearby at Twyford, and the *Anglo-Saxon Chronicle* entries for the early history of the kingdom of Wessex seem to refer to the district around Southampton Water passing into the hands of dynastiuc founder 'Cerdic' (actually a British not Saxon name, ie 'Ceredig') around 500. Cerdic 'took the kingdom' in 500, and was supposed to have fought nearby at Natanleaga' (Netley east of Southampton or Netley Marsh to the West?)

in 508. But Winchester as Arthur's capital was taken up enthusiastically by the mediaeval rulers of England, and the new hall and extended palace built there by Henry III in the mid-thirteenth-century may have been intended to echo Camelot. At some time in the thirteenth-century an appropriate 'Round Table' was built to hang in the hall and presumably be used at 'Arthurian' banquets. In 1486 the Welsh royal descendant and Tudor dynastic founder Henry VII could arrange that his eldest son, to be named 'Arthur', was born in Winchester.

Caerleon – a potential site as it was a Roman fortress?

Caerleon is more probably Arthurian, as it was regarded as his principal court in the twelfth-century legends of the Mabinogi (e.g. '*Culhwch and Olwen*') and in the *Life of St Cadoc*; Arthur's legendary court bishop, Bedwin, has a sandbank nearby named after him.

Geoffrey of Monmouth made it Arthur's principal residence and headquarters, possibly as a logical choice for a major military base due to its legionary fortress and adjoining town. As a local, Geoffrey may have had special access to tradition and his suggestion should not be dismissed out of hand. It has been suggested by Blackett and Wilson that if the Roman legionary camp /city site in the valley at Caerleon had been abandoned by c.500 the Arthurian court was at the nearby hillfort on Lodge Hill, overlooking the bend in the River Usk.[12] This makes more sense for the topography in the Culhwch legend – implying that by the time the latter was written down in its extant form (c.1100?) the author could connect Arthur's court with the site and use its topography. But the hagiography of St Cadoc (see above) seems to imply that Arthur did not rule at Caerleon – at least at one point in his career – as he came to the river from elsewhere in search of a fugitive.

Arthur as a king in Gwent, i.e. the local ruler at Caerleon

The linkage of Arthur to the Silurian ruler of the sixth century was made as early as the later eighteenth-century by John Whittaker (*History of Manchester*, 1775) and later by David Williams in his *History of Monmouthshire* (1796) and William Pughe in *The Cambrian Biography* (1803). Edward Gibbon, citing Whittaker, referred to Arthur as 'hereditary prince of the Silures in South Wales' in his *Decline and Fall of the Roman Empire*.[13]

The earliest but second-hand reference is in a transcript, probably of the Stradling family documents at St Donat's Castle, made in the mid-sixteenth-century by Llewelyn Sion of Llangewydd, Glamorgan, preserved in the Llanover collection. In modern times it has been made at length by Baram Blackett and Alan Wilson, citing the *Llandaff Charters* as more reliable for the sixth-century than most historians would reckon them. Their case is undermined by confusion over their suggestion that Arthur – and Maelgwyn of Gwynedd – should be dated in the 550s and 560s. They also contradict themselves at various points as to where they think Badon should be situated – Mynydd Baedan near Tondu (Glamorgan) or in Scotland? The South Wales case is supported by Chris Barber in *Journey to Avalon* (1993). He conflates this ruler with the Breton saint 'Armel' or 'Arthmael', in a tortuous argument that posits Arthur as recovering from his wounds after Camlann and living on into the 550s as a hermit in Brittany.[14] This does not explain how the Saint's biographers failed to mention his earlier royal career in Britain, as it can be assumed that the earliest hagiographers would have been keen to play up their hero's earlier role as a militant Christian champion in Britain if he had been the victor of 'Badon'. The Saint assisted St Samson (c. 486 – 560) in the overthrow of the tyrannical usurper Conomorus, who had taken over the kingdom of Vannes and exiled its young prince Iudhael, by an alliance of Breton rebels and the Frankish King Chlotar in 560(?). He died in 562. He was apparently of royal Silurian blood according to his Breton biography in the 1490s – rather late, but presumably based on earlier manuscripts – and was referred to as a warrior. Albert Le Grand, in his 1636 biography of Arthmael, claims that he was born in 482 at Boverton in Morgannwg. Barber accordingly suggests that that means that the Saint was the retired soldier-King, now a hermit. But why did not the hagiography specfically say that Arthmael had ruled in South Wales as king of the Silures if he was the same man? It is more likely that he was merely a royal connection of that dynasty, probably through his mother. There may be some confusion here with another 'Artus' remembered in Brittany, the son of a local prince, and/or the Arthmail who was a son of the early sixth-century King Riwal and a princess of Morgannwg.[15]

Chapter 9

'Original' Arthurs. The Silurian Arthur – A Credible Candidate or a Coincidence of Names?

The genealogical connections – Arthwys' sons and the line of Lothian

The crucial argument regarding the Silurian king 'Arthur'/Arthwys, is his dating, as explored above. Which (later) genealogy is the more accurate – that presenting him as a couple of generations later than Pebiau (mid-sixth-century) or the son of a mid-sixth-century Mouric, or that putting Mouric as c.500? The hagiographical evidence of Mouric as earlier than St Samson (b.486?) is seemingly seventh-century, and the later – eleventh-century – account in the 'Life' of St Cadoc putting Arthur's cousin and contemporary Brychan at c500 had no reason to alter dates. How reliable is the evidence in the ' Book of Llandaff' as essentially accurate transcripts, c.1100, of sixth-century detail – and does it put Mouric as alive in the 560s? Is the alleged claim that Mouric outlived this Arthur – or at least lived into his son's middle age – an explanation of the 'warrior Arthur' not being a reigning king? Or is it just a coincidence that this Arthur had the 'right' name and a plausible date to be 'the' Arthur? Come to that, given the evident 820s political 'agenda' and mythologizing of Nennius can we be confident that the 'original' was more than a successful warlord who caught the imagination of later generations? 'King' or not, was he more than winner of a few battles and/or a co-ordinator of a British/Welsh coalition?

But putting this man forward as 'the' Arthur – and thus placing the king of the Silures in the 500s to 530s – presents problems. Not least of these is the etymological one, arising from the widespread poetic attributions of 'Bear'- connections to 'the' Arthur in early Welsh literature and the probability that his name was connected to this. 'Bear-Man' in early Welsh would be 'Arto-wiros' and hence 'Art(h)ur', not 'Arthwys', so were these two separate personal names? If the Silurian ruler was 'the' Arthur, why was he not called straightforwardly 'Arthur' but Arthwys? Or did the latter come to take on qualities of and actions associated with 'the' Arthur only in retrospect, due to the similarity between their names and dates? (And in that case which of the two men was married to 'Gwenhywfar' and by marriage was related to Llew of Lothian?) There is also a problem concerning the dating of Arthwys' son and successor Morgan if he is to be considered as a son of 'the' Arthur. He is recorded (in mediaeval Welsh literature centuries later) as marrying the daughter of Urien/ Urbgen of Rheged (who died c.589) and fighting against Aethelfrith of Northumbria when the latter attacked Powys after the battle of Catraeth c.600, though this data is of uncertain origin. So how was he the son of a man who died around 540? He is claimed to have been the son of Arthwys' third marriage and old age and to have succeeded as an infant. This could reconcile the need to have him active at the end of the sixth-century with the annalistic dating of 'the' King Arthur in the 500s to 530s. But if the information in the early twelfth-century *Book of Llandaff* is to be taken seriously as transcribing genuine early data, Morgan was witnessing charters with his grandfather Mouric[1] – indicating that he was alive before the old King died. If Mouric is to be dated back as adult in the 480s (being grandfather to St Samson, born then) he would have had to be very old to witness charters with someone still able to conduct a campaign c.600 – though it is just about feasible.

In one theory Arthwys' much older elder son, Nowy 'Llacheu'('the Glittering One'?), the intended heir, had been killed in battle at Llongborth as remembered in mediaeval Welsh poems. Nowy is recorded as a son of Arthwys who grants land to Bishop Dyfrig/Dubricius in the *Llandaff Charters*[2] – assuming that the 'revision' of the charters in the early twelfth-century preserved accurate details from this period and that the latter is c.530, both of which Wendy Davies disputes. (This is not the Nowy, son of Arthwys of Dyfed – that man was three generations later than Vortipor, who was alive in the 540s according to Gildas.) The naming of Dyfrig Dubricius in the land-grants however seems to indicate that this Nowy and his father Arthwys *are* dateable to the second third of the sixth-century – the near-contemporary *Life of St Samson* has that Saint, born c.486, ordained by Dyfrig as a young man.[3] The Saint's hagiographer, probably writing in the seventh-century, would have known if it was plausible to date Dyfrig to Samson's time, even if he was – as sceptics claim – associating the two on uncertain evidence.

Another mediaeval claim had it that Arthwys restored Urien and his brothers Llew and Arawn to lands they had lost in Lothian. These men are named in the genealogies of the *Gwyr y Gogledd*, the northern British dynasties of Coel 'Hen's' line, as the sons of Cynfarch 'Oer' – who can be presumed to be the 'St Cynfarch' recorded as a grantee of land from Arthwys in the *Llandaff Charters*. The church of Cynfarch, a.k.a. 'St Kinnemark', presumably his burial-place, is near Chepstow in Gwent. The genealogies place him as fourth in descent from the early-fifth-century Coel 'Hen', along a line of shadowy kings of the Lothian/Northumberland region. He is thus at least early sixth-century in date. Llew married Arthwys' sister Gwyar, daughter of Mouric/Meurig of Siluria, and his sons were Gwalchmai (the original of Gawain?) and Medraut. This marriage must lie behind the legend of 'Lot of Lothian' as Arthur's brother-in-law, and Gwyar is thus presumably the 'original' behind Arthur's legendary sister Morgause – though Geoffrey of Monmouth and his successors did not refer to 'the' Arthur, ally of Llew/ Lot, as a Silurian king.

If Llew had adult sons (Gwalchmai and Medraut) who were the 'originals' of Arthur's eponymous nephews, he was presumably active around 500–530. The *Life of St Kentigern*, founder of the see of Glasgow, presents the Saint (born c. 530) as the daughter's son of 'King Loth of Lothian' who in legend is Arthur's brother-in-law, ie presumably an alternative name for Llew. The eponymous Northern founder-king 'Loth' has been called an invention, but the rest of the details of Kentigern's hagiography are reliable enough so why should this one be different? Urien did not succeed to his kingdom of Rheged until around 560 and was not regarded by the poets celebrating his campaigns as notably aged in the 580s. The father of Llew and Arawn, Cynfarch, is recorded in the 'Gwyr a'r Gogledd' genealogies as marrying Nevyn, the daughter of Brychan (Arthur of the Silures' first cousin), a man who ruled Brycheiniog around 500–20. Nevyn's sister was Gwladys, the mother of St Cadoc who was born around 500; thus logically Gwladys and Nevyn should have been born in the later fifth-century. Thus, Cynfarch is to be located as Nevyn's contemporary, a generation younger than Brychan.[4]

Archaeological evidence for a sixth-century 'Arthur' in Morgannwg: but is this 'the' Arthur?

There are two pieces of archaeological evidence that place a man with a name like 'Arthur' in Morgannwg in the early to mid-sixth century. The 'purists' would argue that as this king was called 'Arthmail' ('bear prince') not 'Arthur' he could not be the same man, and linguistic specialists tie themselves in knots assessing how soon a personal name derived from the Gallo-Brittonic 'Arto' ('bear') could turn into 'Arthur' ('Arto-wiros', 'bear-man'?). The 'Old Welsh' derivation would be 'Arthgur' and only in the ninth-century 'Middle Welsh' would it turn into 'Arthur', according to one version.[5] Other analysts argue for a possible development into 'Arthur' as early as the sixth-century. But how can we be sure that such linguistic 'rules' were universally applied? And the widespread use of names derived from 'arth', 'bear', as personal names in the post-Roman centuries (e.g. 'Arthgen' as well as 'Arthmael') shows that different names were created from one 'root', whether or not the basis was a god's name. It is logical that 'Arthur' could be a nickname for a man with a similar, 'bear'-derived name, and we cannot rule any 'Arthmaels' out as an 'original'.

The 'Ogmore Stone', a record of a land-grant now at the National Museum of Wales found at Ogmore Castle (where a copy was set up), gives 'Arthmail' as granting land to a group of people identifiable as contemporary relatives of St Cadoc – Glywys and Nertat, seemingly Cadoc's brother and aunt – and St Fili (of 'Caerphilly'), traditionally recorded as Gildas' grandson and the son of St Cennyd (of Llangennith in the Gower). The wording runs: 'est omnib(us) quod ded arthmail do et gligws et nertat et fili ep'. '(let it be known that) Arthmail has given this field to God to Glywys and to Nertat and Bishop Fili'.[6]

Arthmail, 'Bear Prince', is likely to be an acronym for 'Arthwys' – and although we cannot be certain how many sixth-century kings were named or nicknamed 'Bear' he is credible as the 'Bear' who Gildas says Cynglas ap Owain served as a charioteer. But is he also the 'Bear' who occupied Dinarth ('Fort of the Bear') in Gwynedd? The likelihood is against it, unless he was a roving warband-leader fighting in other kings' service as a young man. Nertat/Nertan and (St.) Glywys – in this case, Cadoc's grandfather not his brother – are also mentioned in the 'Cunobelinus Cross' stone found nearby at Merthyr Mawr, whose church of the 'Great

Martyr' was connected to a Silurian prince called Poulentius (Paul) who was buried there. Blackett and Wilson claim that this was Arthur's brother, the son of Mouric, due to a stone at the church referring to 'Paul filius Ma...' (i.e. 'Mauricius' / Mouric).[7] Paul of Penychen, Illtud's traditional foe, is another possibility. It is noticeable that the terminology of the 'Ogmore Stone', opening 'let it be known that ...', is similar to that of the land-grants in the *Llandaff Charters*. That would argue in favour of the latter using genuine written information from the sixth-century, however much it was reworked by early twelfth-century monks. Recently claims have been made that the style of the lettering on the Stone is tenth-century not sixth-century; but even if this is correct the extant Stone could just have replaced an earlier one.

The wording of the 'Ogmore Stone' would imply that an 'Arthmail', 'Bear Prince', was ruling in the second third of the sixth century, as a contemporary of Cadoc like the eleventh-century hagiography places him. The only candidate with the right name is the father of Morgan and son of Mouric, as the Arthwys who ruled in Dyfed was a descendant (great-grandson?) of Gildas' contemporary King Vortipor. Dyfed would have had no authority as far East as the Ogwr valley in the early to mid-sixth-century; the area was part of the kingdom of the Silures which became 'Morgannwg'. The 'Arthmail' of the grant may be the same man as the Arthwys who is recorded in the *Life of St Cadoc* (late eleventh-century, but based on earlier sources) as granting Cadoc land at Cadoxton near Neath. But this king could also be the shadowy local sub-king Arthwys ap Einudd, father of Gwrgan 'the Freckled'.[8] It is unlikely that this ruler of the Neath area held authority as far east as Merthyr Mawr either; the rulers who Illtud had to evade when he settled in the area c.500 were 'Paul of Penychen' and Meirchiaun of Gwent. The cantref of Penychen included part of this district.

The Llantwit stone and the alleged burial of Arthur in Glamorgan

An inscription at Llantwit places 'Artmali tecani' – 'Arthmael the dead' or just possibly 'the ruler/overlord' – as a contemporary of the local abbot, St Samson, a South Wales saint mainly active in Brittany who died c.560.[9] The one problem with this inscription is its reference to a king called 'Ithael' who is more likely a seventh-century ruler, son of Morgan who died in 664/5 – this suggests that 'Samson' may not be the Breton Saint. Blackett and Wilson have also argued that the story in the '*Life*' of St Illtud of him receiving the body of a high-ranking personage which had arrived by sea and burying him at his cave on the banks of the River Ewenny (Chapel Hill, Merthyr Mawr) refers to the burial of Arthur after Camlann. They claim that he was reburied in an extant cave in the woods of Coed-y-Mwstwr near Pencoed and ultimately at a site by the Church of St.Peter on the ridge of Mynydd y Caer a few miles away (also linked by them with the monument erected to the councillors of Vortigern massacred by Hengest c. 450) They allege that the 'mystery' ('anoeth') linked to the site of Arthur's burial in the literary tradition is a play on words indicating the name of the site in Coed-y- Mwstwr. But they skirt round the fact that the '*Life*' calls the subject of the burial a 'most holy man' not a king.[10]

The 'anoeth' could also be linked to the cave at Merthyr Mawr's Chapel Hill where Arthur was besieged by the 'Wen Pendragon' (see section on the *Triads*). But it is not certain that the author of the stanzas on Arthur's burial-place – as late as the ninth- or tenth-century? – would have known the local name of the supposed site and been able to make the connection. And if Arthur was taken to the 'island of Afallach' for medical treatment after the battle and died he would more likely have been buried there, or at a nearby church, not smuggled off by sea to Illtud's cave. In any case, as Arthur's cousin Illtud would probably have recognised him – or members of his 'escort' – even if he was not told who he was helping. The king would have been mentioned by name in whatever source Illtud's biographer used – or at least called a king not a holy man if Illtud had kept quiet about his exact identity. Moreover, the placing of the burial in the biography of Illtud puts the event as occurring when the Saint was living in his cave in the lands of the hostile ruler Meichiaun of Gwent, possibly before he founded his school. The pupils at the school included an adolescent Maelgwyn, who was an adult King by c.520, and St Paul Aurelian (born c.486), so the incident probably took place earlier than that date and the deceased is unlikely to have been a King 'Arthur' who died c. 539. If it refers to Arthur, it should come right at the end of Illtud's life. It should also be noted that the – eleventh-century? – *Llandaff Charters* which mention Meurig and Arthwys as witnesses have the 'abbot of Illtud' as a witness and an 'abbot of Cadoc', i.e. of Cadoc's monastery at

Llancarfan near Cowbridge.[11] The references in the charters thus seem to post-date the foundation of these men's monasteries, which in Cadoc's case was some time post-520.

Arthur's father – why was Mouric not identified as such if he was really this man?

Any reliance on the Morgannwg genealogy as evidence of 'the' Arthur's identity comes up against the fact that none of the Arthurian legends record his father as Mouric. His mother is stated to have been Igraine (Ygyr, daughter of Amlawdd 'Wledig') not Mouric's wife Onobrawst. The Welsh sources are in agreement in naming Ygyr, whose sisters are supposed to have been the mothers of the hero Culhwch (in *Culhwch and Olwen*) and of St Illtud; she is never linked to Mouric, nor is Mouric referred to under any sobriquet similar to 'Uther'. The mediaeval Welsh pedigrees, brought together by Rachel Bromwich (R. Bromwich, A. O. Jarman, and B.F. Roberts, eds., *Arthur of the Welsh*, 1991), name Yygyr's parents as Amlawdd 'Wledig' and Gwen, daughter of Cunedda – thus placing Arthur at three generations after Cunedda who lived around either 400 or 440.[12] Amlawdd is unplaceable in date or location, and indeed his name is unusual for a British prince and has been linked to the Danish 'Amleth' (the original of 'Hamlet'). If he was a 'Wledic', why has no tradition survived of the location of his kingdom?

The mysterious 'Uther Pendragon', Arthur's father in all stories from the time of Geoffrey, only appears in the early Welsh traditions as the employer of a certain 'Mabon' or 'Mydron' in a dialogue between Arthur, Cai, and 'Gwlywd'. The reference in this poem may mean that Mabon/ Mydron was the servant of the 'wonderful/awe-inspiring Head Dragon (i.e. over-king)' not of a man called Uther; it is not definitive evidence for the Welsh poet regarding Uther as a personal name. In another poem, 'uter' is used of Arthur himself as a 'wonderful/awe-inspiring councillor' and is clearly not a separate person.[13] As we have seen, in the ninth-century–eleventh-century Welsh poems 'Uther Pen Dragon' is a man known by that name, not a 'wonder-working' epithet for a character with a different personal name; but he is an 'enchanter' not a king. This is far from the persona of King Mouric.

None of Mouric's other sons who are named in early genealogies of the Silurian dynasty seem to have survived into Arthurian legend as connections of the great king. They included Idnerth and Comereg, abbot of Moccas near the Golden Valley in Ewias. Frioc, brother of this Arthwys ap Meurig, was apparently killed by Arthwys' son Morgan – at least according to the grant of lands in penance for it in the *Llandaff Charters*. If Arthur was really the Silurian prince, how come the latter's brothers never appeared in the stories taken up by Geoffrey? His Uther's family is thus clearly not derived precisely from Meurig's. But Mouric's daughter (Anna or Gwyar) and her marriage into the royal house of Coel 'Hen' in Lothian did survive as far as Geoffrey of Monmouth's text and the *Brut Tyssilio*. Her Northern husband Llew ap Cynfarch was turned into 'Lot of Lothian' in the Anglicized stories – the early sixth century 'king of Lothian' who was grandfather of the founder of Glasgow cathedral and bishopric, St Kentigern?

Blackett and Wilson, the major proponents of Arthwys of the Silures as 'the' Arthur, argue that the man named as Arthur's father in all sources, Uther Pendragon, was an honorific not a personal name – it meant 'the awe-inspiring Head Dragon', i.e. chief ruler. A 'Funeral Ode' to a great commander identified as Arthur, the '*Mawrnad Uthyr Pendragon*', was published in the *Myrvyrnian Archaeology* in 1801, and used the word 'Uthyr' in the sense of meaning 'wonderful' not as a personal name. Recent analysis suggests that it is ninth- or tenth-century, i.e. as valuable evidence as the *Triads*. It referred to Arthur as the 'kinsman of Caesar', presumably meaning the dynastic link with Magnus Maximus, and as vanquisher of the family of Caw 'of the Wall', Gildas' father, as in mediaeval Welsh legend.[14]

'Arthur mab uthr', 'Arthur the awe-inspiring', could be misinterpreted as 'Arthur son of Uthr'. The alternative reading is of 'mab uter' – as used by 'Nennius' – as 'wonderful son'. However, 'Uthyr' *was* a personal name – the Welsh derivation of 'Victor', a Roman name whose most famous holder was the eldest son of Emperor Maximus, Arthur's ancestor according to legend. So was Uther active in the later fifth century, as a noble or a 'wise man' wonder-worker? Arthur would then be his (illegitimate?) son, and Geoffrey of Monmouth picked up and expanded this story that he had found in his famous 'ancient book', be it Welsh or Breton. The odds must however be against this 'Uther' as a great king, as an overlord who reigned for around fifteen years and continued Ambrosius' victories would surely have left more of a trace on early Welsh traditions. If 'Victor'/Uther was Arthur's father and also a king, he is unlikely to have been a memorable ruler in the manner of 'Vortigern', Ambrosius, and the North British ruler Urien of Rheged.

Other Candidates

The son of King Aedan of Dalriada

Despite southern Scottish place-names and connections with Arthur, not least Arthur's Seat, it seems likely that the eponymous prince 'Artuir' of Dal Riada in the 570s – promoted as a possible 'original' by Richard Barber in the early 1970s – is too late to have fought the traditional Arthurian campaigns. He was probably named after the 'original' by his ambitious father, the great war-leader King Aedan mac Gabhran who ruled from c.568 to 590. Aedan, the greatest ruler of the century in the new kingdom of Dal Riada established around 500 by Irish settlers from Ulster in Argyll ('Coast of the Gael'), was the pre-eminent ruler of northern Britain in the second half of the sixth-century. The story known today of the establishment and early history of his kingdom owes more to subsequent myth than to sound contemporary evidence, requiring a note of caution in dealing with it. As with the early Welsh evidence, most of it (a few early chronicle entries apart) was written down in its extant form centuries later as a 'foundation myth' for the kingdom and so was a heroic 'saga' to play up the deeds of the listeners' ancestors rather than a scholarly study. Indeed, although the kingdom was allegedly founded by the ancestor of the later dynasty, Fergus 'the Great', c.500 in an emigration from Ulster, there seem to have been Irish settlers in Argyll for centuries before that. (The dynastic legends were also confused over which member of his family was the first to move to Scotland.) It is not clear to what extent his Irish immigrants inter-married with the local Britons, the Epidaii tribe in Argyll, and were thus a mixed Gaelic-British people in the sixth-century; their Irish descent may have been more marked among the nobility (who preserved heroic poetic traditions of their ancestors) than widespread. Despite the best efforts of John Morris, it is an unlikely conclusion that any powerful British overlord like 'Arthur' could have had the influence on Ulster to invite or require a local prince such as Fergus to move to Argyll as an ally against the Picts.

The early history of the kingdom is obscure even by sixth-century standards, but traditionally saw a rotation in the succession among the families of Fergus' son Domangert's sons Comgall and Gabhran. The first powerful ruler was Aedan, son of Gabhran, who succeeded around 574 through the backing of the newly-arrived Celtic Christian mission from Ireland under his distant cousin St Columba (Columcille). The first known ruler in Britain to be anointed as king by a bishop and according to Columba's biographer Adomnan recommended to the Saint by an angel,[15] he clearly ruled in alliance with the Church organization set up in his lands by Columba as a force for stability and divine legitimization. Militarily powerful and backed by the church, he was thus the sort of ruler to be attracted by stories of a similarly successful 'Arthur'. In any event, he called his son (and probable junior co-ruler) by that name. The young man was killed in battle against the Picts ('Maetae') near the Antonine Wall in 596 according to the Irish *Annals of Tigernach* – eleventh-century but probably transcribing early documents – and intriguingly fought his father's Irish overlord Baetan in 574.[16] At best he may have fought battles in the Lennox area which were later attributed to the Welsh 'Arthur', though it would seem unlikely that the heroic deeds of a prince of Dal Riada would have been muddled up with those of a Celtic prince by later bards.

The other Welsh candidates

The 'Arthur'/Arthwys who ruled in Dyfed in the second half of the sixth century, descendant of Gildas' contemporary Vortipor, is also probably too late to be the 'original'. He may have been called after him and/or contributed some of the Welsh place-names associated with him in later tradition, having a son and successor called Nowy like the Arthur of Welsh myth. He might have been the king who clashed with St Padarn, whose monastery of Llanbadarn was in Dyfed, and have been the father of the 'Amhar/Amr' recorded as being buried near Wormelow in Herefordshire. (It is possible that 'Amr' as a name is a mistaken interpretation; the word may refer to the site as being the source of the river 'Gamber'.) But he is too late to have been referred to in the *Gododdin* as a great warrior, and is clearly distinct from the 'Arthwys' of Siluria contemporary with Dyfrig and Cadoc. The later Arthwys, ap Rhys ap Ithael, of Morgannwg is approximately dateable to the late seventh-century to early eighth-century (his great-grandson Ffernfael died in 775) and is far too late, as is Ffernfael's son Arthwys – though Mike Ashley suggests that he may have fought local battles against the Saxons that were taken up by later bards.[17] But how could a minor prince of Morgannwg have ended up as a hero remembered in Powys and Gwynedd as a predecessor to be emulated?

Ashley also suggests that if Wendy Davies' dating of the *Llandaff Charters* is accepted and King Mouric placed at c.600, his son and co-ruler Arthwys could have fought Saxons from Wessex – around the Severn valley in the early seventh-century. This could explain the locale of the final battle of ex-King Tewdric at Tintern, which is far west for a Saxon army fighting around 470–80. The history of the Severn valley in the sixth-century and early seventh-century is largely a blank, though it is assumed that the victory of King Ceawlin of the 'Gewissae'/West Saxons over three British kings at Deorham (Dyrham near Chipping Sodbury?) brought it under the control of his kingdom after c.577. Could a late sixth-century or early seventh-century Arthur of Siluria/ Morgannwg have fought the Saxons here? But in this case, why would evidently minor victories that did not make it into Anglo-Saxon records produce such an inspiring effect that the victor was taken up as a national Welsh hero? Why did the Welsh not take up Cadwallon of Gwynedd, who destroyed the power of Northumbria and killed King Edwin, in 632/3, as their inspiration? Or Urien of Rheged, about whom Taliesin had written inspiring later sixth-century poems so his role as a heroic warlord was clearly known? The court of Gwynedd in the 820s, where 'Nennius' was commissioned to write his works, had no reason to take up the cause of an obscure prince of Morgannwg. At the very least, Arthur was celebrated as a formidable warrior even if not yet an anti-Saxon one, as already known by the composer of the *Gododdin* by c.600. Nor can modern literary experts comfortably write off all post-sixth-century Welsh authors and oral poets as devoid of reliable written or oral sources and so totally ignorant.

There are two 'Arthurs' (or one man entered in two separate lists?) in the genealogies of the 'Men of the North', one of them the father of the mid-sixth-century king Pabo 'Pillar of Britain'. He, and possibly the other Arthur too (Arthwys ap Mar ap Ceneu ap Coel) if they are two men rather than one person, ruled in the Pennines within reach of the Anglian settlers of Deira. Thus they could have fought battles against them, campaigned in Lindsey/Linnuis, or marched north to fight battles around the Forth easier than a South Welsh or Dumnonian ruler. Local enthusiasts have noted that one of the kings of Coel's line ruling York was called Elidyr/Eleutherius 'of the Great Army'. Could this army have been inherited from a successful warlord called Arthur earlier in the century? But both these men appear to be mid- rather than early sixth-century, and neither is connected to the 'original' Arthur in Welsh tradition. Nor are there any local battle-sites with names similar to those on Nennius' list, apart from possible sites for Glein, Dubglass in Linnuis, and 'City of the Legion' (York?). Any Pennines or Yorkshire 'Arthur', 'dux bellorum'/'leader of battles', would have been closely connected to the scattered lordships of the dynasty of Coel 'Hen', not to events and persons in Wales. These Arthurs are more likely to have been called after a great commander of the preceding generation than to be 'the' Arthur.

There is nothing implausible in the theory that 'Arthur' commanded a force of cavalry that used the Roman roads to campaign all over Britain, not least in Scotland, despite the sneers of modern sceptics. King Rhun of Gwynedd could march north to Gododdin in the 570s(?) and king Edwin of Northumbria march south to Wessex in 626. It is unproven that Arthur's name was 'added' to other men's victories to extend his reputation, except with one possible battle of Urien's in Rheged. We do not know for certain that no sixth-century king or warlord had a 'reach' that extended across all of central and northern Britain. But some historians now prefer to argue that the Welsh place-name connections attributed to him only spread after Britons carrying stories of him were driven out of his original area (the north?) and settled there, or that tales travelled along the trade-routes.

Arthur in Cornwall – the finds at Tintagel

One theory places him in Cornwall, where there are strong topographical connections (of uncertain antiquity) though no early literary evidence. How much of this depends on a eleventh- or twelfth-century assumption that 'Cerniw' must be 'Cornwall', following the assumptions of Geoffrey of Monmouth but with no other literary basis, is unclear. The fact that Cornwall was part of the major British kingdom of the south-west in the fifth- and sixth-century, Dumonia, and the amount of modern archaeological discoveries at relevant sites makes it still a major area of investigation. After an initial enthusiasm for digging in the 1920s, led by the pioneer of Glastonbury excavations Ralegh Radford, another burst of activity followed in the 1970s as the discovery of an impressive post-Roman hillfort at Cadbury Castle in Somerset revived optimism about uncovering 'Arthurian' relics in Dumonia.

This was stimulated by the discovery of secular settlement at his legendary birthplace, Tintagel, in recent years, to add to the earlier twentieth-century 'digs' which had uncovered a seemingly monastic site on the rocky peninsula near the thirteenth-century castle. This was accompanied by the finding in 1998 of an inscribed stone referring to 'pater coli avi fecit artognou' – translated as 'Artognou, father of a descendant of Coll'.[18] The name of the latter seems Irish, appropriate for an area open to Irish settlement in the fifth-century, and it is not a direct equivalent of 'Arthur'. But it has revived the local Arthurian claims, as the site now seems to be more of a secular base than the potential monastery that it was initially assumed to be by Ralegh Radford's exacavations. 'Arthur' could have been born at a royal hall on the peninsula, with erosion meaning that substantial parts of the Dark Ages 'royal enclosure' may have fallen into the sea.[19] (The current castle was the work of Henry III's brother Richard, Earl of Cornwall and elected claimant to the Holy Roman Empire.) But it is not clear how old the linkage of Arthur to the area is, even if Geoffrey of Monmouth (the earliest extant source for it) used earlier Welsh or Breton books which mentioned Cornwall. The 'King Arthur's Bed' and 'King Arthur's Hall' on Bodmin Moor may have been named at any time before the eighteenth-century when they were first mentioned. Gorlois/ Gwrleis, the 'Duke of Cornwall' and supposed husband of Ygraine/ Ygyr who, Arthur's father Uther seduced, is suspiciously absent from the Welsh genealogies of the rulers of Dumnonia though local kings' genealogies may not have survived. March/Cunomorus and Tewdric are not in the Dumnonian genealogies either, but their names survived through separate literary traditions. Gwrleis may have been the local king at Tintagel, or at a Dark Ages enclosure at St Dennis near St Austell where the nearby farm of Domellick could be the 'Damelioc' associated with him by Geoffrey of Monmouth. The linkage of Arthur and Mark as foes in the Tristram stories might indicate that they ruled nearby kingdoms, thus locating Arthur to Cornwall, but it is not clear how early this connection arose.

The identity of Arthur's court at Cylliwic/Gelliwig as the hillfort at Killibury (Kelly Rounds) near Wadebridge is fiercely defended by protagonists of a Cornish Arthur, and opposed by the Welsh scholars who insist that 'Cerniw' is Gwent not Cornwall. The Cornish evidently had a fierce pride in Arthur as a local hero by 1113, when Hermann of Laon (in his *Miraculi S. Mariae Laudunensis*) records that a fund-raising tour by canons of Laon Cathedral in 'Dunaxaveria', i.e. the former Dumnonia in the West Country, ran into trouble there. Having had Arthur's 'seat' and 'oven' (still landmarks) pointed out to them by their guides, they caused a riot in Bodmin by refusing to believe that Arthur would return.[20] This does not however mean that he was a local Cornish dynast, as opposed to a British over-king and/or 'national' general whose memory survived strongest in the areas of his activity which were still inhabited by Britons. What it may indicate is that 'Arthur' campaigned in or had personal associations with the Dumnonian kingdom – more likely for a South Wales prince than for the 'Arthur' who appears in the pedigree of the family of Coel 'Hen' in the north. The biographer of St Carantog, c. 1120, certainly associated him with Cador of Cornwall and Dunster.

Arthur of the 470s? The evidence of the Gallic campaign

Geoffrey Ashe, meanwhile, concentrates on the origin of the story in Geoffrey of Monmouth that Arthur fought a campaign in Gaul in the time of the Emperor Leo (reigned 457–474), and links him to a British ruler who fought there in 469. This man, 'Riothamus' ('High King') of the Britons according to Jordanes' *History of the Goths*, brought 12,000 men to a campaign in the Loire valley to assist the Roman authorities as they struggled to reassert their control over northern Gaul against assorted local rulers and roaming brigands. The participants in the chaos included Saxons on the Loire, and it appears that 'Riothamus' moved south-east from Armorica to link up with the Romans in a 'pincer' movement. He achieved initial success, but was defeated and disappeared after a battle at the significantly-named Avallon in Burgundy.[21] This is not the grand invasion of Gaul to take power from the Romans as supposed by Geoffrey; Emperor Leo – the ruler in Constantinople, and patron of the weak Western Emperor Anthemius – was 'Riothamus' ally not enemy, and there is no 'tribune Frollo' or general Lucius Hiberius. But it is the only time when a British ruler is recorded in Continental sources as active in the area.

The 1019 *Life of St Goeznovius*, a Breton saint, portrays Arthur as campaigning in Gaul c.470,[22] and Ashe supposes that Geoffrey used this story in constructing his account of Arthur's Gallic war. Thus Riothamus contributed at least a major part of the Arthurian legend and could have defeated the Saxons in Britain in the 460s. Ashe supposes that if an 'Arthur' fought at battles c.500 he could have been a second man with this name, or else commanded the force set up by the 'original' – the cavalry force known as the 'Arturiani'? Again, the theory presents major problems of dating, given the stronger Welsh traditions linking him to events and personalities of the early sixth-century. 'Arthur' as 'Riothamus' is far too early to have fought at a battle of Badon around 490 to 516, and Badon cannot be dated as early as the 460s by any ingenious theory. Indeed, the story of the intervention in Gaul traditionally comes at the end of Arthur's career, and Riothamus' ally Emperor Anthemius was installed on the Western Roman throne by Emperor Leo of the East in 468 so Badon would be earlier than that. This compresses the events of the seemingly long Saxon wars and the pre-Arthurian career of Ambrosius into too short a period, given that the *Gallic Chronicle*, a contemporary source unlike Gildas or Nennius, dates the main Saxon revolt at 441/2. But it still leaves us with the question as to who 'Riothamus' was if he was indeed a ruler in Britain who came to the aid of Roman Gaul – was he 'Ambrosius', or an unknown king of Dumnonia? The only possible Breton candidate appears to be an obscure fifth-century king called 'Iann Reath', of unknown British connections.[23]

Conclusion – the Silurian ruler is the likeliest candidate. But….

If an 'Arthur', a commander called or known by his nickname as 'the bear', is to be placed in a definite kingdom instead of being a successful general who fought for assorted sovereigns, the obscure Silurian ruler is closest in date. He is the only 'Arthur' in a royal genealogy who can – though distinguished scholars still deny this – be put into the early sixth-century. The Welsh literary evidence shows that 'the' Arthur was not remembered as a placeable 'King' of a well-known 'kingdom', but as a roving warrior-hero. This would argue against the Silurian ruler being 'the' Arthur, unless the legends were distortions of dim memories of his exploits before he gained his father's throne – in which context Mouric's exceptionally long reign would be significant. This Arthur could have fought as a roving commander for assorted kings across Britain as a young man when he was only the heir to his long-lived father in Siluria, and succeeded to his father's throne when already the victor of Badon and in his forties or fifties – or predeceased him if Mouric lived into the 550s? It is possible that too much emphasis has been placed on the fact that some Llandaff charters have Mouric and Morgan witnessing land-grants together, without Arthwys. Might the absent Arthur have been fighting outside Siluria at the time rather than being dead? It is equally possible that no grants by Arthwys as sole King have survived, and this has been wrongly interpreted as meaning that he predeceased his father.

Is it possible that there were two Arthurs active in Wales in the early sixth-century – one the son of Meurig, ie his aged father's colleague in the south-east, who predeceased him or not, and the other a Welsh warlord/general not of (legitimate) royal blood? The latter could have held authority over the Severn valley, lands later lost to the Saxons so no traditions of this survived into Welsh literature, and up via Viroconium into eastern Powys and Gwynedd. He may not have been a legitimate son of an existing dynasty, but a self-made warlord; hence he did not appear in the royal genealogy of Powys or Gwynedd. He would then have been the main rival of Maelgwyn over ruling North Wales, and could have ruled at Dinarth in Clywd as an 'outpost' hillfort keeping guard on his Western frontier (or as a young warlord in Ambrosius' lifetime). In that case he would have centred his campaigns on Viroconium and the Severn valley, using the road-network to travel across Britain, and the later rulers of the area (Eastern Powys) like Cyndylan would have considered themselves his heirs as stated in literature. But he left no sons and was not a legitimate prince of the royal houses of either Gwynedd or Powys, so he does not appear in extant genealogies. It is possible that the prince of Morgannwg named in the Llandaff Charters was named after his older contemporary, 'the' Arthur who won the great battles against the Saxons, and that subsequent genealogists muddled the two up. 'The' Arthur could have been a composite of two men – a wandering heroic 'mercenary', who attracted Fionn-like stories, and Ambrosius the victor of the Saxon wars. But once again, Arthur recedes into the area of ambiguity – in which he has been placed since at least the 820s.

Conclusion. Arthur's Return?

Arthur's departure for 'Avalon' (or wherever) was a staple of myth by Geoffrey of Monmouth's time and was thus present in the Welsh legends that he used, though it does not appear in 'Nennius' despite the latter's openness to other unlikely stories (e.g. that of the dragons in the pool under Dinas Emrys). As we have seen, as early as the ninth-century or tenth-century Arthur was regarded as immortal with his grave nowhere to be found – without any indication of a link to any 'Avalon'. Arthur's miraculous survival in the 'Otherworld' or lying asleep in a cave in Britain did not find their way into his list of 'Mirabilia'. The adventures of the fund-collecting monks of Laon in Cornwall in 1113, when their prosaic denial that Arthur was still alive caused a riot in Bodmin, show that it had penetrated Cornish folklore by then and was a talisman for patriotic local Britons hoping he would return to lead them to victory. This notion was therefore present in popular consciousness by 1113, presumably spread by travelling poets (Welsh or Breton?), but not yet in literature. To Cornish patriots, the 1113 story plus the Tintagel legend showed that Arthur was really Cornish, not Welsh.

To Geoffrey of Monmouth c.1135 Arthur was clearly mortally wounded at Camlann, and his departure for an unlocated island in the company of a party of women did not mean that he was still alive there.[1] The point at which the ambiguous notion of Arthur being 'summoned from human activity' was transformed into his survival is unclear, but was probably enhanced by the increasing 'otherworldiness' attributed to his escorts. Morgan was human to Geoffrey, but Arthur's escort 'Argante the elf-queen' in Layamon's '*Brut*' (c. 1190) was evidently non-human. Once the wounded Arthur was taken to have been carried to a specifically magical location, his survival there became logical. The probable catalyst for this was earlier Welsh and Irish myth related to the 'Otherworld', where sojourners were 'suspended in time' and if they returned to the human world were surprised to discover that a few days or months in the Othrworld had turned into centuries in the human one. The most famous example of this was in Irish myth, where Fionn's son Oisin accompanied an elf-lady to 'Tir na n'Og' in his own time, presumably the third-century AD, and returned to find that it was the fifth-century and the era of St Patrick. Thus the literary story of Arthur's removal to 'Avalon' by the mysterious ladies after Camlann added to the reasoning for his survival which was already present in popular culture by 1113.

The idea was impossible for 'serious' writers of 'factual' histories to accept even in the twelfth-century, which may be reflected in William of Malmesbury's irritation at the ridiculous stories being told of Arthur in his time (c. 1125) as well as Geoffrey's attempted realistic explanation. In addition, it presented a political threat to the 'Celtic' British peoples' new Anglo-Norman sovereigns, both in Cornwall and from the post-1081 invasions in parts of Wales. Would the myth of Arthur's return be used to inspire 'Celtic' resistance to their overlords, and even in a revolt if a 'new Arthur' appeared to lead them? The idea of Arthur as inspiration for a Welsh military revival, as we have seen, was certainly present in the 820s at the court of Gwynedd and was used by 'Nennius' to inspire his countrymen, probably at his patron king Merfyn's request. Similar notions of a heroic Welsh military leader as inspiration for a revival to drive the Anglo-Saxons out of England had been seen in the 'Armes Prydein' prophecies of the 930s, aimed at the new 'empire' of Athelstan – but 'starring' the seventh-century hero Cadwaladr, mythically the last Welsh king of all Britain. Now it took on a religious aura, as the 'Second Coming' of Arthur – a man already implicitly compared to Christ by 'Nennius'. Accordingly, it is clear that the fortuitous 'discovery' of Arthur's alleged remains at Glastonbury Abbey in 1190/1 was politically useful for the Angevin dynasty in showing that he was definitely dead and would not lead the Welsh to victory in a revolt. The current King of England and overlord of much of Wales, Richard I, was away on Crusade at the time and so is very unlikely to have 'stage-managed' the discovery despite its political usefulness (there had been disorders in Wales on the death of his father Henry II in 1189). Richard seemingly saw himself as Arthur, as by 1190 he had a sword believed to be Excalibur in his possession and presented it to his ally King Tancred of Naples and Sicily. The discovery did not however end the Welsh and Cornish stories of Arthur's survival, as Giraldus Cambrensis was still fulminating about them in his '*Speculum Ecclesiae*' around 1215.[55]

The 'official' literary version of the Arthurian story continued to mention the King's departure in a boatload of ladies led by Morgan after Camlann, though now maintaining that he had died. In the French '*Roi Mort Artu*' of c.1230, the third part of the *Vulgate* trilogy and used as the basis for Malory's version, Arthur died of his wounds 'off-stage' and his tomb was shown to Lancelot when the latter arrived from his exile, too late to save his King and fellow-knights. From now on, the location of the tomb could be placed at Glastonbury with the discoveries of 1190/1 as 'evidence'. In 1278 Edward I, the final conqueror of Wales and an Arthurian enthusiast, staged an elaborate re-burial there at a magnificent new shrine – with the added bonus of showing the Welsh that their hero would not return to save them. Five years later he finally annexed Gwynedd, building a string of castles around its perimeter to hold it down – including the grandest at 'Macsen Wledig's mythical residence, Caernarfon. The Glastonbury shrine survived to the Reformation, but so did the popular version of the story in which Arthur lay asleep in a cave somewhere in Britain ready to return and save his people – now not just the Welsh – in their hour of need. Now he was accompanied by his knights with their steeds, and mediaeval stories referred to what happened when a traveller found the cave – accidentally or at the invitation of a 'guardian'. The Welsh version of the tale placed him on Mount Snowdon, in an area with ancient Arthurian associations since the story of him fighting the local giant Ritta Gawr – and within reach of several of the putative sites for Camlann, in Lleyn or Snowdonia.[56] An English version placed him at Alderley Edge, where a local farmer was invited to place his horse at the disposal of the sleeping knights by a mysterious old man (probably the wizard Merlin) in a story still commemorated by an inn-sign and used by the children's author Alan Garner. (The occupant of the cave was not specifically named as 'Arthur' until the local writer Elizabeth Gaskell's time, the early-mid Victorian period.) An alternative south-western version, recorded in the early-mid sixteenth-century by Ellis Gruffydd, linked him to Cadbury Castle and had his men riding out sometimes at night. The Scottish version placed him under a mountain near Melrose, in an area of Arthurian (and Votadini) associations. One Gwynedd story placed him underneath Mount Snowdon, and connected him to a cairn on a high pass there – though the latter might also suggest a story where he had been buried there (after a battle of Camlann in the area?). In the 1210s the writer Gervase of Tilbury also recorded how he had been told while visiting Sicily that Arthur and his knights were asleep under Mount Etna – a story transmitted to the Norman Kingdom of Sicily in the twelfth-century by Anglo-Norman or Breton 'fans' of the legends?

The story of Sir Bedivere being required to cast away Excalibur in a lake near the Camlann battlefield only appears in the early thirteenth-century in French versions, possibly influenced by local pre-Christian practices and/or Alan tribal legend; many swords have been found in 'Celtic' lakes, apparently ritually placed there. This was quickly adapted into local English lore with sites being found for this episode too – the Cornish one being at Dozmary Pool. It formed an appropriate climax for the saga, and was still being used in Rosemary Sutcliff's conclusion to '*Sword at Sunset*' in the 1950s – while the Monty Python team teased their viewers with the reminder that relying on 'ironwork distributed by strange women in ponds' was not an adequate method of selection for government. In that, as in so much else, the Arthurian stories were still being used for contemporary reinterpretation 1500 years after the time of any 'original'.

Notes

Introduction

1. William of Malmesbury, *History of the Kings of Britain*; part 1, as 'The Kings Before the Norman Conquest', trans Joseph Stevenson 1844 (Llanerch reprint 1989) p. 11.
2. *The Gododdin*, edited Kenneth Jackson (Edinburgh 1969).
3. Nennius, *Historia Brittonum*, chapter 50.
4. *Annales Cambriae*, sub. Anno 516, 537.

Chapter One

1. *The Anglo-Saxon Chronicle*, ed Michael Swanton (Phoenix 1996) p. 11.
2. *Ammianus Marcellinus*, History, trans Walter Hamilton (Penguin 1986), book 27, chapter 8 (pp. 342–3).
3. *Archaeology Journal*, vol 102 (1945), p.30; Oliver Rackham, *History of the Countryside* (Phoenix 1986) p. 75; Petra Dark, *Britain and the End of the Roman Empire* (Tempus 2000).
4. Peter Heather, *The Fall of Rome and the End of Civilisation* (Oxford UP 2005).
5. D.N. Brooks, 'A Review of the Evidence for Continuity in British Towns in the Fifth and Sixth Centuries' in *Oxford Journal of Archaeology* no. 5, part 1 (1986) pp. 77–102; on Viroconium, see R. White and P. Barker, *Wroxeter: Life and Death of a Roman City* (Tempus 1998) and R. White, *Britannia Prima* (Tempus 2005).
6. Sidonius Apollinaris, *Epistles*, nos. 3 and 9.
7. Procopius, *Persian Wars*, book 2, chapter 22.
8. Procopius, *Gothic Wars*, book 4, chapter 20.
9. *Anglo-Saxon Chronicle*, ed Swanton, pp. 16–17.
10. Francis Byrne, *Irish Kings and High Kings* (Four Courts Press, Dublin 2001).
11. Gildas, *De Excidio Britanniae*, chapters 18–19; Zosimus, *New History*, book 6, chapter 5.
12. Gildas, chapter 21.
13. Gildas, chapter 26.
14. For the latest opinions on 'settlers, invaders, or peaceful acculturation' see Catherine Hill, *The Origins of the English* (Duckworth 2003).
15. Bede, *Ecclesiastical History*, book 3, chapter 2.
16. Rackham, p. 75; also see Francis Pryor, *Britain AD*.

17. *Journal of Roman Studies*, vol 21, p. 232.
18. *Anglo-Saxon Chronicle*, ed Swanton, pp. 18–19; also eg BL Harleian Mss. 3589. See also collection edited by Peter Bartrum as *Early Welsh Genealogical Tracts* (University of Cardiff Press, 1966).
19. Geoffrey of Monmouth, *History of the Kings of Britain*, trans Lewis Thorpe (Penguin 1966).
20. Nennius, chapter 1.
21. Oliver Padel, 'The Nature of Arthur' in *Cambrian Mediaeval Celtic Studies* vol 27, pp. 1–31.
22. Orosius, book 7, chapter 35.
23. Gildas, chapter 13.
24. *The Mabinogion*, trans Jeffrey Gantz (Penguin 1976) pp. 118–27, especially 118–22.
25. *The Life of St Gildas*, chapters 10–11 (Cymmrodorion Society, London 1899). *Geoffrey of Monmouth*, trans Thorpe, pp. 133–4.
26. V.E. Nash-Williams, *Early Christian Monuments in Wales* (1950) pp. 123–5.
27. Nennius, chapter 62.
28. Gildas, chapter 33.
29. *Geoffrey of Monmouth*, ed. Thorpe, 1966, p. 132 for Helena as daughter of British king 'Coel'.
30. BL Harleian Mss. 3589.
31. Lindsay, *Arthur And His Times*, pp. 70–92.
32. See Rachel Bromwich, ed, *Trioedd Ynys Prydein: the Welsh Triads* (1978): *Triad* 80, series 1; also Nennius, chapter 46.
33. Orosius, book 7, chapter 35.
34. De Situ Brecheniau: *Genealogy* no. 10.
35. Baram Blackett and Alan Wilson, *Artorius Rex Discovered* (Cardiff 1985) pp. 72–4.
36. *Geoffrey of Monmouth*, trans Thorpe, p. 133.
37. John Morris, *The Age of Arthur*, pp. 50–1.
38. *Archaeological Journal*, vol 89 (1932) pp. 202–19.
39. *The Notitia Dignitatum*, ed O Seck (Berlin 1876, reprinted Frankfurt 1962).
40. T.F. O'Rahilly, *Early Irish History and Mythology* (Dublin 1946) p.209.
41. *Ammianus*, p. 342; also A. Parson, *The Roman Saxon Shore Forts: Defences of Coastal Britain* (Tempus 2000).
42. *Anglo-Saxon Chronicle*, ed Swanton, pp. 14–15.
43. *Zosimus*, book 6, chapter 5.
44. *Chronica Minora*, quoted in Lindsay, pp.167–8.
45. *Anglo-Saxon Chronicle*, ed Swanton, pp. 12–13; Gildas, chapter 20.
46. Morris p. 51.
47. *Salvian, De Gubernatio*, book 4, chapter 21; book 5, chapters 18 and 51–6; book 7, chapter 91.
48. *Fastidius, De Re Christiana*, book 4, chapters 11 and 14 (Trans R.S. Haslehurst, *Society of SS Peter and Paul*, 1927).

49. Gildas, chapter 21.
50. R.G. Collingwood and J.N. Myres, *Roman Britain* (Oxford UP 1932).
51. Bromwich, ed, Trioedd Ynys Prydein, p. 444; also discussion in M.P. Charlesworth, *The Lost Province.*
52. *Geoffrey of Monmouth*, trans Thorpe, pp. 200–01.
53. Lindsay, pp. 125–40.
54. Rhigyfach, *Life of St David*: chapter 22 on his austerity.
55. Constantius, *Life of St Germanus*, chapters 17–18.
56. A. Barrett, 'St Germanus and the British Mission' in *Britannia*. Vol 40 (2009) pp. 197–217.
57. T O'Rahilly, *The Two Patricks* (Dublin 1957); J. Carney, *The Problem of St Patrick: A History of Christianity in Fifth Century Ireland* (Dublin 1961).
58. Rhigyfach, chapters 2–4.
59. Blake and Lloyd, pp. 135–8, quoting the *Triads* (NLW Peniarth Mss. 16).
60. Constantius, *Life of St Germanus*, chapter 26.
61. Gildas, chapter 21.
62. C Snyder, article in *Arthurian Studies*, vol 64.
63. T. Wilmott, *Birdoswald: Excavations of a Roman Fort on Hadrian's Wall and Its Successor Settlements 1987–92* (London 1997).
64. W.F. Skene, *The Fourt Ancient Books of Wales*, Edinburgh 1868; Rachel Bromwich, 'Concepts of Arthur' in *Studia Celtica*, vol 10/11, 1973–4, pp. 167–81. For the 'Artuir of Dalriada' theory, see Richard Barber, *The Figure of Arthur*, Totura, New Jersey, 1972. See also summary in Mike Ashley, *Mammoth Book of King Arthur*, pp. 294–303.

Chapter 2

1. Nennius, chapter 48.
2. See P. Bartrum, *EarlyWelsh Genealogical Tracts* (Cardiff 1966).
3. Nicholas Higham, *King Arthur: Myth-Making and History* (Routledge 2002)
4. Nennius, chapters 31, 43–7.
5. Ibid, chapter 44. And see David Dumville, 'Nennius and the Historia Brittonum' in *Studia Celtica*, vol 10–11 (1975–6), pp. 78–95.
6. Nennius, chapter 31.
7. Bede, *Ecclesiatical History of the English People* (ed Judith McClure and Roger Collins, Oxford UP 1969) pp. 26–7.
8. Nennius, chapters 32–5. Mike Ashley, *The Bumper Book of King Arthur*, pp. 119–21. *Anglo-Saxon Chronicle*, ed Swanton, pp. 12–13.
9. David Dumville, 'Sub-Roman Britain: History and Legend' in *History* vol 62 (1977) pp. 173–92; J.E. Turville-Petre, 'Hengest and Horsa' in *Saga-Book of the Viking Society* (1953–7) pp. 273–90.
10. Gildas, chapters 25–6.
11. *Geoffrey of Monmouth*, trans Thorpe, pp. 150–1.
12. *Vita Pauli Aureliani*, in Albert Le Grand's *Breton Saints' Lives* (Paris 1636, revised edition 1901).

13. Gildas, chapter 25.
14. Nennius, chapter 66.
15. *Anglo-Saxon Chronicle*, ed Swanton, pp. 12–13.
16. *Geoffrey of Monmouth*, pp.166–9.
17. Ibid, pp. 196–7.
18. Ibid, pp. 198–200.
19. *Brut Tyssilio*, ed Manley Pope (London 1862) p. 96.
20. Steve Blake and Scott Lloyd, *Keys to Avalon*, pp. 85–6.
21. As note 17.
22. P. Sims-Williams, 'Gildas and the Anglo-Saxons'.Green, pp. 145–6.
23. As implied in *Geoffrey of Monouth*, p. 212, Uther must have reigned for 15–16 years as Arthur was conceived early in his reign and succeeded him aged 15.
24. *Geoffrey of Monmouth*, pp. 199–211. 25.
25. Blackett and Wilson, pp. 162–5 from *Artorius Rex Discovered.*
26. Green, p. 145.
27. J.T. Koch
28. Green, pp. 145–6.
29. As n. 23.
30. *Lives of the Cambro-British Saints*, ed Reverend William Jenkins Rees (1853), 'Life of St Carantog' chapter 4; also Jack Lindsay, *The Age of Arthur*, pp. 274–5.
31. Green, pp. 145–6.
32. Brut y Brenhinedd: *Llanstephan Mss.* version, ed B.F. Roberts (Dublin 1971) and BL Harleian Mss. 3589 pedigrees.
33. National Library of Wales: Peniarth Mss. 183, no. 24.
34. A.O.H. Jarman, 'Arthurian Allusions in the Black Book of Carmarthen' in P Grout et al, eds, *The Legend of Arthur in the Middle Ages* (Cambridge UP 1983) pp. 99–112. P. Sims-Williams in R. Bromwich, A.O.H. Jarman, B. Roberts and D. Huws, eds, *The Arthur of the Welsh* (Cardiff 1991) pp. 46–7; J Rowlands, *Early Welsh Saga Poetry: A Study and Edition of the Englynion* (Cambridge UP 1990).
35. *Anglo-Saxon Chronicle*, ed Swanton, pp. 13–14.
36. As n. 53; and Green, pp. 78–9.
37. Green, pp. 78–9. Barber and Pykitt, pp. 111–12.

Chapter 3

1. *William of Malmesbury*, ed Stevenson vol 1: *The Kings Before the Norman Conquest* (Llanerch reprint 1989) p. 11. William, *De Antiquitate Glastoniae Ecclesiae*, ed. and tr. John Scott, Boydell 1981.
2. *Geoffrey of Monmouth*, tr. Thorpe, p.51. See also J.E. Lloyd. 'Geoffrey of Monmouth' in *English Historical Review*, vol lviii, 1942, pp. 460–8; Stuart Pigott, 'The sources of Geoffrey of Monmouth' in *Antiquity*, vol xv, 1941, pp. 269–86.

3. Ashley, pp. 335–9.
4. Geoffrey Ashe, *Avalonian Quest*, pp. 58–9, 68–72.
5. *Gesta Henrici II et Ricardi I*, by Roger of Hoveden, ed W. Stubbs (Rolls Series, 2 vols, 1867) vol ii p. 159.
6. E.K. Chambers, *Arthur of Britain* (1927) pp. 280–1.
7. A. Allan, 'Yorkist propaganda: pedigree, prophecy and the 'British History' in the reign of Edward IV' in C. Ross, ed, *Patronage, Pedigree and Power in Later Mediaeval England* (Goucester 1979).
8. Ashley, pp. 343–4.; pp. 445–6, quoting 'Histoire de Guillaume le Marechal'; pp. 356–62. C. Hardyment, *Malory: The Life and Times of King Arthur's Chronicler* (Harper Perennial 2006) pp. 279–316.

Chapter 4

1. R.G. Collingwood and J.N. Myres, *Roman Britain*, 1932.
2. Ashe, pp. 68–73.
3. Rodney Castleden, *King Arthur: The Truth Behind The Legend* (Routledge 2000) pp.225–6.
4. Tacitus, *Annals of Imperial Rome*, trans Michael Grant (Penguin 1956) pp. 327–8. '*Anglo-Saxon Chronicle*, ed Swanton, pp. 14–15.
5. R.W. Hanning, *The Vision of History in Early Britain* (London 1966).
6. D. Kirby and J. Carwyn Wilson, 'Review of "The Age of Arthur"' in *Studia Celtica* vol 10–11 (1975–6) pp. 454–86.
7. David Dumville, 'Sub-Roman Britain: History and Legend' in *History*, vol 62 (1977) pp. 173–92.
8. Philip Ratz review of C. Thomas book on Tintagel in *Cornish Archaeology* (1993) pp. 178–80; Oliver Padel, 'The Nature of Arthur' in *Cambrian Mediaeval Celtic Studies*, vol 7 (1994) pp. 1–31.
9. T.M. Charles-Edwards 'The Authenticity of the Gododdin: A Historian's View' in R. Bromwich and R.B. Jones, eds, *Studies in Old Welsh Poetry* (Cardiff 1978) pp. 44–71; also his 'The Arthur of History' in R. Bromwich, A.O.H. Jarman, B. Roberts, and D. Huws, *The Arthur of the Welsh: The Arthurian Legend in Mediaeval Welsh Literature* (Cardiff 1991) pp. 15–32.

Chapter 5

1. *The Mabinogion*, trans Jeffrey Gantz (Penguin 1976) pp. 66–82.
2. P. Mac Cana, The Mabinogion (Cardiff 1982) pp. 39–42. Also P.K. Ford 'On the Significance of some Arthurian names in Welsh' in *Bulletin of the Board of Celtic Studies*, vol 30 (1983) p. 272. Albert of Aachen, *Historia Ihersolimitana*, trans and ed S. Edgington (Oxford UP 2007), chapter 46; *Gesta Francorum*, trans Rosalind Hill (Penguin 1962), book 14; analysis in T. Asbridge, 'The Holy Lance of Antioch: Power, Devotion and Memory in the First Crusade' in *Reading Mediaeval Studies* vol 33 (2007) pp. 3–36.
3. R. Baigent and H. Lincoln, *The Holy Blood and The Holy Grail.*
4. Procopius, *The Wars.* Ashe, *Avalonian Quest*, pp. 258–62.

5. M. Ashley, pp. 411–18.
6. R. Bromwich, 'First Transmissions to England and France' and I. Lovecy, 'Historia Peredur ap Efrog' in Bromwich, Jarman, Roberts and Huws, *The Arthur of the Welsh*, pp. 273–98 and 171–82.
7. *Mabinogion*, ed Gantz, p. 86.
8. Ashley pp. 436–7.
9. Ibid, p. 333.
10. Ibid, pp.332–3.
11. Baram Blackett and Alan Wilson, *The King Arthur Conspiracy* (Cardiff 2003).
12. Ibid.
13. *Navigatio Sancti Brendani.*
14. Tim Severin, *The Brendan Voyage* (McGraw Hill and Co. 1978); Barber and Pykitt, p. 138.
15. National Library of Wales, Peniarth Mss. 4; *Mabinogion*, trans Gantz, p. 156.
16. Jesus College Oxford Mss. 119 (*Life of St Beuno*), chapter 24.
17. Ashley, p. 424.
18. Ibid, p. 423.
19. Wolfram von Eschenbach, *Parzival*, ed Andre Lefevre (Continuum 1991), p. 124.
20. Geoffrey de Villhardouin.
21. Jacobus de Voragne, *The Golden Legend*, trans William Granger Ryan, 2 vols (Princeton UP 1993).
22. See article on Lugh in Peter Beresford Ellis, *Dictionary of Celtic Mythology* (Oxford UP 1998).
23. *Britannia Internet Magazine* 2000 article on the Marian Chalice.
24. Ashley pp. 429–36.
25. David Keays, Catastrophe: An Investigation into the Origins of the Modern World (Random House 1999).
26. Mabinogion, trans Gantz, pp. 178–91.
27. BL Harleian Mss. 3589 genealogies; as reinterpreted by Baram Blackett and Alan Wilson in their series of books especially *Artorius Rex Discovered* (Cardiff 1985).
28. Ashley p. 437.
29. Ashe, *Avalonian Quest* pp. 30–1.
30. Ibid.
31. Ifor Williams, *Lectures in Early Welsh Poetry* (Dublin 1954) and J.T. Koch, 'When Was Welsh Literature First Written Down?' in *Studia Celtica*, vol 20–21 (1985–6) pp. 43–66; also Roger Loomis, 'The Spoils of Annwn: AN Early Welsh Poem' in his *Wales And The Arthurian Legend* (Cardiff 1956) p. 131; and J.T. Koch, 'Gleanings From the Gododdin and Other Early Welsh Texts' in *Bulletin of the Board of Celtic Studies* vol 38 (1991) pp. 111–18.
32. See Green, *Concepts of Arthur*, pp. 47–8, 55–9, 80–981, 112–14, 118–22.

33. Green, pp. 80–1, 84, 112–15, 119–21.
34. Green, pp. 84 and 121.
35. *Mabinogion*, trans Gantz, pp. 140–8.
36. P. Sims-Williams, 'The Early Welsh Arthurian Poems' in Bromwich et al, *The Arthur of the Welsh* (1991) p. 50.
37. Oliver Padel, *Arthur in Mediaeval Welsh Literature* (Cardiff 2000) pp. 50–1.
38. Padel, 'The Nature of Arthur' in *Cambridge Mediaeval Celtic Studies* vol 35 (1994) pp. 1–31.
39. Green, pp. 47–8, 63–6, 157–9, 167–8, 251–2.
40. Green, pp. 55–6, 165–7.
41. *Geoffrey of Monmouth*, p. 223.
42. Blake and Lloyd, p. 118, 224, 233; Barber and Pykitt, p. 72: Ashley, p. 384.
43. Ibid, pp. 382–4.
44. Linda Malcor, *From Scythia To Camelot* (1999).
45. Padel, as note 38; also Padel, 'Recent Work on the Origins of the Arthurian Legend: A Comment ' in *Arthuriana*, vol 5, no. 3 (1995); Kemp Malone, 'The Historicity of Arthur' in *Journal of German English and Germanic Philosophy* vol 23 (1934) pp. 463–9; Malone, 'Artorius' in *Modern Philology*, vol 22 (1924–5) pp. 367–74.
46. Green pp. 181–2.
47. Padel, p. 31; Green, pp. 182–3.
48. David Dumville, 'Sub-Roman Britain: History and Legend' in History, vol 62 (1977) p. 173–92; ibid, *Histories and Pseudo-Histories of the Insular Middle Ages* (Variorum Press 1990). Green p. 188.
49. Green, as n. 46 and ibid, p. 188.
50. Nicholas Higham (2002). *Nennius*, chapters 40–2.

Chapter 6

1. P.K. Ford, 'On the significance of some Arthurian names in Welsh' in *Bulletin of the Institute of Celtic Studies* vol 30 (1989) pp. 268–73.
2. *Mabinogion*, trans Gantz, pp. 68, 154.
3. In *Triad* series 3, no. 109, in the *Red Book of Hergest.*
4. Nennius, *Historia Brittonum*, ch. 73.
5. Green, pp. 160–1, 168–9.
6. Rachel Bromwich, *Trioedd Ynys Prydein* (Cardiff 1978) pp. 417–18.
7. P. Sims-Williams, 'The Early Welsh Arthurian Poems' in Bromwich et al, *The Arthur of the Welsh* (1991) p. 199; Morris p. 104–6; Green pp. 78–9.
8. *Triad* no. 47.
9. P. Bartrum, *A Welsh Classical Dictionary* (1993) p. 212.
10. Steve Blake and Scott Lloyd, *The Keys to Avalon*, pp. 202–5.
11. *Myvyrian Archaeology*, 2nd edition (Gee and Son, 1870): transcript of 'Conversation Between Arthur and his Second Wife Gwenhwyfar'; also translation by Mary Williams in *Speculum* vol 13 (1938) pp. 38–51.
12. Geoffrey of Monmouth, *History of the Kings of Britain*, trans Thorpe, p. 257.

13. Blackett and Wilson, pp. 204–5.
14. Ashley p. 457.
15. Ibid p. 454.
16. P. Sims-Williams, 'The Earliest Arthurian Poems' in Bromwich et al (1991), as note 10; and 'Culhwch and Olwen' in *Mabinogion*, trans T. Jones and Jones (1948) pp. 107–8.
17. Green, pp. 80–3, 136.
18. Ashley p. 467.
19. Green pp. 82–3.
20. Roger Loomis, 'The Spoils of Annwn: An Early Welsh Poem' in Loomis, *Wales and the Arthurian Legend* (Cardiff 1956) pp. 161–4; I Foster, 'Culhwch and Olwen and Rhonabwy's Dream' in Loomis, ed, *Arthurian Literature in the Middle Ages* (Oxfod 1959) p.34; A.O.H. Jarman, 'The Arthurian Allusions in the Black Book of Carmarthen' in *An Arthurian Tapestry* (Glasgow 1983); Rachel Bromwich and D.S. Evans, ed, *Culhwch and Olwen: An Edition and Study of the Earliest Arthurian Tale* (Cardiff 1992) p. 74.
21. Ashley pp. 441–2, quoting Joseph Lot.
22. Lleminawc also appears in the *Triads* (Trioedd Ynys Prydein, no. 65) as one of the 'Three Wanderers of the Isle of Britain', and in the Stanzas of the Graves (no. 50).
23. Ashley p. 573.
24. Linda Malcor and C Scott Littleton, *From Scythia to Camelot* (1999).
25. Ashley pp. 443–4.
26. *Mabinogion*, trans Gantz, pp. 158, 163–6.
27. Green, pp. 58, 156.
28. P.K. Ford (1983) p. 271.
29. *Mabinogion*, trans Gantz, p. 140; *Geoffrey of Monmouth*, trans Thorpe, p.212.
30. Ashley p. 334, quoting Linda Malcor.
31. Barber and Pykitt, pp. 131–4; Blackett and Wilson, pp. 88 and 133–4.
32. Ashley p. 402.
33. Geoffrey Ashe, *The Quest for Arthur's Britain* (Pall Mall Press 1968) p. 21.
34. Barber and Pykitt, pp. 132–3, 151.
35. As note 34..
36. C. Groome, *The Giants of Wales: Cewri Cymru* (Lampeter 1993) pp. 249–316. P.T. Koch, 'Further To Tongu Do Dia Toinges: Mo Tuath etc' in Etudes Celtique, vol 29 (1992) pp. 255–6, and ibid, 'The Celtic Lands' in M. Lacey, ed, *Mediaeval Arthurian Literature: A Guide To Recent Research* (New York 1996), p. 261. Blackett and Wilson p. 243.
37. *Life of St Illtud*, chapter 18.

Chapter 7

1. Gildas, chapter 32.
2. K Jackson, 'Gildas and the Names of the British Princes' in *Cambridge Mediaeval Celtic Studies* vol 3 (1982).

3. Gildas, chapter 27.
4. J Morris, in *Arthurian Sources* vol 6 (Phillmore 1977) p. 77.
5. Gildas, chapter 27.
6. Gildas, chapter 10.
7. Ibid chapter 24; and see Petra Dark, *Britain and the End of the Roman Empire* (Tempus 2000).
8. P. Dark article in *Antiquity*, 2004, see Bibliography
9. See Michael Jones and John Casey, 'The Gallic Chronicle Exploded?' in *Britannia*, vol 22, 1991, pp. 211–16.
10. Gildas, chapter 25.
11. Bede, chapter 16.
12. Castleden, p. 108.
13. Analysis in David Dumville, 'The Welsh Latin Annals' in *Studia Celtica* vol 12–13 (1977–8) pp. 461–7.
14. Gildas, chapter 26.
15. Bartrum, *A Welsh Classical Dictionary* (National Library of Wales 1993) pp.112–13, and A Wade-Evans, *Welsh Christian Origins* (1934) p. 181.
16. Blake and Lloyd p. 208.
17. See Hugh Williams, trans, *Two Lives of Gildas* (LLanerch 1990) and Higham, *The English Conquest: Gildas and the Sixth Century* (1994) pp. 90– 6.
18. K. Jackson, 'The Arthur of History' in Loomis, *Arthurian Literature of the Middle Ages* (1959).
19. *The Gododdin of Aneirin*, ed J.T. Koch (Cardiff 1997) p. 23.
20. *The Gododdin*, ed Ifor Williams (Cardiff 1938)
21. As surmised by J. Stuart Glennie in his history of early Scotland in 1869.
22. K. Jackson in *Antiquity* (March 1939).
23. J.T. Koch 'Gleanings from the Gododdin and other early Welsh literature' in *Bulletin of the Board of Celtic Studies* vol 38 (1991) pp. 111–18.
24. Oliver Padel, *Arthur in Mediaeval Welsh Literature* (Cardiff 2000).
25. Alistair Moffat, *Arthur and the Lost Kingdoms* (Edinburgh 1999).
26. J.B. Coe and S. Young, *The Celtic Sources for the Arthurian Legend* (Llannerch 1995) pp. 100–01.
27. Green, pp. 48–9.
28. Kathleen Hughes, 'The "A" Text of the Annales Cambriae' in N Lacey, ed, her *Celtic Britain in the Early Middle Ages* pp. 80–6.
29. J.T. Koch, 'The Celtic Lands' in *Mediaeval Arthurian Literature: A Guide to Recent Research* (New York 1996) pp. 239–327.
30. *Annales Cambriae*, ed J. Morris, in his *Arthurian Sources*: volume 8 (Phillimore 1980): entry for AD 518.
31. Ibid, entry for AD 539.
32. *Geoffrey of Monmouth*, trans Thorpe, p. 217.
33. T.M. Charles-Edwards, 1970.
34. Bromwich and Evans, eds, *Culhwch and Olwen* (Cardiff 1992).

35. J.T. Koch, 'Gleanings from the Gododdin' (1991), and ibid, *The Gododdin of Aneirin: Text and Context from Dark Age Britain* (197) pp. cxxviii, 90–3, 208–9.
36. National Library of Wales; Peniarth Mss. 77.
37. In Rachel Bromwich, ed, *Trioedd Ynys Prydein* (3rd edition, Cardiff 2006).
38. Ashley pp. 224–31.
39. *Lives of the British Saints*, ed Rev. William Jenkin Rees (Cardiff 1853):Life of St Cadoc.
40. Ibid, Life of St Illtud, chapter 2.
41. Ibid, Life of St Carantog.
42. Ibid, Life of St Padarn, chapter 21; see also J.P. Tatlock, 'The Dates of the Arthurian Saints' Lives' in *Speculum* vol 14 (1939) pp. 349 ff.
43. As note 40.
44. Green, p. 103: Coe and Young (1995) p. 39.
45. As surmised in Oliver Padel's theory of Nennius referencing the Old Testament. Oliver Padel, 'The Nature of Arthur' in *Cambridge Mediaeval Celtic Studies* vol 27 (1994).
46. David Dumville, 'Nennius and the Historia Brittonum' in *Studia Celtica* vol 10–11 (1975–6) and Peter Field article in *Studia Celtica* vol 30 (1996). N. Higham, *King Arthur: Myth-Making and History* (Routledge 2002).
47. *Nennius*, chapter 73.
48. *Nennius*, chapter 50.
49. H.M. and N.K. Chadwick, *The Growth of Literature* (Cambridge UP 1932).
50. Guy Halsall, *Worlds of Arthur*, pp. 169–71.
51. K. Jackson, 'Once Again Arthur's Battles' in *Modern Philology* vol 43 (1945/6) pp. 44–57.
52. W.F. Skene in his *Chronicles of the Picts and the Scots* (Edinburgh 1867).
53. Blake and Lloyd, pp. 103–9.
54. P. Sims-Williams in Bromwich, Jarman, and Roberts, *The Arthur of the Welsh* (1991) pp. 33–71.
55. Ashley, pp. 184–5, 287–8.
56. *Anglo-Saxon Chronicle*, tr. Michael Swanton, pp. 14–15.
57. Blake and Lloyd, p. 106; Barber and Pykitt, p. 116; Ashley, pp. 135–8; Green, pp. 210–14.
58. Blake and Lloyd, ibid; Barber and Pykitt, ibid; Ashley pp. 138–9.
59. Green, p. 207.
60. Blake and Lloyd, p. 106; Ashley, p. 143; Green p. 208.
61. Ashley, pp. 143–4; Barber and Pykitt, p. 120.
62. Blake and Lloyd, p. 108; Barber and Pykitt pp. 121–2; Ashley pp. 144–6.
63. Green, pp. 84–5, 9–21; P. Sims-Williams, in Bromwich et al, *The Arthur of the Welsh* (1991) pp. 40–2.
64. K. Jackson, 'Arthur's Battle of Bregouin' in *Antiquity*, vol 23 (1949) pp. 48–9;
65. Barber and Pykitt, pp. 122–3.

66. A. Anscombe, 'Local Names in the "Arthuriana"', in *Zeitshchrift Fur Celtische Philologie*, vol 5 (1904) pp. 103–23.
67. *Nennius*, chapter 56.
68. *Gildas*, chapter 16.
69. Barber and Pykitt, pp. 125–30; Blake and Lloyd, pp. 108–10; Blackett and Wilson, pp. 113–20; K. Jackson, 'The Site of Mount Badon' in *Celtic Studies* vol 2 (1953–8) pp. 152–5.
70. Listed in Nennius' 'Mirabilia'.
71. Jesus College Oxford Ms. 111: *The Red Book of Hergest.* Interpretations in Blackett and Wilson, pp. 117–18.
72. Malory, *Morte d'Arthur* (Oxford UP 1998), p. 39.
73. Ashley, pp. 47–8.
74. Barber and Pykitt, pp. 49-50, 100–01, 105; Ashley, pp. 155-6, 611.
75. Blake and Lloyd, pp. 119–24 and 184-6.
76. Philip Holmes, *King Arthur: The Military History* (1996) and Morris, *Age of Arthur* (1973).
77. Barber and Pykitt, pp. 131–5.
78. Castleden, pp. 183–8.

Chapter 8

1. Blackett and Wilson, pp. 138–47.
2. *Mabinogion*, trans Gantz, pp. 140–7.
3. Ashley, pp. 565–7.
4. Blackett and Wilson, pp. 30–7 and 48–58.
5. Barber and Pykitt, pp. 46–9; Blake and Lloyd, p. 116.
6. Castleden pp. 149–50.
7. J. Morris, pp. 138, 283.
8. Blake and Lloyd, pp. 116–17.
9. P. K. Ford (1983) pp. 268–73; Ashley p. 206.
10. Blake and Lloyd, pp. 42–3; Blackett and Wilson pp. 64–70.
11. Blake and Lloyd, pp. 53, 119.
12. *Mabinogion*, tran Gantz, pp 147–8.
13. Gibbon, vol 4 p. 94.
14. Barber and Pykitt, pp. 145–55, 168.
15. Ibid, p. 87.

Chapter 9

1. *Liber Landavensis*, ed W.S. Rees (Cardiff 1983), list of charters: notably the phraseology 'Be it known that…' is the same as that on the Ogmore Stone.
2. Ibid, book 2, section 10.
3. *Life of St Dubricius*, chapter 4.
4. *The Chronicle of the Kings of Britain translated from the Welsh copy attributed to Tyssilio*, trans P. Roberts (1881, Llanerch reprint 2000) p. 146. R. Bromwich et al, *The Arthur of the Welsh* (1991) pp. 5–6; A. Ross, *The Folklore of Wales* (2001) p. 46; Coe and Young (1995) p. 11.

5. Green, p. 190; P. Schrijver, Studies in *British Historical Phonology* (Amsterdam 1995) pp. 151–2; K. Jackson, *Language and History in Early Britain* (1953) pp. 392–3; Higham (2002) p. 74.
6. Blackett and Wilson, pp. 171–2.
7. Ibid, p. 216.
8. Blake and Lloyd, pp. 116–17.
9. Barber and Pykitt, p. 99.
10. *Life of St Illtud*, chapter 22.
11. Barber and Pykitt, pp. 80–2.
12. Quoted in Bromwich et al, *The Arthur of the Welsh* (1991).
13. *Ymddiddan Gwyddneu Garanhir a Gwynfab Nudd*, verse 22: see Green pp. 160–2.
14. Ibid, lines 10 and 12.
15. Adomnan, *Life of St Columba*, book 3, chapter 6.
16. Ashley pp. 296–7.
17. Ibid, pp. 298–303.
18. Castleden, pp. 64, 225–6.
19. Ibid, p. 170.
20. Lindsay, *Arthur and his Times* p. 102.
21. Jordanes, *Getica*, book 45, chapters 237–8.
22. G. Ashe, 'A Certain Very Ancient Book' in *Speculum*, vol 56 (1981) pp. 301–23.
23. Ashley, pp. 62, 127.

Conclusion

1. *Geoffrey of Monmouth*, trans Thorpe, p. 261.

Bibliography

Leslie Adams and James Carley, eds, *The Archaeology and History of Glastonbury Abbey*, Boydell and Brewer, 1991.
Leslie Alcock, 'South Cadbury Excavations 1968' in *Aniquity*, vol 43, 1969, pp. 52–6.
——, 'South Cadbury Excavations 1969' in *Antiquity*, vol 44, 1970, pp. 46–9.
——, *Arthur's Britain*, Penguin 1971.
——, *Cadbury Castle, Somerset*, Univ. of Wales Press 1995.
Ammianus Marcellinus, The Later Roman Empire AD 353–78, tr. Walter Hamilton, Penguin 1986.
The Anglo-Saxon Chronicles. tr. and ed. Michael Swanton, Phoenix 1996.
Geoffrey Ashe, *King Arthur's Avalon*, Collins 1957.
——, *From Caesar to Arthur*, 1960.
——, *The Quest for Arthur's Britain*, Pall Mall Books 1968.
——, 'A Certain Very Ancient Book', *Speculum*, 56 (1981), pp, 301–23.
——, *The Discovery of King Arthur*, Bebretts, 1985.
——, 'The Origins of the Arthurian Legends', *Arthuriana* vol 5, no. 4, aut. 1995, pp. 1–24.
Mike Ashley, *The Mammoth Book of King Arthur*, Constable 2005.
Chris Barber and David Pykitt, *Journey to Avalon: the Final Discovery of King Arthur*, Blorenge Books (Abergavenny), 1993
R. Barber, *The Figure of Arthur*, London/Totura, New Jersey, 1972.
——, *King Arthur: Hero and Legend*, Boydell Press, 1986 edition.
——, *The Holy Grail: Imagination and Belief*, Allen Lane 2004.
S. Baring-Gould, *A Book of Brittany*, Methuen, 1901.
S. Baring-Gould and J. Fisher, *Lives of the British Saints*, Society of Cymmrodorion, London 1913.
P. Barker, *Wroxeter: Roman City Excavations 1960–80*, 1981.
W. Barron and S. Weinberg, ed, *Layamon's Arthur: the Arthurian Section of Layamon's 'Brut'*, Longmans 1989.
R.C. Barrowman, C.E. Batey, and C.D. Morris, *Excavations at Tintagel Castle, Cornwall 1990–1999*, London 2007.
P.C. Bartrum, *Early Welsh Genealogical Tracts*, University of Wales Press 1966.
Steve Bassett, ed, *The Origins of Anglo-Saxon Kingdoms*, Leicester UP, 1989.
Martin Biddle, *King Arthur's Round Table*, Boydell Press 2000.
Baram Blackett and Alan Wilson, *Artorius Rex Discovered*, Cardiff 1986.

Steve Blake and Scott Lloyd, *The Keys of Avalon: the Compelling Journey to the Real Kingdom of King Arthur*, Rider 2003.
G. Bowen, The Travels of St Samson of Dol, *Aberystwyth Studies* vol xiii, 1934.
——, *The Settlements of the Celtic Saints in Wales*, University of Wales Press, 1956.
——, *Dewi Sant* (St David), University of Wales Press, 1963.
A. Breeze, 'Historia Brittonum and Arthur's Battle of Mons Agned', in *Northern History* vol 40, no. 1, March 2003, pp. 167–70.
R. Bromwich, *Armes Prydein*, Institute of Advanced Studies, Dublin 1972.
——, 'Concepts of Arthur', in *Studia Celtica*, vol 10–11, 1975–6, pp. 163–81.
——, *Troedd Ynys Prydein: the Welsh Triads*, University of Wales Press, 1978.
R. Bromwich, A.O.H. Jarman and B.F. Roberts (eds), *The Arthur of the Welsh*, University of Wales Press 1991.
R. Bromwich and D.S. Evans, *Culhwch and Olwen: an Edition and Study of the Oldest Arthurian Tales*, University of Wales Press 1992.
The Brut y Brenhinedd, Cotton Cleopatra Version, ed. J.J. Parry, *Mediaeval Acedmey of America*, 1937.
The Brut y Brenhinedd, Llanstephan Mss. 1 Version, ed. Brynlle Roberts, Institute for Advanced Studies, Dublin 1971.
Brut Dingestow, ed. Henry Lewis, University of Wales Press, 1942.
A. and T. Burkitt, 'The frontier zone and the siege of Mount Badon: a review of the evidence for their location', in *Proceedings of the Somerset Archaeological and Natural History Society*, vol 134, 1990, pp. 81–93.
Francis Byrne, *Irish Kings and High Kings*, Four Courts Press, Dublin 2001.
J. Carney, *The Problem of Patrick: A History of Christianity in Fifth Century Ireland*, Dublin 1961.
Rodney Castleden, *King Arthur: the Truth behind the Legend*, Routledge 2000.
Richard Cavendish, *King Arthur and the Grail*, Weidenfeld and Nicolson 1978.
Nora Chadwick, *Celt and Saxon*, Cambridge UP, 1963.
——, 'The Colonization of Brittany from Celtic Britain', in *Proceedings of the British Academy*, vol 51, 1965, pp. 235–99.
E.K. Chambers, *Arthur of Britain*, Sidgwick and Jackson, London 1927.
Jon Coe and Simon Young, *The Celtic Sources for the Arthurian Legend*, Llanerch 1995.
R.G. Collingwood, 'Arthur's Battles', in *Antiquity*, vol 3, 1929, pp. 292–8.
R.G. Collingwood and J.N. Myres, *Roman Britain*, Clarendon Press 1932.
R. Collins and J. Gerrard, eds, *Debating Late Antiquity in Britain AD 300–700* (Oxford UP 2004).
J. Cotterill, 'Saxon raiding and the role of the Late Roman coastal forts' in *Britannia*, vol 24 (1993) pp. 223–39.
J.C. Crick, 'The British Past and the Welsh Future: Gerald of Wales, Geoffrey of Monmouth and Arthur of Britain', in *Celtica*, vol 23, 1999, pp. 60–75.
Michael Curley, *Geoffrey of Monmouth, Twayne's English Author Series*, New York 1994.

K.R. Dark, *Civitas to Kingdom: British Political Continuity AD 300–800*, Leicester UP, 1994.
——, 'A Famous Arthur in the Sixth Century' in *Reading Mediaeval Studies*, vol 26 (2000), pp. 77–95.
Petra Dark, 'Farming in the First Millenium AD', *Antiquity* vol 78, 2004, pp. 222–4.
——, 'The Environment of Britain in the First Millenium AD'
——, *Britain and the End of the Roman Empire*, Tempus 2000.
Wendy Davies, *The Llandaff Charters*, National Library of Wales, 1979.
——, *Wales in the Early Middle Ages*, Leicester UP, 1982.
P.H. Dixon, 'The Anglo-Saxon Settlement at Mucking: An Interpretation' in *Anglo-Saxon Studies in Archaeology and History*, vol 6, 1993, pp. 125–47.
David Dumville, 'Some Aspects of the Chronology of the Historia Brittonum', *Bulletin of the Board of Celtic Studies*, vol 25, 1974, pp. 439–45.
——, 'Nennius and the Historia Brittonum', *Studia Celtica* vol 10–11, 1975–6, pp. 78–95.
——, 'Sub-Roman Britain: History and Legend', *History*, vol 62, 1977, pp. 173–92.
——, 'The Welsh Latin Annals', *Studia Celtica*, vol 12–13, 1977–8, pp. 461–7.
——, 'The Historical Value of the Historia Brittonum', *Arthurian Literature*, no. 6, 1986, pp. 1–26.
——, *Histories and Pseudo-Histories of the Middle Ages*, Variorum Press, 1990.
David Dumville and M. Lapidge, *Gildas: New Approaches*, Boydell Press 1984.
Robert Dunning, *Arthur – the King in the West*, Sutton 1988.
D. Edel, ' The Arthur of Culhwch and Olwen as a figure of Epic-Heroic Tradition', in *Reading Mediaeval Studies*, vol 9, 1983, pp. 3–15.
Peter Beresford Ellis, *Celt and Saxon: The Struggle for Britain AD 410–937*, Constable 1993.
John Gwenogfryan Evans (ed), *The Book of Taliesin: Facsimile and Text*, Llanbedrog 1910.
——, *The Book of Aneirin*, vol ii, Llanpedrog 1922.
J.G. Evans and John Rhys, eds, *The Text of the Book of Llan Dav*, Clarendon Press, 1983.
P.K. Ford, 'On the Significance of Some Arthurian Names in Welsh', *Bulletin of the Board of Celtic Studies*, vol 30, 1983, pp. 268–73.
——, (ed), *Ystoria Taliesin*, University of Wales Press, 1992.
J. Frazer, *The Golden Bough: A Study in Magic and Religion*, London 1922..
Sheppard Frere, *Britannia*, London 1967.
Maureen Fries, 'The Arthurian Moment: History and Geoffrey of Monmouth's "Historia Regum Britanniae"' in *Arthuriana*, vol 8. no.4 (winter 1998) p. 88–99.
Laurence Gardner, *Bloodline of the Holy Grail*, Shaftesbury 1996.
R. Gardner, 'Gildas' New Testament Models' in *Cambrian Mediaeval Celtic Studies*, vol 30 (1995), pp. 1–12.
Alan Garner, *The Weirdstone of Brisingamen*, Collins 1960.

Margaret Gelling, 'Why aren't we speaking Welsh?' in *Anglo-Saxon Studies in Archaeology and History*, vol 6 (1993) pp. 51–6.
Geoffrey of Monmouth, The History of the Kings of Britain, tr. Lewis Thorpe, Penguin 1966.
Edward Gibbon, *The Decline and Fall of the Roman Empire*, 1966 Everyman edition (6 vols).
Adrian Gilbert, Baram Blackett and Alan Wilson, *The Holy Kingdom*, Bantam Press 1998.
Gildas, De Excidio Britanniae, ed. M. Winterbottom, *Arthurian Sources* vol 7, Phillimore 1978.
Norma Goodrich, *King Arthur*, Franklin Watts, New York, 1986.
G. Hall Gerould, 'King Arthur and Politics', *Speculum* vol 2, Jan 1927, pp. 33–51.
A. Gransden, 'The Growth of Glastonbury Traditions and Legends in the Twelfth Century', *Journal of Ecclesiastical History*, vol 27, 1976, pp. 337–58.
Miranda Green, *Dictionary of Celtic Myth and Legend*, Thames and Hudson 1992.
Thomas Green, *Concepts of Arthur*, Tempus 2007.
R. Gruffydd, 'From Gododdin to Gwynedd: Reflections on the Story of Cunedda', in *Studia Celtica*, vol 24–25, 1989–90, pp. 1–14.
R.W. Hanning, *The Vision of History in Early Britain*, London 1966.
Christina Hardyment, *Sir Thomas Malory: the Life and Times of King Arthur's Chronicler*, Harper Perennial 2005.
M. Haycock, 'Preiddiau Annwn and the Figure of Taliesin', in *Studia Celtica* vol 18–19, 1983–4, pp. 53–78.
W.S. Hewins, *The Royal Saints of Britain from the Latter Days of the Roman Empire*, Chiswick Press 1925.
Nicholas Higham, *Rome, Britain and the Anglo-Saxons*, London 1992.
——, *The English Conquest: Gildas and Britain in the Fifth Century*, Manchester UP, 1994.
——, *King Arthur: Myth-Making and History*, London 2002. *King Arthur: The Making of the Legend* (Yale UP 2018).
Katherine Hill, *The Origins of the English*, Duckworth 2003.
D.R. Howlett, 'The Literary Context of Geoffrey of Monmouth', in *Arthuriana* vol 5 np. 3, aut 1995.
——, *The Celto-Latin Tradition of Biblical Style* (Dublin 1996).
——, *Cambro-Latin Compositions: their Competence and Craftsmanship*, Four Courts Press Dublin, 1998.
Kathleen Hughes, 'The Annales Cambriae and Related Texts', *Proceedings of the British Academy* vol 59, 1973, pp. 233–58.
——, *Celtic Britain in the Early Middle Ages: Studies in Scottish and Welsh Sources*, Boydell Press 1980.
David Lloyd Isaac, *Siluriana*, Newport, 1859.
Kenneth Jackson, 'Once Again Arthur's Battles', *Modern Philology* vol 43, 1945–6, pp. 44–57.

——, 'Arthur's Battle of Breguoin', *Antiquity* vol 23, 1949, pp. 48–9.
——, 'The Site of Mount Badon', *The Journal of Celtic Studies*, vol 2, 1953–8, pp. 152–5.
——, *Celt and Saxon: Studies in the Early British Border*, Cambridge UP, 1963.
——, (ed), *The Gododddin*, Edinburgh 1969.
A.O. Jarman (ed), *Llyfr Ddu Caerfyrddin: The Black Book of Carmarthen*, 1982.
Elizabeth Jenkins, *The Mystery of King Arthur*, Michael O'Mara Books, 1975.
Jocelyn of Furness, *The Life of St Kentigern*, Llanerch reprint 1989.
Michael Jones,'The Appeal to Aetius in Gildas' in *Nottingham Mediaeval Studies*, vol 32, 1988, pp. 141–5.
——, 'St Germanus and the "Adventus Saxonum"' in *Haskins Society Jounral*, Vol 2, 1990, pp. 1–11
Thomas Jones, Brut y Tywysogion: the *Red Book of Hergest Version*, University of Wales Press 1955.
——, 'Stanzas of the Graves', the John Rhys Memorial lecture, *Proceedings of the British Academy* vol liii, 1967, pp. 97–137.
Marian Kalinke, ed, *The Arthur of the North: the Arthurian Legend in the Norse and Rus' Realms* (University of Wales Press 2011).
Martin Keatman and Graham Philipps, *King Arthur: the True Story*, 1992.
E.D. Kennedy, 'John Hardyng and the Holy Grail', in *Arthurian Literature* vol 8, Boydell and Brewer 1989, pp. 185–206.
D.P. Kirby, *The Earliest English Kings*, Unwin Hyman 1991.
J.T. Koch, *The Gododdin of Aneirin: Text and Context from Dark Age North Britain*, University of Wales Press, 1997.
——, Celtic Culture: *A Historical Encyclopedia*, Oxford UP 2006.
Norris Lacy, *The Arthurian Encyclopedia*, Boydell Press, 1986.
——, *The New Arthurian Encyclopedia*, New York, 1996.
Stuart Laycock, *Britannia: A Failed State?*, Tempus 2008.
Albert Le Grand, *Les Vies des Saintes de la Bretagne Armorique*, Quimper, 1901 edition.
John Leland, *Itinerary*, ed. Lucy Toulmin Smith, Arundel 1964.
V.M. Lagorio, 'The Evolving Legend of Joseph of Arimathea', *Speculum*, vol 46, 1971, pp. 209–31.
Liber Landavensis: *The Ancient Register of the Cathedral Church of Cardiff*, ed. William Rees, Longmans 1839.
Jack Lindsay, *Arthur and His Times*, Frederick Muller 1958.
L. Scott Littleton and Anne Thomas, 'The Sarmatian Connection: New Light on the Origin of the Holy Grail Legends' in *Journal of American Folklore*, vol 91 (1978) pp. 512–27.
L. Scott Littleton and Linda Malcor, *From Scythia to Camelot: a Radical Reassessment of the Legends of King Arthur, the Knights of the Round Table and the Holy Grail*, New York, 1994.
Roger Loomis, *Celtic Myth and Arthurian Romance*, Columbia University Press, 1927.

——, 'Edward I, Arthurian Enthusiast', *Speculum*, vol 28, 1953, pp. 114–27.
——, 'Arthurian Tradition and Folklore', *Folklore* vol 69, March 1958, pp. 1–25.
——, *Arthurian Literature in the Middle Ages*, Clarendon Press, 1959.
——, *The Grail from Celtic Myth to Christian Symbol*, Columbia UP, 1963.
The Mabinogion, tr. and ed. Jeffrey Gantz, Penguin 1976.
Hugh Macdougall, *Racial Myth in English History: Trojans, Teutons and Anglo-Saxons*, Montreal 1982.
Kemp Malone, 'The Historicity of Arthur' in *Journal of English and Germanic Philology* (1924) pp. 463–91.
Sir Thomas Malory, *Le Morte D'Arthur* (Caxton Text), 2 vols, Penguin 1969.
Caitlin Matthews, *Arthur and the Sovereignty of Britain*, Arkana, 1989.
John Matthews, *An Arthurian Reader*, Wellingborough 1988.
Garrett Mattingley, *An Imperial Possession: Britain in the Roman Empire.*
Keri Maund, *The Welsh Kings*, Tempus 2000.
Alastair Moffat, *Arthur and the Lost Kingdoms*, Weidenfeld and Nicolson, 1999.
Iolo Morgannwg (Edward Williams), *The Iolo Manuscripts*, Longmans 1848.
John Morris, *The Age of Arthur: Britain AD 350–650*, Weidenfeld and Nicolson, 1973.
Michael Mountney, *The Saints of Herefordshire*, Hereford 1976.
The Myrvynian Archaiology, 2nd edition, Gee and Son, 1870.
Nennius, Historia Brittonum, ed. John Morris, *Arthurian Sources*, vol 8, Phillimore, 1980.
E. Nicholson and B. Williams, 'The Dynasty of Cunedda and the Harleian Genealogy' in *Y Cymmrodor*, vol 21, 1908, pp. 63–105.
W. Nitze and T. Jenkins, eds, *Perlesvaus*, 2 vols, Chicago, 1937.
Edwin Pace, 'Athelstan, 'Twist-Beard', and Arthur: tenth-century Breton origins for the 'Historia Regum Britanniae' in *Arthuriana*, autumn 2016.
Oliver Rackham, *The History of the Countryside*, Phoenix 1986.
T.F. O'Rahilly, *Early Irish History and Mythology*, Dublin 1946.
——, *The Two Patricks*, Dublin 1957.
Oliver Padel, 'The Nature of Arthur', in *Cambrian Mediaeval Celtic Studies* vol 27, summer 1994, pp. 1–31.
——, 'Recent Work on the Origins of the Arthurian Legend: a Comment', *Arthuriana*, vol 5 no. 3, autumn 1995, pp. 103–14.
——, 'A New Study of the Gododdin', *Cambrian Mediaeval Celtic Studies*, vol 35, summer 1998, pp. 45–55.
J.C. Parsons, 'The Second Exhumation of King Arthur's Remains at Glastonbury, 10 April 1278', *Arthurian Literature* vol 12, Boydell and Brewer, 1987, pp. 173–7.
A. Pearson, 'Construction of the Saxon Shore Forts', *British Archaeological Report* no. Oxford 2003.
——, *The Roman Saxon Shore Forts: Defences of Coastal Britain*, Tempus 2000.
H.D. Phillimore, 'The Annales Cambriae and Old Welsh Genealogies', *Y Cymmrodor*, vol 9 (1888), pp.

Graham Phillips, *The Search for the Grail*, Random House 1995.
Howard Reid, *Arthur the Dragon King*, Headline 2001.
Frank Reno, *The Historic King Arthur*, Mc Farland, Jefferson North Carolina, 1996.
Joseph Ritson, *The Life of King Arthur from Ancient Historians and Authentic Documents*, London 1825.
John Rhys, *Studies in the Arthurian Legend*, Clarendon Press, 1891.
——, *Celtic Folklore*, Clarendon Press, 2 vols, 1901.
Peter Salwey, *Roman Britain*, Clarendon Press, 1971.
P.H. Sawyer and Ian Wood, eds, *Early Mediaeval Kingship*, Leeds UP, 1977.
W.F. Skene, *The Four Ancient Books of Wales*, Edinburgh 1868.
F.M. Stenton, *Anglo-Saxon England*, Clarendon Press 1971.
CE Stephens, *Sidonius Apollinaris and His Age*, Clarendon Press, 1933.
Mary Stewart, *The Crystal Cave*, 1970.
——, *The Hollow Hills*, 1973.
——, *The Last Enchantment*, 1979.
——, *The Wicked Day*, 1983.
Rosemary Sutcliff, *The Lantern Bearers*, Hodder and Stoughton, 1959.
——, *Sword At Sunset*, Hodder and Stoughton, 1963.
Charles Thomas, *Christianity in Roman Britain to AD 500*, Batsford 1981.
——, *Tintagel: Arthur and Archaeology*, London 1993.
Kenneth Tiller, *Layamon's 'Brut' and the Anglo-Norman Vision of History*, University of Chicago Press, 2007.
J.R.R. Tolkien, *Finn and Hengest: the Fragment and the Episode*, Houghton Mifflin, Boston 1983.
R.F. Treharne, *The Glastonbury Legends*, Cresset 1967.
The Vulgate Version of the Arthurian Romances, ed. H.O. Sommer, 7 vols, Washington 1908–16.
A. Wade-Evans, *The Life of St David*, SPCK, London 1923.
——, *Welsh Christian Origins*, Oxford 1934.
——, *Vitae Sanctorum Britanniae et Genealogiae*, University of Wales Press, 1944.
A.E. Waite, *The Holy Grail: its Legends and Symbolism*, Rider, 1933.
T.H. White, *The Once and Future King*, Collins 1958.
William of Malmesbury, The Antiquities of Glastonbury, ed. Frank Lomax, Llanerch reprint 1992.
The Early History of Glastonbury: An Edition, Translation and Study of William of Malmesbury's "De Antiquitate Glastoniae Ecclesiae", ed. John Scott, Boydell 1981.
David Williams, *The History of Monmouthshire*, Monmouth 1796.
Ifor Williams, ed, *The Poems of Taliesin*, Institute for Advanced Studies, Dublin 1975.
——, Ymddiddan Arthur ar'r Eryr, *Bulletin of the Board of Celtic Studies*, vol 2, pp. 279–86.
V.E. Williams-Nash, *The Early Christian Monuments of Wales*, University of Wales Press, 1950.

Index